BURT FRANKLIN: RESEARCH & SOURCE WORKS SERIES 760
Selected Essays in History, Economics and Social Science 274

# THE LIFE AND WRITINGS OF TURGOT

FROM THE MEDAL IN JOINT HONOUR OF TURGOT

AND ADAM SMITH STRUCK BY THE SOCIÉTÉ

D'ÉCONOMIE POLITIQUE PARIS IN 1876

LONDON & NEW-YORK. LONGMANS GREEN & C°

F. JENKINS HELIOG. PARIS

# THE LIFE AND WRITINGS

OF

# TURGOT

COMPTROLLER GENERAL OF FRANCE 1774-6

EDITED FOR ENGLISH READERS

BY

W. WALKER STEPHENS

BURT FRANKLIN
NEW YORK

Published by LENOX HILL Pub. & Dist. Co. (Burt Franklin)
235 East 44th St., New York, N.Y. 10017
Originally Published: 1895
Reprinted: 1971
Printed in the U.S.A.

S.B.N.: 8337-44518
Library of Congress Card Catalog No.: 74-161008
Burt Franklin: Research and Source Works Series 760
Selected Essays in History, Economics and Social Science 274

Reprinted from the original edition in the New York Public Library

# PREFACE

THIS attempt to provide English readers with a fuller and more exact knowledge of Turgot and his writings than they have hitherto possessed needs not much justification. The only Life of Turgot in English is the translation of Condorcet's work, published in London in 1787, which is now to be found only in some of the greater libraries and a few old book stores.

Except to special historical students, the merit of Turgot's writings remained here unknown until in 1870 Dr. W. B. Hodgson delivered and published his two excellent Lectures. Meanwhile Mr. John Morley had been maturing the admirable study of Turgot, which afterwards appeared in his 'Critical Miscellanies,' vol. ii., in 1886. This work, like all others from Mr. Morley's pen, is so artistically complete in the treatment of its subject, that it may seem almost presumptuous, at least in me, to further cultivate the same field. One of my apologies is that some may possibly desire to know more about Turgot's conduct as Minister than they can gather from Mr. Morley's essay. It is true that his ministerial career, as Mr. Morley remarks, 'belongs to the general history of France,' and was an 'attempt to extend, over the whole realm, the kind of reform which had been tried, on a smaller scale, in the Limousin.' Yet I am disposed to think that a short history of his twenty months' arduous struggle, as Minister, to save France from the dangers to which she was madly rushing, might, for some minds, have a certain interest, and especially as this struggle, passed amidst more critical circumstances than those of his previous career, afforded a still better test of Turgot's character.

Almost contemporaneously with Mr. Morley's essay, M. Léon Say, the distinguished French statesman and economist, published in 1887, in the series of 'Les Grands Écrivains Français,' the volume on Turgot, small in bulk but of wonderful comprehensiveness. As a summary of the principal facts of Turgot's life, and as a true and lively presentment of many features of his character, nothing better could be given. An English translation appeared the year following, from the competent hand of Mr. Gustave Masson. The original work, however, was written by a Frenchman for Frenchmen, and was, as the translator himself has observed, in some degree an *ouvrage de circonstance*, with the prominence given in it to economical questions. It presumed a greater acquaintance with French history than that possessed by the ordinary English reader, and, by the necessary limits of its plan, it could not give to the leading events of Turgot's time that explanatory detail which is almost necessary in order to excite interest in them and to render them intelligible.

My remaining apology for publishing this volume is that a large portion of it consists of selections of Turgot's writings given for the first time to an English public. This portion will, I trust, prove to be of such value as to redeem all imperfections in the other.

In France so much has been written about Turgot, and so much study devoted to the history of his time, that the field for any original research has now been almost exhausted. My object has thus been limited to condensing into one volume, from many volumes treating of the period, all matter of sufficient importance and interest for general readers of the present day. I may say that I have spared no pains in endeavouring to carry with me, throughout the narrative, a confidence in its substantial accuracy, by referring, in every important case, to the sources of information, and, as often as possible, by giving the words of the original texts themselves. While this has involved in some degree a loss of uniformity in literary construction, it will, I am sure, be welcomed as a gain by all studious readers who love to deal with the facts of history at first hand.

ROSEHALL LODGE, EDINBURGH:
*March* 1895.

# CONTENTS

## *THE LIFE OF TURGOT*

### CHAPTER I

**1727–1761**

**DIVINITY STUDENT. MASTER OF REQUESTS**



### CHAPTER II

1761–1774

INTENDANT OF LIMOGES

## CHAPTER III

### 1774–1776

### COMPTROLLER-GENERAL

## CHAPTER IV

### 1776–1781

### IN RETIREMENT

## *SELECTED WRITINGS*

# THE LIFE OF TURGOT

'So great is the value, even in our more advanced times, of Turgot's history, and especially of his writings, that there is room, if not need, for more than one attempt to redeem them from unmerited and almost unaccountable neglect.'

W. B. HODGSON, LL.D. (*Turgot: his Life, Times, and Opinions.* London, 1870).

'The times which, above all, are the most important to study are those when dangers ought to have been avoided, when reason struggled against the passions, when men were yet masters to choose between the counsels of wisdom and the lessons of misfortune.'

JOSEPH DROZ (*Hist. du Règne de Louis XVI.* Paris, 1839–1842).

'I speak of Turgot not as a defeated man but as a victor. Because, if he failed in the eighteenth century, he has in fact dominated the century following. He founded the political economy of the nineteenth century, and, by the freedom of industry which he bequeathed to us, he has impressed on the nineteenth century the mark which will best characterise it in history.'

LÉON SAY (*Turgot.* Paris, 1887).

# CHAPTER I

1727–1761

## DIVINITY STUDENT—MASTER OF REQUESTS

ANNE ROBERT JACQUES TURGOT, third son of Michel Étienne Turgot and Madeleine Françoise Martineau, was born in Paris May 10, 1727. His ancestors for many generations had occupied high positions in several departments of the State. His grandfather was Intendant of the Generality of Metz, afterwards of that of Tours, under Louis XIV. His father was President of the second *Chambre des Requêtes*, afterwards *Conseiller d'État Ordinaire* (1737), and (1741) President of the *Grand Conseil.* He earned most honour, however, in the capacity of *Prévôt des Marchands*, by his active and beneficent management of the sanitary affairs of Paris; many of the best improvements in the city, during that period, being due to his administration.

The home education of young Turgot was not fortunate. His father, probably, was too deeply involved in his laborious public duties to afford much time to his son's upbringing. Between the mother and the son there was some want of sympathy. Probably she disliked his fondness for books and for serious studies. With her, as with most French women, a graceful carriage and refined manners in a youth were almost everything. Unfortunately these were wanting in her son, and he made no effort to acquire them. She was continually upbraiding him for his *gaucherie*, and this made him only more nervously sensitive. He endeavoured to avoid, as much as possible, occasions which might put his deportment on trial. When visitors came he would skulk under a sofa, or behind a screen, and would have to be dragged forth to be presented. This shyness in an intellectual and excessively studious boy is not difficult to understand. He considers his life to be devoted to a great purpose, and that the whole world of knowledge lies before him to be gained. Every hour, every minute spent otherwise than in thinking, in reading, in noting his studies, in self-culture, is for him lost time. The sports of boyhood, the amenities of household life, the rules of social life, are all to be despised, or hated as robbing him of the precious time, once lost never regained, which might be given to the conquest of a new province of knowledge, or to the intercourse with minds (speaking through books) far above the commonplace level of the family circle or their visitors! A boy with these tendencies overindulged could not fail to make himself often disagreeable to those about him, and especially to a mother whose theory of life was very different from his. This 'awkwardness,' for which she was continually blaming him, was, long afterwards, in public life, often imputed to him by his enemies, and was sometimes apologised for by his friends. His manner to strangers, and to those with whom he did not much sympathise, was felt to be stiff and reserved. It is possible that the seeds of this constrained manner were sown by the unnatural seclusion and the excessive devotion to study of his boyhood, and that, instead of being then gently eradicated by parental care, they were subjected to a treatment which gave them only firmer root.

He had a tutor who, it appears, was not very efficient, and when the time came for his being sent to college, although his multifarious reading had filled his mind with ideas, the nature of his knowledge was far from being exact. But the *Collège Louis-le-Grand,* the one selected for him, was at that time under the ablest direction, and here he soon made a very decided a vance. A characteristic story has been told of his college-life at this time. Although he was allowed a liberal supply of pocket-money, it always soon disappeared. Very little of it was spent on himself, and he did not seem inclined to tell in what way the rest went. This caused some uneasiness at home, and his father thought it advisable to mention the matter to the principal. An inquiry was quietly made and the secret came out. The pocket-money, as soon as received, had been distributed among those of the day-scholars who had not the means to buy their necessary class-books.

Afterwards, for the higher classes, he attended the *Collège du Plessis*. Here he was fortunate in having most distinguished masters. One of these was the Abbé Sigorgne, who was the first professor in France to substitute for the fanciful theories of Descartes the sublime and mathematically demonstrable physics of Newton. Turgot enthusiastically embraced the new doctrine. A deep friendship grew up between the teacher and his pupil.

As customary for the youngest son of the family, Turgot, being intended for the Church, left the *Collège du Plessis* for the seminary of *Saint-Sulpice*. There he gained the distinction of being admitted to the degree of Bachelor of Theology (1747), before the usual period, by special sanction of the Faculty. His next step was to enter (1749) the House of the Sorbonne in order to study for his licence.

The Sorbonne

The 'Society of the Sorbonne' was a select ecclesiastical body, consisting of about a hundred members, mostly dignitaries of the Church. There were thirty-six apartments for the residence of the thirty-six oldest doctors, members of the Society. But, as seldom more than twenty-five made use of the privilege, accommodation remained which was turned to educational account in favour of ten or twelve young men, already Bachelors of Theology, who lived two years or more in the House, having their studies directed by the six doctors, professors of the Faculty. The Society was broken up at the Revolution; but unjustly so, for it had little of the nature of a monastic institution. It was in fact a combination of club for the elder, and college for the younger members, having its garden-grounds, its chapel, lecture-rooms, and ample library, common-hall and dining-room, with tariff at fixed prices. Turgot was one of the bachelors admitted in 1748.

In the Society of the Sorbonne he was fortunate to have as fellow-students several highly cultivated young men, with many of whom he contracted a warm and lifelong friendship. Among these were Morellet, afterwards the distinguished *littérateur* and economist; De Boisgélin, afterwards Archbishop of Aix, and who died Archbishop of Tours and Cardinal; De Cicé, afterwards Bishop of Auxerre; and Loménie de Brienne, afterwards Archbishop of Toulouse and Cardinal; whom readers of Carlyle's 'French Revolution' are not likely to have forgotten.

He was now one-and-twenty. Morellet, who entered the House in the same year, mentions in his 'Memoirs' the impression made on him by his fellow-student:—

> The remembrance of Turgot is sweet to all who have known him personally. Already (at the Sorbonne) his mind announced all the qualities it afterwards unfolded of sagacity, penetration, and profoundness. He had the simplicity of a child, yet it was compatible with a kind of dignity; he was respected by his comrades and even by his *confrères*, of an age much beyond his own. His modesty and reserve would have reflected honour even upon a maiden. It was impossible to risk with him the slightest *équivoque* on certain subjects without making him blush to the eyes and placing him in extreme embarrassment. This did not prevent him having a frank and naive gaiety, and from laughing into fits at a pleasantry, a point, or an absurdity. . . . He had a prodigious memory; I have known him to repeat pieces of 120 verses, after having heard or read them twice, or even once. . . . His mind was in a continual activity, but when he set himself to work and there was need of writing or of acting, he was slow and dawdling (*musard*). . . . He would lose time in arranging his bureau and trimming his pens. I do not say that he did not think while giving himself up to these triflings, but by thinking only his work was not advanced.

Turgot certainly never acquired the facility that enabled Morellet to publish his forty or fifty volumes, but the critic himself accounts in some degree for Turgot's shortcoming in a way quite intelligible to us. 'Turgot,' he says, 'wished to give the highest degree of perfection to what he had conceived, he was particular even to minutiæ, he would in no respect have his work done for him, being never content unless he had mastered it and completed it himself. . . . He was never satisfied (with his work) and,' repeats the facile writer of contemporary literature, 'this difficulty caused him to lose much precious time.'[1] But, taking a longer view, was the time really lost? For it may be said that of Morellet's fifty volumes, however serviceable some of them were in their day, nearly all are now forgotten. In Turgot's five volumes, on the other hand, there are few pages which do not possess an interest for us still.

Turgot's two years in the House of the Sorbonne were the seed-time of his life. Without neglecting the studies absolutely necessary for the ecclesiastic profession, he set himself upon a course of self-culture, as remarkable for its comprehensiveness as for the unflagging diligence with which it was followed out. In order the better to assimilate to his own mind the principles and ideas he was imbibing from his studies, it was his practice to select the most important of them for special analysis, and, after submitting these to a rigidly unprejudiced criticism from every side, to cast them into written expression in his own words.

It was in accordance with his high aims, and with the serious spirit in which he pursued his studies, that the earliest literary work to which he gave a deliberate treatment, at a considerable length, was a treatise 'On the Existence of God.' Only three fragments of it remain. As Turgot's religious views have been often misrepresented, it may be as well to record at once, that at no time of his life did he ever waver from the belief in God, to which he gave

[1] Morellet, *Mémoires*, i. 10–17.

eloquent utterance in this essay of his early youth. Afterwards, when the reforming policy of his administration created for him many enemies, 'Atheist' was one of the harsh epithets they did not scruple to hurl at him; but if some of them believed it to apply to him, most of them knew better, and used the word just as a handy rhetorical weapon.

In December 1749 Turgot was unanimously elected Prior of the Society of the Sorbonne for the following year. This office was mostly an honorary one, conferred generally on the most promising young student, who had not already held it. In this capacity it was his duty to deliver two Latin discourses, one at the summer, the other at the winter session. Again he selects the highest themes to which human reason can address itself, as if planning to develop his ideas on the greatest questions in the order of their importance. The First Discourse was 'On the Advantages which the Christian Religion has conferred on the Human Race.' (July 13, 1750.) The Second was 'On the successive Advances of the Human Mind.' (December 11, 1750.)

His Discourses

The First Discourse, although certainly above the average of young theologians' essays, would not, at the present day, be held to merit much distinction, but it had characteristics—a breadth of view, and a freedom from the tone of clericalism, remarkable in a discourse delivered by an ecclesiastic before an ecclesiastical audience. It is, besides, interesting to us as an indication that already Turgot's mind was gradually leading him on a road deviating somewhat from that to the Church.

The Second Discourse is more notable in every respect, and especially as being one of the earliest enunciations given of the doctrine of the 'perfectibility of the human race,' which was so enthusiastically proclaimed by many of the leading men of France a quarter of a century later, and was, through them, twelve years later still, to receive its first great practical application in the great Revolution. Like other principles, true in themselves, it has become discredited through the excesses of its wild votaries, but, in reasonable minds, a belief in 'perfectibility' was nothing more than the well-founded opinion that existing society was capable of enjoying greatly improved conditions, and that, step by step, stage by stage, century by century, these conditions might be still further improved. This belief was so earnestly held by Turgot that it became a part of his being, and we should fail to understand the man were the characteristic lost sight of. His belief in a great purpose of existence and in the laws of human progress not only gave an impulse to his work of self-culture, but, when the time arrived, the belief inspired as well his whole public life. We may read this between the lines of every letter, every memorial, or every decree that came from his pen. In this discourse he gave expression to his ideas on what has since been called the 'philosophy of history' in these words, which have often been quoted: 'All the ages are linked together by a sequence of causes and effects, which connects the existing state of the world with all that has preceded it. The multiform signs of language and of writing, by giving to men the means of insuring the possession of their ideas, and of communicating them to others, have made of all the individual funds of knowledge a common treasure, which one generation transmits to the next, along with an inheritance always increased by the discoveries of each age. Thus the human race, seen from its origin, appears to the eye of a philosopher as one vast whole, which itself, like each individual composing it, has had its infancy and its development.' [1]

As a deduction from the principles set forth in the discourse he, incidentally, boldly predicts the independence of the American States. In October 1774, less than two years before the Declaration of Independence, Washington wrote to a friend that independence 'was not desired by any thinking man in all North America.' Those close to events are often blindest to their coming. Twenty-three years

[1] *Œuvres de Turgot* (Daire, 1844), ii. 597.

before this the young Prior of the Sorbonne, recognising the law that like causes in the world's experience produce like effects, saw the event to be inevitable.

Self-culture

Meanwhile he was earnestly strengthening his intellect, and extending his knowledge, by the help of the excellent library of the Sorbonne. He gave much of his time to making at considerable length translations into French of the masterpieces in other languages. Dupont de Nemours gives us particulars of these, which introduce us to Turgot's favourite authors at this period. The translations include Homer, Seneca, Cæsar, Ovid, Tacitus, Horace, Tibullus, Virgil, Tasso, Klopstock, Gessner. Of contemporary English authors he translated copious selections from the Essays of Hume, Addison, and Johnson, and, in full, Pope's 'Essay on Man' and 'Universal Prayer'; afterwards, when his mind was drawn particularly to politico-economical subjects, he translated Hume's Essay 'On the Jealousy of Trade,' and some of Dr. Josiah Tucker's Essays. His knowledge of languages is seen to have been considerable. His two discourses before the Sorbonne were delivered in Latin; his translations include works in that language, in Greek, Hebrew, German, Italian, and English. Later on in life, if not already, he wrote in English with ease and correctness. To these acquirements he added a remarkable facility of writing in verse, and this with some epigrammatic point. He did not limit himself to the study of literature and of Political Economy. His knowledge of Chemistry and Physical Science generally, and especially of Astronomy, was far beyond that possessed by the majority of educated men.[1] The ambitious student claimed the whole world of Thought as his domain. Among his papers was found a list, in his own handwriting, drawn up at the Sorbonne period, of the literary projects he had then in view, which comprised a

[1] Dupont states his having made 'observations on the laws of Heat,' which were held to be valuable by a scientific specialist. In 1760 he is mentioned in the Transactions of the Academy of Sciences, as being the first to spot in Orion the comet of that time.

grand course of treatises on Language, History, Sciences, Metaphysical Philosophy, Theology, Morals, Laws, Politics, and Principles of Administration. It is pleasant to know that this scheme was never really shelved, that he kept working at it, more or less, all his life, even while involved in pressing public duties. Considering that he died when just past middle life, the fact is almost surprising that 'of the works he proposed to himself' while a student, 'he lived to write, in whole or in part, fifteen, and that he wrote besides several of which he did not then dream.'[1]

Turgot's earliest literary work, remaining to us in an entire state, is his letter to Buffon, the celebrated naturalist. He had been reading the 'Theory of the Earth,' and some parts of the speculation appeared to him to be inconsistent with strictly scientific and Newtonian principles. He was little over nineteen when he first formed an opinion on the subject, but the lapse of two years only confirming it, he, while still an obscure student in the *Séminaire Saint-Sulpice*, summoned courage to address in October 1748 a critical letter to the world-famous Buffon, then in his full glory. The letter is anonymous, being merely signed 'Admirateur,' the writer naively mentioning that he has no intention of publishing it. The kind of reception Buffon gave to it is not known. The progress made in Geology and Biology has at the present day put the particular discussion out of court. But, curiously enough for young Turgot's credit, *savants* of the time came to admit that Buffon's theory was faulty in many points, including those questioned by Turgot. Early writings

His next essay that we know of was his first work in the field of Political Economy—a science whose birth dates from scarcely a generation before Turgot, and of which, in its larger and modern acceptation, he became one of the founders. It was a short treatise on 'Paper-Money' in the form of a letter dated April 7, 1749, addressed to his comrade

[1] Dupont, *Œuvres de Turgot* (ed. 1811), i. 21.

of the Sorbonne the Abbé de Cicé.[1] It exposes the fallacies of the theories brought into vogue by John Law, and aims at demonstrating the true functions of money as an instrument of exchange. Unfortunately, there is but a fragment left of this letter. There is enough, however, to enable us to see how thoroughly Turgot had apprehended the real question at issue, and how vigorously he could give expression to his own well-considered thoughts. To one given to the study of this branch of economic science in our own time, there will indeed, in the 'letter on paper-money,' be found little with which he is not already familiar; but when he takes into account the fact that it was written in the middle of last century—almost in the time of politico-economical darkness—he will read Turgot's words with the interest which belongs to the earliest announcement of a great truth.

During 1750 he set himself to refute the metaphysical doctrines of Berkeley in two short essays which are published in his collected works, and which he threw into a more succinct form for the 'Encyclopédie' in the article 'Existence.'

In the same year he attacked another metaphysician of note, Maupertuis, mostly with reference to the philosophy of language.

Among Turgot's papers, when examined after his death, were found considerable portions of two important treatises which also belonged to the Sorbonne period. The one on 'Political Geography' is the outline of a larger work on the subject, which is sketched in a very comprehensive manner. It is remarkable for embracing the plan of an historical atlas, a kind of publication which has not been ventured upon, at all events on a proper scale, until almost the present day. Turgot's scheme goes into considerable detail and specifies several maps. It occupies forty-three pages octavo in his published works. It is worth reading if only as an evidence of the breadth of his views, and of the thoroughness

[1] Abridged *infra*, pp. 204–9.

he is accustomed to give to the treatment of any subject he took in hand. The other treatise was 'On Universal History,' being an attempt to supply some of the defects in Bossuet's celebrated 'Discours'; for this work Turgot had laid a vaster plan than he was able to carry out. We have, however, an admirable Introduction, and a valuable chapter 'On the History of the Progress of the Human Mind,' the two, along with detached thoughts, intended to be worked in, occupying 142 printed pages in his works.[1]

Clerical career renounced

Amidst all these various and suggestive studies his mind had taken a development which could no longer adapt itself to the narrow sphere of the Sorbonne Society, nor to the greater ecclesiastical sphere beyond it.

§ 2. He was now over three-and-twenty. Some of his comrades in the Society already suspected his growing repugnance to the Church and his growing preference of the State for a career. There was great commotion among them at this. Dupont narrates a most interesting incident that occurred:—

His resolution was not approved of by his friends and comrades the Abbés de Cicé, de Brienne, de Véry, and de Boisgélin. In order to dissuade him from taking the step he contemplated, they requested an interview in his chamber. The Abbé de Cicé, speaking for them all, said to him: 'Turgot, we are unanimous in thinking that you are about to commit an act completely contrary to your interest and to the great good sense that distinguishes you. You are a younger son of Normandy, and consequently poor. The magistracy, which you are thinking of making your profession, exacts a certain competency, without which it loses the consideration generally attached to it, and without which one can look for almost no advancement. Your father has enjoyed a great renown, your relations have much influence. By keeping to the career in which they have placed you, you are certain to have your choice of excellent abbeys and in good time of a bishopric. It would be almost easy for your family to procure for you an episcopal see in Languedoc, Provence, or Brittany. Then you would be able to realise your noble dreams upon public adminis-

[1] Abridged *infra*, pp. 174–92.

tration, and, without ceasing to be a churchman, you would become a statesman. Instead of which, if you shut the door upon yourself, if you break the plank that is under your feet, you will be confined to judge law-suits, you will exhaust in the discussion of petty private matters your genius which is fit to deal with the most important affairs.' Turgot replied: 'My dear friends, I am deeply touched by the zeal of your friendship for me, and by the feeling that dictates this appeal to me. There is great truth in your observations. Follow then for yourselves the advice that you have given to me; for *you* can follow it. But for myself, it is impossible for me to give myself up, all my life, to *wearing a mask*.'[1]

Turgot had laid before his father the reasons he had for renouncing the profession of the Church, and had requested permission for adopting, instead, that of the Law. The father's consent had been obtained, and his influence was about to be exerted to gain for his son a favourable introduction, when in February 1751 he died. This event brought to a close Turgot's residence at the Sorbonne.

The rest of the year was employed by his relations in efforts to obtain for him such a position as would give prospect of advancement in the State. Fortunately, Law had been in some measure included in his curriculum at the Sorbonne; this, and the reputation he had gained there for intellectual activity and ability, encouraged his friends in their expectations. Turgot, in the meantime, exerted himself diligently to supply the deficiencies in his legal education, but without denying himself due relaxation.

In society

At no period of his life, probably, did he see more of what is called 'society' than at the one we have reached. He had just abandoned the secluded life of the Sorbonne, and the death of his father had naturally brought him to take a more prominent part in the family circle, and beyond it. In a short time he found himself launched upon a world almost new to him, consisting of those select assemblies of cultured and brilliant men and women for which Paris has always

[1] Dupont, *Œuvres de Turgot*, i. 28, *note*.

been famous. He had not the self-possession, the audacity, and the several social graces of a young Duc de Fronsac, but he succeeded, nevertheless, in winning recognition from a higher set than the merely fashionable—the intellectual, the literary and scientific sections of the Paris world. Among his associates were Montesquieu, D'Alembert, Helvetius, Morellet, Galiani, Raynal, and Marmontel. But now, as well as during all the rest of his life, he instinctively recoiled from surrendering himself entirely to any literary or other *coterie*. His dislike to the spirit of party or of sect was always ready to be expressed. 'It is the spirit of sect,' he has said a hundred times, 'that makes enemies to useful truths. When an independent man proposes modestly what he believes to be the truth, if he has reason with him, we listen to him; if we find him wrong, we forget him. But as soon as the *savants*, in their pride, give themselves up to form a *body*, to say WE, to believe themselves able to impose laws upon public opinion, thoughtful public opinion revolts against them, for it wishes to receive laws from truth only, and not from any authority.' [1]

But he did not absent himself from that inner court of all, where the celebrated goddesses of the day held their receptions, giving the law to manners and even to literature. Now, and for many years afterwards, he was assiduous in his attendance at the drawing-rooms of Mme. Geoffrin, Mme. Helvetius, and Mme. Graffigny. His intellectual relations with the last-named lady are specially interesting. She had shortly before obtained great celebrity by her 'Lettres d'une Péruvienne.' She had probably been struck with some observations Turgot had made on her work, and she requested him to write out for her his views more fully. This he did in a remarkable letter of considerable length, touching critically upon nearly every subject dealt with in her work, and advancing from his own side many ideas on education, marriage, &c., very different from those at that time prevailing, but some of which acquired signal notoriety, ten

[1] Dupont, *Œuvres de Turgot*, i. 47–48.

years afterwards, through the matchless eloquence of Rousseau.[1]

Master of Requests

Turgot seems to have had in view for himself the office of 'King's Advocate at the Châtelet,' which would have given him practice in public speaking, but there being this year no resignation, he decided to accept (January 5, 1752) the position of 'Deputy Councillor' of the Procurator-General. The 30th December of the same year he was admitted as Councillor in the Parliament of Paris, and shortly afterwards he was appointed Master of Requests (March 28, 1753), which position he held until he was promoted to be Intendant of Limoges in 1761.

These nine years and a half, as far as spent in the magistracy, are necessarily uneventful for us. The fulfilment of his official duties was characterised by the most painstaking study of the cases brought before him, by the exercise of a mind nervously conscientious and anxious to clear itself from all prejudice, and by a benevolence in his decisions which was checked only by a strict sense of justice. There occurred a case in which he considered he was not free from blame for neglect of duty, and he made of it a lesson to himself for life. It is related by Condorcet. He had to report upon the affair of an employé in the office of the Farmers-General of the Revenue, prosecuted for some misconduct. From the circumstances that appeared, Turgot, as well as others, thought there was little doubt of the man's guilt, and as the punishment would be one of great rigour according to the law then in force, he felt disinclined to take up the case any sooner than absolutely necessary. Afterwards, when he went into it, he found that *the man was actually innocent.* 'He at once felt himself compelled to repair the injury his delay had occasioned, and ascertaining what income the accused had lost, pending the process, Turgot insisted on making it up to him, taking care at the same time to mark his act as one not of generosity but of justice.'[2]

[1] The letter is translated (slightly abridged) *infra*, pp. 193–203.

[2] Condorcet, *Life of Turgot* (English translation), pp. 21–22.

In May 1753 Turgot, as a Master of Requests, accepted a seat in the new 'Royal Chamber,' which was created in the place of the Parliament then exiled. By this step he incurred some unpopularity, to account for which it is necessary to explain how these matters stood.

There were thirteen parliaments in France, twelve provincial, besides that of Paris, which is indeed the one generally understood when the *Parlement* is alluded to. There is no analogy between them and our Parliament. They had no representative character whatever. Their function was not legislative, but judicial. From time to time the Parliament of Paris claimed a veto on edicts of the king, but it was never allowed to be one practically. The office, being of great honour and influence, was always much coveted, and a needy monarch set the example of making the nominations to it for a consideration in money. In course of time this became the rule. The members acquired the right to sell or to bequeath the office they had bought, and thus the parliaments came to consist of men of rank and means, including the princes, dukes, and peers and other dignitaries *ex officio*.

Since 1730 the Parliament of Paris had attracted to itself much popularity by its opposition to the Jesuits, although in this, and in other respects, its proceedings were not characterised by prudence, nor were they of any real service to liberty or the public good.

Turgot, by taking his seat in the new Chamber, thus, at the very outset of his career, made himself conspicuous as an opponent of the political influence of the Parliament. He held that the true function of the judicature was to administer the laws, and not to make them, nor even to interfere with their making. He could not recognise a self-elected, limited, aristocratic body, actuated too often by class interests and class prejudices, as possessing any just claim to represent public opinion. We shall find his estimate of the Parliament too well confirmed by circumstances in which he became the chief actor twenty-three years later.

Letters on Religious Liberty

During the period of his judicial office he found time to make some valuable contributions to the discussion of public questions. The first of these, in order of time and of importance, was his 'Letters on Toleration,' suggested by the commotion which had been caused throughout France by the controversy between the Church and the Parliament of Paris upon their respective spheres of jurisdiction. Turgot could take the side of neither the Church nor the Parliament, for he was the advocate of toleration, which was detested by both. Dealing impartially with the questions in dispute between the parties, where they involved matters of fact, he, on the other hand, appealed to higher principles than were held by either body, and propounded a doctrine which we may safely say no party in Church or State at that time was advanced enough to accept. Away from the dust and heat of the common road, he betook himself to the mountain summit, to think out there, amidst its serene sky and bracing air, the claims of the individual man to absolute liberty of thought—to anticipate the 'voluntaryism' of a later time, involving the separation of Church from State.

The first of the letters was written in 1753, shortly after he had been appointed Master of Requests; the second was written about a year later.

'Le Conciliateur'

This was followed (May 1, 1754) by the publication of a short tract entitled 'Le Conciliateur,'[1] taking its name from a proposal made to effect the reconcilement of both Jesuits and Jansenists to the action of the State, by its sacrificing to them their common enemy, the Protestants. The attempt to deprive the small body of Protestants of the limited rights they enjoyed, and the unprincipled character of the policy suggested, raised his indignation. In his plea for tolerance in this work he does not attempt ascending to first principles, as he did in his previous one, but contents himself with arguing from grounds admitted by his opponents, and with appealing to the authority of Christ and His Apostles, the Fathers and others. The 'Conciliateur'

[1] See *infra*, pp. 210–18.

went through three editions. It is said that the king read the work and was favourably impressed by it. At all events, the project of persecuting the Protestants was abandoned.

During his leisure from magisterial duties he translated, annotated, and published an essay by one of our own political writers of that time—Dr. Josiah Tucker[1]—on 'Questions on the Naturalisation of Foreign Protestants.' He contributed five articles to the 'Encyclopédie,' viz. 'Étymologie,' 'Existence,' 'Expansibilité,' 'Foires,' and 'Fondations.' They were all lengthy articles, and would together make up a good-sized volume. 'The appearance of the article "Existence,"' says M. Léon Say, 'was a real literary and philosophical event. The world of the *literati* and the *encyclopedists* was struck by the precision and clearness of the style, the originality and depth of the ideas. . . . [In our own day] Cousin admired it much, and assigned to it a special place in the philosophical outcome of the eighteenth century.'[2] But the last-named article on the list is the most important to us. In it he boldly asserts the right of the State to modify and even to annul the terms on which old foundations were made in order to use their endowments in accordance with the changed conditions of society.[3] Much of Turgot's article,[4] written a century and a quarter ago, is still good reading for ourselves, for, in spite of the repeated attacks we have seen successfully made in our country, during the last two generations, against the superstitious respect for the will of the 'pious founder,' we have still remaining many institutions which have outlived their 'reason for existence.'

Articles in the 'Encyclopédie'

§ 3. In 1755, or earlier, Turgot had attached himself, as nearly as his independent spirit would permit, to the party of the 'Economists,' then rising into importance, which was eventually to influence so profoundly the intellectual and political movements in France and Great Britain. He had for

Joins the 'Economists'

[1] See *infra*, p. 291.
[2] Léon Say, *Turgot*, p. 36.
[3] 'Mirabeau afterwards drew from Turgot his best arguments against the "*biens*" of the clergy.' (*G. d'Hugues.*)
[4] See *infra*, pp. 219–28.

his friends the two great founders of the school—Quesnay, the author of several works in propagation of its doctrines, and Gournay, Intendant of Commerce, the author of the celebrated formula of *laissez-faire et laissez-passer*. With Gournay he formed a very deep and tender friendship. It was one of the official duties of the Intendant of Commerce to inspect different provinces of the kingdom. Turgot accompanied him in his tour of 1755 by Rochelle, Bordeaux, Montauban, the rest of Guienne and Bayonne, and through part of Gascony. In 1756 they followed the course of the Loire from Orleans to Nantes, then through Maine and Anjou, and the coast of Brittany from Nantes to St. Malo, returning by Rennes. We can imagine what an education these travels were to a mind like Turgot's, alive to every important and interesting fact bearing upon the condition of his fellow-creatures, and how much his pleasure and his profit were increased by the thoughtful, methodical spirit in which he would prepare himself for his journeys, and the wise use he would make of every experience gained to illustrate the economical principles he had already formed, or to modify them into accordance with facts. Throughout his travels, now and afterwards, he made it his rule to study the geology, natural history, and agriculture, as well as the commerce and manufactures of each province, and to record his observations on all such matters. Gournay resigned the office of Intendant of Commerce in 1758. He died the following year. The loss was felt by Turgot as irreparable. He raised a lasting memorial to his friend by composing his *Éloge*.[1] Marmontel had been officially charged with the duty, and Turgot's paper was modestly offered as furnishing some materials for the academician's use, but there remained little, if anything, to be added to it. The note to Marmontel accompanying it is dated July 22, 1759. It alludes to the paper having been finished some days before, and as Gournay died on June 22, its composition must have been completed within three weeks at most. It is a very elaborate estimate

Travels with Gournay

*Éloge* of Gournay

[1] See *infra*, pp. 229–48.

of the man, his life, and his doctrine, and it has all the qualities of a profound philosophical treatise presented in finished literary form. It occupies a space of more than fifty printed octavo pages. The reflection is naturally suggested to us, either that Morellet must have exaggerated in describing Turgot's habitual slowness of composition, or that Turgot must have gained considerable facility in practice since the days of the Sorbonne.

Gournay had had a friend of longer standing than Turgot, and also greatly valued, M. Trudaine, one of the Intendants of Finance and Director of Roads and Bridges. A feeling shared by the remaining two suggested their drawing together in sympathy in their common loss, and Turgot became Trudaine's guest for some time at his country seat of Montigny. Their intercourse on this occasion deepened the attachment between them, and Trudaine became a powerful support to him in the Government during his subsequent provincial administration.

He left Montigny for a tour in Switzerland and the east of France, saddened as it must have been by thoughts of the loved companion now lost to him with whom he had enjoyed his former travels. He went by Lyons and Geneva into Vaud, and returned by Zurich and Bâle to Alsace.

It was when passing through Geneva on this tour that he made the acquaintance of Voltaire. He brought a letter of introduction from D'Alembert. Voltaire writes to Count d'Argental, October 10, 1760: 'We have at present with us M. Turgot, who is worth more than all the Bar. He has no need of my instructions, he is fitter to instruct me; he is a most lovable philosopher. We performed for him "Fanime" and the "Ensorcelés." He confessed he had not wept at "Tancrède," but I saw him in tears at "Fanime," moved perhaps by the touching tones of Mme. Denis.' Five weeks later he writes to D'Alembert: 'I am still full of M. Turgot. I did not know that he had written the article "Existence"; he is still better than his article. I have scarcely ever met a man more lovable or better informed, and, Visit to Voltaire what is very rare with our metaphysicians, he has the finest and most correct taste.'

There were essential differences between the mental character of Voltaire and that of Turgot, but these did not prevent Turgot from recognising Voltaire's brilliant, versatile, and altogether astonishing genius, and his signal services to civil and religious freedom, in spite of his frequent bitterness, his intemperance in controversy, and occasional malice with which Turgot had no sympathy. Turgot, with a tithe of Voltaire's genius, had a much better balanced moral character, and looked at things in a serious, never in a mocking spirit. It is possible that Voltaire appreciated the presence in Turgot of qualities in which he was himself deficient. At all events, throughout Turgot's whole career, Voltaire paid him constant enthusiastic homage. It was to Turgot, on his retiring from public life, that Voltaire addressed the epistle in verse bearing the title—itself one of the noblest of tributes—'To a Man.'

**Appointed Intendant of Limoges**

He had not long returned to his judicial duties when he received, August 8, 1761, the appointment to a high office of State, the intendancy of the provinces of Limousin, Angoumois, and Basse-Marche (shortly called the 'intendancy of Limoges'). To obtain an intendancy had been the aim Turgot's ambition had in view when he entered the magistracy. He had now obtained it, after nine years' State service, and while still comparatively young—having just turned four-and-thirty.

The position of an intendant, under the old *régime* in France, is thus defined by De Tocqueville: 'The central administration had but a single agent in its province. Nobles were still to be found in the eighteenth century bearing the title of Governor of Provinces; they were the ancient and often hereditary representatives of feudal royalty. Honours were still bestowed upon them, but they no longer had any power. The intendant was in possession of the whole reality of Government. All the powers which the Council of State itself possessed were accumulated in his hands. Like the Council he was at once administrator and judge. He corresponded with all the Ministers, and in the province was the sole agent of all the measures of the Government. . . .' The Marquis d'Argenson relates in his 'Memoirs' that one day Law said to him, 'I never could have believed what I saw, when I was Comptroller of Finance. Do you know that this kingdom of France is governed by thirty intendants? You have neither Parliaments, nor Estates, nor Governors. It is upon thirty Masters of Requests, despatched into the provinces, that their evil or their good, their fertility or their sterility entirely depend.'[1]

A position of this importance and responsibility presented to Turgot the very work that would gratify his earnest and never-resting ambition to do something before he died (and he knew that his life would be a short one) to relieve the misery he saw throughout France, and to help on in some effective manner the world's general advancement. Here was a sphere subject almost to his sole control. What might he not make of it! What schemes of beneficence might he not plan, with the confidence of being able to have them actually carried out!—schemes for the relief of the oppressed peasantry, embracing better remuneration for them, less uncomfortable dwellings, some little leisure, or at least margin of existence, to be given to the mind and the affections, in which they could realise themselves to be human beings, created for a higher purpose than a life of incessant toil to gain a bare subsistence.

It was indeed a great field, and one to test a statesman's capacity, but few men could have entered upon it better equipped than Turgot. We have seen how sedulously he had educated himself for the work he had before him. He had laid his foundation on wide observation of facts, a patient personal observation, for several years, of agricultural life over the most part of France. He had endeavoured from these facts to rise to the knowledge of those economical laws, obedience to which operates for man's happiness, and

[1] De Tocqueville, *L'ancien Régime et la Révolution*, book ii. chap. 2.

disobedience to which operates for his misery. Feeling confident that he knew the remedies for much of the wretchedness of provincial France, and having the good fortune to have power placed in his hands, he determined to make use, unflinchingly, of his whole power, in order to raise the condition of the people committed to his care. We shall see how faithfully, during the thirteen years of his government, this great object was carried out.

# CHAPTER II

1761—1774

## INTENDANT OF LIMOGES

§ 1. THE lines of territorial division throughout France are considerably altered since Turgot's day. In endeavouring, on a modern map, to mark out the 'generality' of which he was appointed administrator, we should not, however, greatly err from the old boundaries by taking the present departments of Haute-Vienne and Corrèze and adding to them a portion (north-east) of Charente. The largest and most important province in the generality was that of Limousin, of which the old historic town of Limoges was the capital, and the office was thus commonly known as the 'intendancy of Limoges.' Contemporary published records, descriptive of the province as it existed in Turgot's time, are rather scanty. The territory and people

A geographical work,[1] dated 1765, specifies its productions: 'The country is in great part covered by forests of chestnut trees. The rest produces rye, buckwheat, and in some places good wine. There are mines of copper, tin, lead, and iron. These last are very abundant. Its commerce consists chiefly in cattle and horses, which are much valued.'

Arthur Young, who travelled through the country in 1787, in his journal dwells with great delight upon its picturesque features. Upon Limoges, the town itself and seat of Government, he remarks: 'June 6. View Limoges, a Roman station, some traces of its antiquity still remaining. It is ill built,

[1] *Dictionnaire géographique de la France.* Paris, 1765.

with narrow and crooked streets, the houses high and disagreeable. They are raised of granite, or with wood with lath and plaster—lime, an expensive article here, being brought from a distance of twelve leagues; the roofs are of pantiles with projecting eaves and almost flat—a sure proof that we have quitted the region of heavy snows.'[1]

As for the condition of the people over whom Turgot was placed as governor, it differed only for the worse from that of the agricultural and industrial classes in France generally. Like other provinces, owing to the miserable appliances in the art of agriculture, and the grievous oppression of a system of taxation, which left the cultivator no saving to form capital, and bereft him of all hope of improvement, Limousin was subject to a chronic state of agricultural distress, varied periodically by acute outbreaks of famine. And of all the provinces of France, Limousin was perhaps the most unfortunate, for its soil was naturally about the poorest.

M. Taine's description of the poor cultivator's life in France may be quoted as applicable here:—

> On the failure of a crop, this portion remains untilled; its occupant is too poor to purchase seed: the intendant is often obliged to distribute seed, without which the disaster of the current year would be followed by sterility the following year. . . . The fields lie fallow one year out of three, and often one year out of two. The implements are poor; there are no ploughs of iron; in many cases the plough of Virgil's time is still in use. . . . The yield is slight.'[2]

The Marquis de Mirabeau reports:—

> In Limousin the basis of food is buckwheat, with chestnuts and radishes. . . . There is no wheat-bread. . . . There is no butcher-meat; at best the farmer kills one pig a year. His dwelling is built of raw clay roofed with thatch, without windows, and the floor is the beaten ground. Their clothes are rags.

An authority of a later date, but whose knowledge was

[1] Arthur Young, *Travels in France*, 1787–89 (ed. 1889), p. 22.
[2] Taine, *Ancien Régime* (English translation), 1876, p. 338.

gathered from family documents and family history of that time, M. Boudet, draws the following impressive picture :—

> On his arrival Turgot found a poor country without cultivation, without trade, without roads, with an ungrateful soil, whose products could scarcely suffice to defray the numerous charges with which the properties were burdened. The taxes, fixed upon an unjust basis, were collected as unsystematically as they were assessed. . . . The pale inhabitants of the country uselessly impoverished the ground, gathering for fruit of their labours only a coarse and black bread as disagreeable to the taste as to the sight. This was their only nourishment during half the year, the chestnuts supplied for the other half. Fortunate for them if this too precarious fruit was not insufficient for their needs, for otherwise the most extreme misery became their lot. The Militia was the scourge of the country which it depopulated, the *corvée*, more odious still, crushed man and beast, and left the fields uncultivated. No activity, no industry, everywhere desolation—crowds of beggars and vagabonds inundated the town and the country places and fatigued one's feeling of pity and sense of sight. Everything in these God-forsaken provinces reflected the image of ignorance and of barbarism in the middle of the eighteenth century.[1]

Such was the state of the province, with a population of about 500,000, subjected to Turgot's administration. Certainly it has few features of an attractive kind. But it is a province that must be administered by some one ; and if he can succeed, amidst such hopeless circumstances, in making it in some measure more productive, and improving, in some degree at least, the condition of its people, he will, besides, have given a needful encouragement to those intendants of France who are less unfortunately placed.

It is, of course, impossible to review adequately even the most important acts of an administration which lasted for thirteen years, and had its every day full of work. The most we can do is to endeavour to form some idea of the spirit in which Turgot accepted his mission, and of some of the means he used to prosecute it.

[1] Quoted by M. Gustave d'Hugues in his *Essai sur l'Administration de Turgot dans la Gén. de Limoges.* Paris, 1859.

Self-instruction on the condition of the province

Bound always, by the necessity of his mind, to possess himself with a clear knowledge of the facts with which he has to deal, one of his first acts is, with that view, to address a circular to his 'sub-delegates' (the officials under his control), specifying the points on which he requires information, while he anxiously endeavours to inspire them with his own earnestness. As the double object of this book is to unfold the character of Turgot by means of his own thoughts impressed directly upon its readers, and to assist them at the same time to form for themselves a picture of the condition of France in his time, I make no apology for quoting largely from documents of his own composition, as well as from other documents, which may illustrate the history of each period.

Do not neglect [he writes to each sub-delegate] to instruct yourself upon the state of agriculture in each parish, the quantity of lands in waste, the reclamation of which these are susceptible, the principal productions of the soil, the object to which the industry of the inhabitants is applied, and any others that might be suggested to them; the place where they can find the best market for their commodities, the state of the roads, and if they are practicable for carts or only for beasts of burden. . . . The position of the locality, the salubrity of the air, the most frequent maladies of men and of animals, and the causes to which these are attributed, are also worthy of your study. You should always listen to the complaints of individuals on all matters. You should endeavour, as far as possible to you, to discover the abuses of every sort by which people may suffer, the disorders in different parts of the administration, grievances more or less characterised, popular prejudices which might be baleful to the tranquillity or to the health of mankind. You could confer on all these subjects with the *curés* of your canton (to whom I have also applied for similar enlightenment), with the nobles and the gentlemen whom you will have occasion to see, with the principal shopkeepers and traders of the canton. . . . I shall be very happy to be acquainted with all persons who are able to give me useful information. You will give me pleasure by indicating to me those in whom you have recognised this ability. You will acquaint yourself carefully, above all, with the physicians, the surgeons, and the charitable persons who concern themselves with medicine, and who distribute remedies to poor sick people. . . .

Officials to be guided by rules of justice

If you meet any men who are distinguished by some special talent, or who show peculiar dispositions for some science or some art, whatever it may be, you will oblige me by not leaving me ignorant of them. I shall seek occasions to employ them, so that their talent may not remain buried.

You will gratify me by taking note of the inhabitants in whom, in the course of your official relations, you observe the most intelligence, and who have the highest reputation for probity. . . .

Although the part of your functions which I have here dwelt upon is connected only in a distant manner with the direct object of your circuit, I feel persuaded that it will become to you more and more valuable, and I doubt not that it will also serve you greatly in conciliating the affection and the confidence of the inhabitants.[1]

Not content with using, for the amelioration of his province, all the machinery belonging to his own administrative office, he sought to enlist the influence of every volunteer agency procurable for the same end, particularly the influence of the district clergy.

Letters to the *Curés*

He had no sympathy with the intolerant feeling towards the clergy so common among the class of 'enlightened' minds of France at that time. He had, indeed, long before this come to recognise no authority but his own conscience and his own judgment on religious matters; but the same tolerance that he claimed for himself he unreservedly allowed to others. Above all, the followers of practical Christianity had always his reverence, however much their minds might be imbued with ideas he could not but consider irrational. He knew that while, as a class, the country clergy of France were miserably educated and grossly superstitious, there were yet many of them of a superior character, and that, even amongst the lowest of them, there were many hard-working, simple-hearted men, their narrow-mindedness being greatly redeemed by an earnest devotion to the poor people of their parish. In this sense Turgot felt they were fellow-workers with himself, and in this spirit he addressed, from time to time, during his intendancy, circulars 'to the *curés* of the

[1] *Œuvres de Turgot* (ed. 1844), i. 510–11, *note.*

Generality of Limoges,' to which allusion is made in the preceding letter. There remain to us five of these circulars, reaching from May 1762 to January 1770, each of them of considerable length.

His first circular to the *curés*[1] is dated May 3, 1762, and opens as follows :—

No one has greater opportunities than the *curés*, by their position, by the special education which that position exacts, and by the confidence which their ministry inspires in the people, to know well the people's situation and the means to render that situation better. The administration ought to have no other end than this, and it is certain that the *curés* could furnish to it much assistance and very valuable enlightenment. They could also render great service to science, to the arts, to commerce, and above all to agriculture, since it is peculiarly within their reach to make a number of observations that necessarily escape the inhabitants of towns. All that would be required of them is to take the trouble of informing either the persons charged with the administration or the bodies which cultivate the sciences of the interesting facts which chance might present to them. The instructions which they could give to the peasantry, in communicating to them the discoveries and the new methods of proved utility, would also be very advantageous to the progress of economic science. Persuaded that their zeal embraces everything tending to the public good, I propose to myself to have often recourse to MM. the *curés*, in order to request of them enlightened information of every kind, or to beg of them to help me in dispensing to their parishioners real justice. I trust then, sir, that you will expect that I shall address myself more than once with confidence to you as well as your brother *curés*, and I hope even that they and you will not content yourselves with a mere reply to me, for I earnestly desire of you to keep me informed directly of all matters on which you might think it useful for me to be instructed. You would also do me a great pleasure by engaging those of your vicars, who might have taste for the different kinds of observations I have spoken of, to make of them a relaxation to themselves, and to communicate them to me. You may be assured that I shall always

[1] 'Those impetuous and peremptory spirits who see in Frederick or Napoleon the only born rulers of men, might find in these letters, and in the acts to which they refer, the memorials of a far more admirable and beneficent type.' (J. Morley, *Crit. Misc.* ii. 137.)

take a delight to distinguish on every occasion, and to oblige those whose correspondence shall have procured for me any useful information. I feel confident that MM. the Bishops cannot but be well pleased that the *curés* should take part in such good work as here presented, and I shall beg of them to be kind enough to give evidence of their satisfaction.

The first thing that I request of you at present is to inform me, or the nearest sub-delegate, of any serious accidents to which your parish is subject, and particularly of any contagious maladies that might spread there among men or even among animals. These occasions require help that cannot be too prompt, and I am able to provide help if I am warned in time.

I have also to ask of you to render a service to your parishioners in regard to the petitions which they are in the practice of presenting to me for different objects. I know that they often apply to MM. the *Curés* to compose these petitions for them. I cannot too highly acknowledge the kindness of those who undertake this care; I beseech of them to continue it. I shall be very happy if *they* would take the trouble of laying these petitions before me, and if they would persuade the peasants not to break off their work, as it often happens, in order to come to me to present the petitions themselves. The audiences which I feel obliged to give them are a loss of time to myself, but I still much more regret the loss of theirs, and the expense that these journeys occasion them. . . . You can, at the same time, assure them that I would not give the least less attention to reply promptly and exactly to the petitions. By means of the expedient I have taken in causing to be registered and numbered in my office all the petitions and the decisions made, it becomes almost impossible for them to be forgotten, and, when granted, to remain without being carried out.

Whatever trouble these particulars which I request may give you, the good which will result from them convinces me that you will with pleasure undertake to furnish them, and I shall be obliged if meanwhile you give me an earnest of your disposition to assist me by kindly acknowledging the receipt of this letter.[1]

This appeal to the *curés* for their co-operation in the work of raising the condition of the poor country-people seems to have been met in the spirit he had hoped for. We find him, six to seven weeks afterwards, addressing to them

[1] *Œuvres de Turgot*, i. 633–51.

a second circular, prefacing it by expressing the 'very great satisfaction' it gave him to see 'the zeal with which MM. the *Curés* gave themselves to the public good.' Alluding to certain memorials and returns he had received upon matters of administration, he remarks: 'I have seen with pain that in some parishes the *curé* has, alone, signed because no one else could write; this excess of ignorance in the people appears to me a great evil, and I exhort MM. the *Curés* to concern themselves with the means of spreading a little more instruction in the country places, and to propose to me such measures as they would judge to be most efficacious.' The rest of the letter is occupied in requesting their assistance for arriving at some improved basis for the assessment throughout the province of that direct tax known as the *taille*.

As the oppression suffered by the people of France under the operation of the *taille* and the *corvées* formed one of the most important factors in the production of the French Revolution, a short study of these two burdens, in their connection with Turgot's work, will not be unprofitable.

The *taille*

§ 2. The *taille*, a personal tax of feudal origin of variable amount, had in the changed conditions of France, under a succession of expensive Governments, become grievously arbitrary and burdensome. It was levied upon the individual by the official authorities of the province, who were guided in fixing the amount merely by their own estimate of his ability to pay it. First, the Comptroller-General of Finances in Paris finds that he requires so many millions for the service of the State, which he will obtain, so much by one channel, so much by another—so much by the *taille*. He divides this lump sum fixed for the *taille* over the several generalities in the kingdom to the best of his arbitrary judgment. He advises each intendant of the amount set down against his province, which will have to be furnished during the coming year. Then the intendant has to act the same part on the smaller scale. In order to make up the lump sum charged against his province, he sets so much down against each parish, and then advises *his* inferiors, the collectors, accordingly. They again have to do their part, in an equally arbitrary way, in their own districts. The immense field here for the play of injustice, vexation, and oppression can be easily imagined.

De Tocqueville informs us: 'The whole sum to be paid by each parish was fixed every three years; it perpetually varied, so that no farmer could foresee a year beforehand what he would have to pay in the year following. In the internal economy of each parish any one of the peasants named as the collector was entrusted with the apportionment of the tax on the rest. The Provincial Assembly of Berri explains the condition of the collector: 'As everyone seeks to evade this office, each person in the parish must fill it in turn. The levy of the *taille* is therefore entrusted every year to a fresh collector, without regard to his ability or his integrity; the preparation of each rôle of assessment bears mark therefore of the personal character of the officer who makes it. The collector stamps on it his own fears, or foibles, or vices. How, indeed, could he do better? He is acting in darkness, for who can tell with precision the wealth of his neighbour or the proportion of his wealth to that of another? Nevertheless the opinion of the collector alone is to decide these points, and he is responsible with all his property and even his person for the receipts. He is commonly obliged for two whole years to lose half his days in running after the taxpayers. Those who cannot read are obliged to find a neighbour to perform the office for them. This unhappy officer,' continues De Tocqueville, 'was armed with the most arbitrary powers; he was almost as much a tyrant as a martyr. Whilst he was discharging functions by which he ruined himself, he had it in his power to ruin everybody else. 'Preference for his relations,' to recur to the language of the Provincial Assembly, 'or for his friends and neighbours, hatred and revenge against his enemies, the want of a patron, the fear of affronting a man of property who had work to give, were at issue with every feeling of justice.' Personal fear often hardened the heart of the collector; there were parishes in which he never went out but escorted by constables and bailiffs. 'When he comes without the constable,' said an intendant to a minister in 1764, 'the persons liable to the tax will not pay.' 'In the district of Ville Franche alone,' says the Provincial Assembly of Guienne, 'there were 106 officers constantly out to serve writs and levy distraints! Under this system of taxation each taxpayer had in fact a direct and permanent interest to act as a spy on his neighbours, and to denounce to the collector the progress of their fortunes. The whole population was thus trained to delation and to hatred.'[1]

The amount of *taille* paid on the average by the small peasant proprietor was about a sixth of his income, after allowing for his mere necessaries of life, and it was only a part of the burden of taxation that pressed upon him. 'The class which was taillable,' says Mr. Lecky, 'and which consisted chiefly of the farmers of the country, paid on an average out of every 100 francs of their net revenue no less than 53 fr. in direct taxation, 14 fr. 28 in tithes, and 14 fr. 28 in feudal duties, leaving less than a fifth part for the support of themselves and their families.'[2]

But the ugliest feature of the *taille* remains to be named. While it bore, with such aggravated severity, upon the poor, hard-working peasantry, it was a tax from which their superiors in rank and wealth were exempted. It was levied on 'all *roturiers* not privileged.' The privileged classes were estimated at 270,000 persons—being nobles 140,000, clergy 130,000. Although possessing the great bulk of the wealth in the country, it was one of their 'privileges' to contribute a mere fraction to the revenue of the State, and while dividing among themselves the greater part of its expenditure.

This hateful tax it was now Turgot's duty to raise from

[1] De Tocqueville, *Ancient Régime and the Revolution* (Eng. trans. 1873), pp. 155–57.

[2] *History of the Eighteenth Century*, i. 380.

his poor province. He never ceased to condemn its iniquity. But it was beyond the power of an intendant to abolish or reform a law of State; the utmost he could do was to administer it with as much fairness and as little injustice as possible.

His first step was to gather material to form some consistent foundation for the assessment of the *taille.* His object was the compiling of a register, to be based on equitable valuations and on a complete survey of the province. The pre-existing state of things is described by Dupont: 'About two-thirds of the province had been surveyed, but no maps had been drawn out. On the simple rough drafts of the surveyors, official reports on the parishes had been made, and abstracts made intended to represent the *quota* of each individual. It was found that, by the mistakes of copyists, these abstracts did not agree with the official reports, and it was impossible, in the absence of maps, and without the original rough drafts, which had not been kept, to know whether the official reports or the relative abstracts deserved the most confidence. Appraisers had been guided by no fixed principles. . . . The inherent inaccuracy of all the parts of this operation was enormously increased by the fact that for twenty-two years no verification had been made, nor any care taken to note the changes of property by successions, sales, exchanges, or abandonment. . . . The other third of the province had not been surveyed at all. The basis of assessment there was the old declarations of the proprietors upon the state and quality of their heritages. . . . The heritages had all varied in this part of the province as in the other, and still less means had been taken to follow the changes of the property. . . . In fine, the most profound ignorance of the real situation of the taxpayers prevailed, not the least reliable element remained to assist the judgment formed on their appeals or their complaints. The intendants, besieged by those who obtained access to them, would yield sometimes to demands always plausible, but the justice of which it was impossible to verify The great majority of the unhappy taxpayers, being unable to get their case heard, or, if heard, unable to have it proved, sank into hopeless discouragement.'[1]

The *taille* partially reformed

But, about four months after he had been appointed intendant, Turgot was successful in obtaining a Declaration of the king (December 30, 1761), in which a foundation was laid for a more regular assessment of the *taille* in his province. Among other reforms made, it cleared away the overlapping of different departments, claiming or disclaiming responsibility, by fixing the responsibility for the supervision of the tax upon certain officials, and it laid down clear and precise rules for the guidance of the returning officers. Much confusion had been caused by the existence of two separate bureaux for the two divisions of the province. In place of this he established a body of commissioners for the whole province (serving under one and the same authority), to each of whom he assigned a small *arrondissement*, and charged him to verify on the spot the real state of the parishes.

His first circular letter to the commissioners for the *taille*, enclosing a copy of the Declaration of the king, is mostly taken up with instructions on matters of detail, now become of little interest; we may, however, give its conclusion: 'I could expatiate on the different means that might be employed in order to perfect the operation of a registered survey (*cadastre*) and valuation of properties, but my object is to request your own reflections, and not to overburden you with mine; I would rather know your own way of thinking than insinuate my own ideas. I will with pleasure receive information, not only from you, but from all well-informed people influenced by love of the public welfare to take an interest in this matter. You will see that I conceal none of my own opinions, but I hold to them only in as far as they appear to me to be practically useful. The more the public can be convinced of their utility, the more the public will be disposed to concur with them in practice,

[1] Dupont, *Œuvres de Turgot*, i. 486, *note.*

and the greater will be my success. For this reason I intend to give to all my operations the very greatest publicity, in order to obviate, if possible, all distrust on the part of the people. I cannot too earnestly beseech you to work in concert with me to inspire the people with this confidence, not only by rendering scrupulous justice in the exercise of your functions, but, still more, by treating the peasants with kindness, by occupying yourselves with their interests and their needs, and by enabling me to succour them.'[1]

Our next available document illustrative of this period is his letter written some six months later to General Bertin, then Comptroller-General, the minister to whom the intendants, in respect to their financial duties, were specially subject. It throws light on the attitude taken by Turgot towards the Government regarding the administration of his province. The letter gives so interesting a view of the existing state of affairs, and is so characteristic of the writer, that we give it without much curtailment.

Angoulême, August 10, 1762.

Letter to the Ministry

SIR,—My mother has written to me that she had the honour to solicit for me from you the intendancy of Lyons. That place would appear to me very desirable in itself; I should gain from it a considerable increase of income, a residence much more agreeable, and, by the difference in the circumstances of the two generalities, a great diminution of work. In any other conjuncture I would not hesitate to join with my mother in soliciting you for the appointment very earnestly. But all these advantages are outweighed by considerations which I mentioned to you when, on a former occasion, you kindly proposed my promotion to Rouen.

You are aware of the situation in which I found the Generality of Limoges. . . . It was in these circumstances that I had the honour to propose to you the Declaration of December 30, 1761, which you had the goodness to sanction. To propose this was to provide myself with much work, and I confess that if I had then known, as distinctly as I know to-day, the excess of disorder in which this system of the *taille tarifée* existed since its establishment, and the immensity of labour necessary, not only to perfect its operation in the future, but to draw out of confusion the

[1] *Œuvres de Turgot*, i. 510.

existing system, I should, perhaps, never have had the courage to undertake the work. . . . I feel more strongly than ever the absolute necessity, if we would establish in this province a just assessment, to save it from a return to the arbitrary *taille*. . . . The difficulties are so great and so numerous that I dare not promise to you that everything shall be perfectly in order this year. I have, however, taken steps to be instructed in all the details which can enable me to form a definitive plan of operation. Such are, Sir, the circumstances in which I now find myself.

I confess that, notwithstanding the trouble the work must give me, I should abandon it with regret. . . . If I renounced it, it would be necessary for my successor to give himself up to the same prolonged study which I have had to make of it, and thus to leave things for a period in a state of forced suspension, always dangerous; or, what is not less so, he would have to decide for some time much at random. If then, as I have ground to hope, you hold to the intention of establishing in Limousin the system of the *taille tarifée* on principles more solid than acted on in the past, I would sacrifice with great pleasure the advantages and the agreeableness to be found in the intendancy of Lyons, and I would beg of you to leave me at Limoges to carry out the work you have allowed me to undertake. . . . Meanwhile I encounter in the execution of the work a difficulty attached to an operation of this nature, which can be overcome only by you—this is the expense. It is essential that all expense should be made at the charge of the Government. . . .

If you are not disposed to grant to me other resources for this operation than a new imposition on the province, the discontent that I foresee would make me wish that I had never been charged with its administration. . . . But, at the same time, I cannot help insisting with you on the wrong that you would be doing to the province by abandoning such an operation after having commenced it. . . . There is no doubt that, if the apportionment of the tax were once acted upon in a province, with the precision of which it is susceptible, the clear advantages that would result from it would dissipate the greater part of the difficulties, and would reduce to silence most of the opposition. Then we could extend the operation into other provinces with the security given by success. It is certain that Government never had an occasion more favourable to make this trial than the one now presented to it in Limousin. The apportionment there is in so anomalous a state that it cannot remain as it is. . . . What is more, the king has just announced by a Declaration the project of this reform. . . . The work I have already done can at least be reckoned as a beginning, and, although you might find in many others greater talents than mine, I presume to say that you will find no one having more zeal and more patience in giving himself up to an unthankful work, in which only the belief in the utility which should result from it can sustain me.

The object of this long letter is to beg of you to enable me to effect all the good of which I believe my province to be capable: this is the only consideration that attaches me to it. But, in the event of your not believing yourself able to give me the necessary help, then I must think of myself, and I would beg of you to solicit for me from the king the intendancy of Lyons.[1]

The province still left overburdened

This firm and disinterested appeal to the minister was favourably received. Twelve more years, comprising the very prime of his life, were devoted to Limoges, years of incessant uphill work. His annual reports to the Government, during the whole period, 'on the assessment of the *taille*' may still be read. The struggle was renewed, each year, of imploring the apathetic ministry to reduce, in some degree, their exactions from the poor province. In his very first report (1762) to the Council of State, he writes: 'All the information I have been able to gather serves but to impress on me the sad certainty of the misery existing here. In the description of it I present to the council I make it a principle to bring forward no fact of which I have not made myself certain; fortunate would it be if this picture could be traced in colours faithful enough to move his Majesty's heart, and if, while I am in these provinces, bearing a title to make his authority respected, I may, at the same time, be able to spread there the proofs of his paternal goodness.'

He proceeds to give evidence that Limousin and Angoumois had lost much of their former prosperity, 'The inhabitants drew formerly, from their soil and their industry, considerable profits, which enabled them to support easily the charges of the State. It is more than probable that the

[1] *Œuvres de Turgot*, i. 511–16.

excessive burden laid upon them in their prosperity has been, more than anything else, the cause of their present misery. But whatever be the cause, it belongs to the justice of his Majesty to grant to them some remission appropriate to their losses.' He concludes by supplicating the king to grant to the generality a reduction of the *taille* of 400,000 livres.

We find, by his next year's report, that he obtained only 190,000. This may serve as an example of every year to come—renewed petitions to the Government to spare an overburdened people, but petitions never granted to anything like an adequate extent. After ten years, we find him in his very last report as intendant, for the year 1774, writing: 'We conclude by repeating, as we have not ceased doing for several years, that, in order to place the province in the just position it ought to hold, it is indispensable to reduce its burden by about 700,000 livres.' This claim for relief he based on the most unquestionable ground. Year after year he had furnished proof that the annual contributions of the province to the State were about equal to the whole revenue of the proprietors of the land, and he urged that, 'in order to restore the taxation of the Generality of Limoges to the same proportion as in the other provinces (which paid to the king not more than a third of their total revenue),' the deduction he claimed was really due. But 'the demand for a permanent reduction of 700,000 francs always remained without response.' [1]

'At the end of thirteen years,' says M. Morley, 'of indomitable toil, the work [of the apportionment] was still unfinished, chiefly owing to want of money for its execution. The Court wasted more in a fortnight on the easy follies of Versailles than would have given to the Limousin the instrument of a finished scheme of fiscal order.' [2]

Turgot, however, was not the man to permit this want of sympathy in the ministry for his oppressed province to dis-

[1] Dupont in *Œuvres de Turgot* (1844), i. 627.
[2] *Crit. Misc.* ii. 120.

hearten him in his general work for its welfare and its improvement. As much as an intendant could possibly do, that at least would be done.

**Emancipation of the tax-collector**

One of his reforms, apparently small regarded by itself, yet so far-reaching in its beneficial effects that it may be counted among his best, was his creation of a new order of provincial tax-collectors. This office, as formerly mentioned, had to be taken, in turn, by the cultivators themselves. The character and position of the collector we have already seen sufficiently described by De Tocqueville. Turgot's reform, as may be predicated from his treatment of similar disorders, consisted in forming a body of officials, set apart for the particular work. By uniting in the same *arrondissement* six or eight parishes, a moderate percentage on the collections was found sufficient to remunerate a qualified man.

**The *corvée***

The most glaring abuse that existed in the agricultural districts of France was the institution of the *corvée*, the forced employment of the peasantry, and without payment, upon the making and repairing of the roads. Each province having the management of its own roads, Turgot was able here to achieve for Limousin a reform which, had it been followed by the other intendants over the kingdom, would have saved France from incalculable turmoil.

The principle of the *corvée* belonged to feudal times. Among the exactions of the lord from his villeins was included their obligation to render to him a certain number of days' or weeks' labour without payment. That labour would often be employed upon such roads as existed within the lord's domains. As civilisation advanced, the kingdom became intersected by a few great roads—the 'highways'—between certain important points, which were maintained at the king's expense. When the necessity came for branch roads throughout the country, in order to communicate with the king's highway, the intendants, having no funds at their disposal, unfortunately resorted to demanding from the local peasantry contributions of their labour for this purpose, defending the act as accordant with ancient usage, the king, whom they represented, having succeeded to the rights of the feudal lord. 'This expedient,' says De Tocqueville, 'for making roads without paying for them was thought so ingenious that in 1737 a circular of the Comptroller-General Orry established it throughout France. The intendants were armed with the right of imprisoning at pleasure the refractory, or of sending constables after them.'[1]

It seems almost incredible that, not much more than a century ago, a system so senseless, so extravagant, so oppressive, and in every sense so pernicious as the *corvée* could have existed. Its inherent vices were exposed by the elder Mirabeau in his 'Lettres sur les Corvées' (1760) in so thorough a manner that the system stood condemned ever after in the mind of every thinking man. The propositions which Mirabeau undertook to prove were indeed almost self-evident: that society should be served at the least expense, and with the least possible loss to its members; that men engaged in agriculture (a work so important for society) cannot have their time, as well as their horses or oxen, carts, &c., taken up with other work, without discouraging their operations on the farm and effecting a loss in their harvest greater than the value of their labour on the roads; that men who have just travelled three or four leagues, lose a part of their time on the way; that men who are not paid, work without energy; that men who have no regular practice at a handiwork, perform it ill, &c.

The crowning injustice of this institution was that it set a burden on the back of the poor peasants, whose lot was already wretched enough, for the sake of a work from which they derived very little advantage. The 'privileged classes,' that is to say, the principal landowners, &c., though more interested than any in the construction of the roads, contributed nothing to the *corvée*. 'Nothing can better demonstrate the melancholy fate of the rural population. The progress of society, which enriched all other classes,

[1] De Tocqueville (Eng. ed.), p. 160.

drove them to despair, and civilisation itself turned against that class alone.'[1]

But this exemption of the privileged classes, Turgot, being but an intendant of a province, could not touch. Ten years afterwards, as Comptroller-General, when he gained the consent of the king to abolish the *corvée* throughout all France, he was bold enough to call upon the 'privileged' to bear their share in the necessary taxation—an act which they never forgave, and for which his overthrow was to be their revenge. His mode of dealing with the *corvée*, in his own province, was a very simple one, but it was the beginning of a revolution. He put competent workmen on the roads, had them sufficiently superintended, paid them a fair wage, and defrayed the charges by a moderate tax on the ratepayers. The incidence of the tax was necessarily unjust, but the peasants could, at all events, now give all their time to make the most of their poor holdings.[2] The roads of Limousin became roads indeed. As a contrast to the other roads of the kingdom, they were the wonder of all travellers, and, like all good roads, their characteristic was their durability.

The *corvée* abolished in the province

Laharpe writes at this time to the Grand Duke of Russia: 'A benefit which will cause the name of Turgot to be blessed by succeeding generations is the abolition of the *corvées*. These are deeds on which we do not compose an ode, as on a battle gained, but which are worth more than victories.'[3]

[1] De Tocqueville, p. 160.

[2] We are told by Dupont that Turgot was his own chief engineer. In all states of the weather he was out, seeing the work planned and executed under his own eyes.

[3] Laharpe, *Correspond. litt.* x. p. 75. Not only were the old roads permanently improved, but 160 leagues of new roads were constructed. More than twenty years afterwards Arthur Young, passing through the district, notes in his journal: 'The roads through this country are truly noble, far beyond anything I have seen in France or elsewhere.' As he proceeds on his way: 'the road is incomparably fine, and much liker the well-kept alleys of a garden than a common highway'; and again at another stage—'the finest road in the world, everywhere formed in the most perfect manner.' (A. Young, *Travels* (ed. 1889) p. 23.)

*Corvée* of military transports

He had followed up his abolition of the *corvée* for the roads in Limousin by the abolition of another *corvée*—that of the military transports. It was the same in principle as the other. On the occasions of the movements of troops through the province the farmers were compelled to supply the necessary wagons or oxen, for their transport, at a very unremunerative rate. This obligation, it can be easily understood, was at certain seasons of the year a serious interruption to their farmwork. His letter to the Comptroller-General (April 19, 1765), in which he very earnestly represents their case, is a good example of his thoughtful manner of dealing with matters of detail, as well as of his ever-ready sympathy for those he considers to be suffering injustice. It never occurs to him that, as a Government official, he will be expected to defend things as they are. 'The payment,' he states, 'for the use of the horses (20 sous each) has no proportion to the charge borne upon their owners. The journeys are from five to eight leagues, and there are some of from ten to twenty leagues. It is necessary to reckon three days to go to the *rendez-vous*, to make the transport, and to return. The horses must be accompanied by a conductor, to bring them back. Every item of expense is far beyond the payment given. It is about the fourth part of what is really due, and the excess is really an imposition. The burden upon the farmers is infinitely increased by the want of time and of liberty to arrange for it. A contractor has made his calculations and his arrangements before concluding his bargain. His horses and his wagons have no other destination, and the wages paid him are a gain to him; but an unfortunate peasant, whose horse is required from him at the time he has need of it for his work, or his harvest, would be far from being compensated, even by the gain the contractor would accept. Now, the service of the transport of troops is made at all times; the seasons the most important for the work of the farm form no exception. It is above all in the districts where oxen, instead of horses, are used [as in Limousin] for work and carriage that these inconveniences are most felt. These animals are feebler and slower than horses, and much more subject to the accidents of a long route. . . . It is not uncommon for them to die on such heavy journeys. It results that everyone tries to escape from this *corvée*. . . . Those nearest to the place of departure suffer for others. . . . Pardon me for giving so many details in order to demonstrate a thing, the evidence for which is almost sufficient at first sight, but it appears as if the Government has been, for a long time, ignorant how important it is not to sacrifice the liberty of the king's subjects to the exactions and caprices of private interests. There is no part of the administration which has not fallen into this fault, actuated by a most unintelligent idea of economy. I hold that it is most advantageous for the Government to pay for everything in money, because by that method only they know how much exactly an operation costs, and because, by that means, it will always cost infinitely less. Expenditure in money is always taken out of the Revenue, expenditure in kind diminishes often the very source of wealth. Expenditure in money spreads itself over all the king's subjects, in proportion to their means; expenditure in kind strikes exceptionally at individuals, and attacks liberty, which is certainly the most precious property of all.'[1]

He was allowed to make the reform he recommended, and it was carried out with conspicuous success. He made arrangements with a contractor to do gladly and expeditiously the transport work that had been done by the peasant farmers unwillingly and dilatorily. The service was in every way better done, and did not cause a quarter of the loss under the old system.

He had, afterwards, the satisfaction to legalise for the whole kingdom this improvement first introduced into his own province.

§ 3. Hitherto his reforms had been of methods of provincial taxation. These had been framed in the interest

[1] *Œuvres de Turgot*, ii. 98–105.

of the agriculturists, the bulk of his own people, and no class had been especially interested in opposing them. On the question now to be mentioned, he had against him, not only the important interests which are always wedded to things as they are, but (and this caused him more vexation) he had also against him the prejudice and the short-sighted selfishness of his own agricultural population, for whose relief he had fought so earnestly and so constantly.

Freedom of the corn trade

It has been almost forgotten that the great politico-economical question which agitated our own kingdom in 1840–46—*the freedom of the corn trade*—was prefigured in great degree in the history of France three-quarters of a century before. Although the question took action on a smaller scale, and belonged more to internal than to external trade, yet in the discussion of it really the same principles were involved, and doubtless it was clearly seen by Turgot and others that if Free Trade be the right policy between one parish and another, one canton and another, one province and another, it must also be (as he clearly demonstrated) the right policy between one nation and another.

There were few provinces in France free from periodical famines, and, as we have already mentioned, Limousin was subject to these oftener than any other province. Turgot, believing that, at all events, a mitigation of them would be found in a perfectly free circulation of corn throughout the kingdom, before and during the occurrence of scarcity, obtained a Declaration of the king (May 25, 1763) which established this liberty. This was followed by an edict of July 1764, having the same object. But the harvest in the province this year proving to be a short one, although better in some places than in others, discontents arose among the people of certain districts when they saw some supplies of grain leaving their district for another. They feared a consequent rise, and claimed that the good fortune of their own harvest should be for themselves, instead of going to the mitigation of the general scarcity. By stopping the transport of corn they wished to make it abundant and cheap at their own door, not troubling themselves with the reflection how they would stand when *their* time of scarcity came.

The prevalence of these discontents gave him considerable trouble. He at once took steps to allay them as much as possible. He caused to be reissued the Declaration of 1763 and edict of 1764, and widely circulated them throughout the province, along with copies of a pamphlet by M. Letrosne (entitled 'The Liberty of the Corn Trade always useful and never hurtful'). These were accompanied by a letter to the officers of police of Limoges, in which he, with great patience, endeavours to enlist their influence, in order to impress on the people the principle—as elementary in economical as in moral science—that we should do to others as we would that they, in like circumstances, should do to us; it was dated:

**Limoges, February 15, 1765.**

. . . The work of M. Letrosne shows, with as much clearness as force, the wisdom and utility of these laws [establishing freedom in the trade] in all times and in all circumstances. I do not doubt that, impressed, like the author, by the beneficent principles which dictated the well-devised law establishing the full liberty of commerce in corn, you will make it a duty and a pleasure to aid in spreading the same conviction among all minds. The means to succeed in this is to reply with suavity, and in detail, to the popular complaints you every day hear; to speak more in the language of reason than in that of authority; to suggest to the *curés*, to the men of distinction, to all persons who, by virtue of their social or intellectual position, are enabled to influence the people in their way of thinking, that they should read the work of M. Letrosne, of which I send you several copies with that view, in order that, persuaded themselves, they may work in concert with you to persuade others.

Without entering into the principles which M. Letrosne develops with so much clearness, it is sufficient to refer to simple common sense in order to see that all harvests are not equal; that corn being in the same places sometimes very abundant, and at other times very scarce, and in the same years deficient often in one canton, while in others there is much more than can be consumed, subsistence can only be sustained, in those years and in those cantons in which wheat is deficient, by the wheat which may be transported from the places where it is more abundant, or by what has been saved from the harvest of better years.

It is necessary, then, that the transport and the storage of grain should be entirely free, for if the inhabitants of a particular town arrogate the right to prevent the grain going elsewhere, the other towns will believe themselves to have the same right, and thus the places where the dearth is greatest, not being succoured by the others, will be condemned to suffer famine. Also, if merchants who form magazines of wheat are exposed to the insults, to the violences, of the populace; if the magistrates by their suspicions, by imprudent inquisitions, by injunctions to sell at a low price, sanction the popular prejudice against this commerce; if they who undertake it cannot count on a sure profit to recompense them for the charges of storing, of waste, of the interest on their money, no one will give himself to it. The surplus grain of abundant years will be dissipated and be entirely lost for the years of scarcity. This is what was actually seen to occur when the hindrances placed by the police to the commerce in grain existed. There was in France a famine almost every ten years, while in England, where the commerce was not only free but encouraged, there happened scarcely one in a hundred years.

What design have the people in their blind excitement? That the merchants should be obliged to sell cheap? That they should be forced to lose? In this case who would bring grain to them? The pavements of the towns would not produce it. Soon, in places of mere scarcity, a famine would ensue.

In the villages, where the proprietors of the lands in the neighbourhood gather at times the products of their harvest—there the popular cry is most heard. But, if this cry were listened to, if we forced the proprietors to sell at a less price than they could obtain for their grain in places where it was scarcer, then, in depriving those who most suffered by the scarcity of the succour they had the right to expect, the proprietors would be deprived of their wealth, of their income, and thus, by diminishing the value of harvests, all agriculture would be discouraged.

When we shall have enjoyed for some years this precious liberty, when the corn trade shall become the object of the enterprise of a large number of merchants, when agencies shall be established, stores multiplied—then we shall enjoy all the advantages of this new commerce, and then we will acknowledge them.

The price of grain, maintained at a reasonable rate, equally distant from extreme dearness and extreme cheapness, will excite cultivation, will assure the rent of land, will procure for artisans wages in better proportion to their needs.

This is the end you have to aim at, which you must hasten, by combating, in the first instance, the effect of the old popular prejudices, enfeebling them by sound argument, and, above all, by employing all the strength of the administration and of justice to protect against every kind of attack the liberty which the laws have guaranteed to every man engaged in this commerce.[1]

His vigour in protecting the corn-merchants, and in adopting at the same time every means to disseminate just ideas among the people to counteract their ignorance and prejudice, succeeded (for the time) in gradually calming the effervescence in the province, and allowing its provisioning to be made in a manner peaceful and effective. But we have not heard the last of *la liberté du commerce des grains*. The question came up again and again in the province, and we shall see it breaking out, on a more extensive ground, and presenting some new aspects, when Turgot has become Minister of Finance.

**Famine in the province**

He had been intendant about eight years when a crisis occurred which put to the severest trial his capacity as a ruler, his prudence and his moral strength. The crisis involved questions of greater magnitude than the *taille* or the *corvée*, or even Free Trade, for it was a matter literally of life or death—in 1770 and 1771 a FAMINE devastated the province.

In his report of September 17, 1769, 'on the assessment of the *taille*, to be fixed for the following year, he renews his appeal for a considerable reduction of the amount, giving four substantial reasons in his justification. The last one is: 'The bad harvest the province has just had, and the fears too well founded that it may have to endure a famine.' In his next year's report we find how terribly these fears had been confirmed :—

[1] *Œuvres de Turgot*, i. 664–72.

Everyone has heard of the terrible dearth that has just afflicted this generality. The harvest of 1769 in every respect proved to be one of the worst in the memory of man. The dearths of 1709 and 1739 were incomparably less cruel. To the loss of the greatest part of the rye was added the total loss of the chestnuts, of the buckwheat, and of the Spanish wheat—cheap food stuffs with which the peasant sustained himself habitually a great part of the year, reserving as much as he could of his corn, in order to sell it to the inhabitants of the towns. . . . The people could exist only by exhausting their resources, by selling at a miserable price their articles of furniture and even their clothes. Many of the inhabitants have been obliged to disperse themselves through other provinces to seek work or to beg, leaving their wives and children to the charity of the parishes. It has been necessary for the public authority to require the proprietors and inhabitants in better circumstances in each parish to assess themselves for the relief of the poor people; nearly a fourth of the population is dependent upon charitable contributions. After these melancholy sufferings which the province has already undergone, and with the reduced condition in which it was left by the dearth of last year, even had the harvest of the present year been a good one, the poverty of the inhabitants would have necessitated the greatest efforts to be made for their relief. But we have now to add the dismal fact of our harvest being again deficient. . . . We can scarcely think without shuddering of the fate that menaces this part of the province, already so cruelly exhausted by the misfortunes of the past year.[1]

Measures for relief

To mitigate the sufferings induced by this dreadful calamity, his whole energy was called forth. Every means of relief at his command, or within his reach, was at once turned to account. He obtained from the Government, besides a remission of the provincial taxes, some direct assistance in money. This gave him breathing-time to organise a scheme, to be acted upon by the province for its own relief.

He called together for this purpose an assembly of the proprietors, of all men in easy circumstances and all those known to be charitably inclined. To save long and useless discussions, he submitted to them a programme of operations

[1] *Œuvres de Turgot*, i. 590–96.

and of ready-made instructions for the Government agents and the *curés*, which was speedily sanctioned. It was to the effect that—

1. The authorities in each parish, by a house-to-house visitation, were to make up a roll of the really necessitous people. Means were first taken to clear the province of those not belonging to it. This was not done harshly; the 'strangers' moved on having assistance given to carry them to their own parish, and those unfit to travel being sent to the hospital. To obviate overlapping of charities, every form of begging was rigidly suppressed, and the income of established charitable institutions was gathered into the general fund.

2. Boards of Charity were established for the management of each district. The Boards began with a voluntary assessment. But this had to be supplemented by a compulsory tax, by the authority of the intendant, on those who had not volunteered contribution, and on the 'absentees,' 'privileged or not privileged.'

3. Charitable works were opened, suitable for giving employment to all men, women, and children really destitute. A condition was that these works must be useful. They provided mostly for unskilled labour, such as making and repairing the ramparts and streets of the towns, or the roads in the country. As far as possible the labourers were arranged into family groups, 'in which the father employs each according to his strength, and watches and checks each of his co-workers better than the most vigilant overseer.' Special bakeries, eating-houses, and general stores were opened for supplying all articles of necessity at the lowest possible price. Piecework was the rule, and instead of money the workers were paid in tokens, interchangeable for provisions, &c. These tokens could circulate only between the workers and these special establishments and the Board of Charity who retired them. No tokens could be cashed to keepers of *cabarets* (public-houses) or to any private person. Soup kitchens of the modern kind were not allowed. 'It is not intended to assemble the poor in order to give them dis-

tributions of soup or bread or other aliments; these distributions have the defect of accustoming the people to mendicity. It is, besides, very difficult to preserve order in them and to avoid the abuse of double almsgiving, for people without claim can slip through with the crowd,' &c.

4. Arrangements were made to employ picked women and girls in clothesmaking and general serving work for the poor workers, and in teaching sewing to those ignorant of it. Ladies of independent means were asked to act their part also in the circumstances. 'As it is not usual for ladies to attend the parochial meetings, the *curés*, each in his own parish, can arrange for a particular assembly to which shall be invited the ladies who have no husband or representative in any of the Boards, in order to assist in the work of charity.'

Les pauvres honteux

Turgot's sympathetic consideration for a particular class of the indigent is shown in the following instruction: 'We know that there are some who have only temporary needs, occasioned by unforeseen circumstances, but whose necessity is not made known. Public charity would degrade them in some respect below the position which they have held, and many of them would rather suffer the severest misery than be assisted in that way. This class of poor is very common in the larger towns. Their just delicacy ought to be gently dealt with. It is not possible to include them in the rolls, yet it is desirable that they should receive assistance. There does not appear to be any other means of meeting this difficulty than to set aside out of the general income of the Board a particular fund for the relief of the *pauvres honteux* and to entrust its distribution to the *curés*, or through them to one or two members of the Board, who will keep their own counsel.'[1]

The selfish classes summarily dealt with

His energetic measures dealing with the famine were threatened to be thwarted, or, at all events, rendered much less effective, by two causes to which allusion must now be made. These were: The obstructions still made to the circulation of corn, and the selfishness of certain of the land-

[1] *Œuvres de Turgot*, ii. 12.

lords, in exacting undue rents, and neglecting to bear their share in relieving the prevalent misery. But these difficulties he encountered with unmistakable firmness. The existence of the people under his care was beset with such serious danger, that, in the steps he felt compelled to take, he did not scruple to exceed, in some degree, his legal powers as intendant.

A decree of the Parliament of Bordeaux (January 17, 1770) had forbidden proprietors to sell their corn elsewhere than in the local markets, and imposed on them the obligation to supply these with a 'sufficient quantity' each week. He at once secured an order in Council cancelling this decree. He repressed by the same means a similar abuse of authority on the part of the municipal officers of the town of Turenne, and summoned to the bar of the Council, to answer for his conduct, the lieutenant of police of Angoulême, who had followed this example.[1]

Those landlords who neglected to bear their share in the relief of distress were thus plainly told their duty: 'It has sometimes happened that in times of difficulty, when the cultivators (*métayers*) have not had a sufficient harvest for their subsistence, the landlords, to save themselves from claims being made upon them, have turned the unfortunate labourers adrift, doubtless in the hope that they would find resources in the public charities when, struck down by misery, they had exhausted themselves in the hardest works, increasing the value of the lands of their masters, who owe all they possess to the labour of these poor people. If these labourers, abandoned by their masters, were to be included in the roll of those under the charge of the present Board of Charity, this item alone would absorb a great part of the funds. Nothing could be more unjust. The labourers must find resources in the advances from, or in the gratuitous assistance of, their *masters*, who owe to them this support not less on the score of charity than on that of justice, and as landlords, for their own interest, rightly understood.'

[1] Daire, in *Œuvres de Turgot*, ii. 2.

And by his ordonnance issued February 28, 1770, he proclaims that: 'For these causes we order that the proprietors of domains, of whatever quality or condition they may be, privileged or not privileged, shall be held to keep and to maintain, until the next harvest, the labourers whom they had on October 1 last, as well as their families, men, women, and children.'[1]

The precarious condition of the poor *métayers* was aggravated by the rent of most of them being payable in *grain*. This mode of payment became an impossibility, for, owing to the wretched harvest, there was not grain enough even for the tenant's own consumption. The landlords then demanded the money value of the measure of grain fixed at the existing market price. This famine-price of grain was four times the average. The landlords were requiring no more than their legal right, and they upheld the principle of the inviolability of contract. But Turgot considered that Justice had her claims as well as Law, and even, in some cases, before Law.

Justice preferred to Law

But he might well have been doubtful of the Council of State's consenting to promulgate a new law affecting the rights of property, for the special benefit of his own province and its peasantry; at all events, he knew that, even if he succeeded in obtaining such a reformed law, there would necessarily be such a waste of circumlocution, and such a lapse of time before the law could operate, that meanwhile the poor tenants would be brought to ruin. He thus felt himself driven to take an unusual course. His earnest will contrived a way.

In concert with the Procureur-Général of Bordeaux, it was arranged to search out, and turn to account, an almost forgotten Royal Declaration of October 8, 1709, allowing,

[1] Alluding to Turgot being commonly called a *doctrinaire*, Michelet observes: 'Quite on the contrary I see in his intendancy of Limoges, and above all in his ministry, that he very often set himself free to consult facts only, and took, on such occasions, steps that the economists would never have approved.' (*Hist. de France*, Louis XVI.)

rather vaguely, some discretion to the parliaments, in certain cases, to 'ordain as required by local circumstances.' The Procureur-Général was successful in getting the Parliament of Bordeaux to sanction a decree regulating the grain-rents for 1770 by the price current during the month of August of the previous year. At this selected month the scarcity had reached only its first stage, and the price then, although much above the average of past years, was considerably below the famine-rates succeeding. Turgot despatched a copy of this decree to the Council, imploring them to sanction his own action in accordance with it. In his letter addressed to the Chancellor (May 14, 1770) he calls upon the Government to use the law, not to the aggression of the strong, but in defence of the weak. 'In times of scarcity it is humane, and even just, to bring the law to the assistance of the overburdened tenant. The proprietor whom the scarcity enriches cannot, without showing most odious greed, attempt to draw, from the cruel circumstances in which his tenant is now placed, a profit still more exorbitant than before.[1]

A large part of the intendancy was not subject to the rule of the Parliament of Bordeaux, but to that of Paris. However, it does not appear that the Government called in question the stretch of authority taken by him in the circumstances.

The bakers of Limoges at this time wished to raise the price of bread above the proportion indicated by the price of wheat. He suspended their exclusive privileges by permitting anyone to bring bread and sell it in that town. It arrived from all quarters. Experience at once confirmed the wisdom of his act.[2]

'Red-tape' practices not tolerated

There was one other obstacle to his effective administration of the work of charity which he was compelled to overcome, also in rather a high-handed manner—an obstacle presented by officers of a Government department. It is wonderful how the routine of stolid officialism asserts itself in all ages, demanding absolute obeisance to its fetish of

[1] *Œuvres de Turgot*, ii. 71. [2] Dupont, *Œuvres de Turgot*, i. 99.

red tape. All the documents of the Board of Charity, issued as they were in the process of relieving the distressed poor, were declared to be subject to taxation. They should have been written on *stamped* paper! The claims of the Exchequer were duly lodged against the Board. We may readily imagine the height of Turgot's indignation. He at once boldly published an ordonnance (March 7, 1770) suspending in this respect the stamp-laws.

The difficulties at last overcome

At last he is able to report to the Comptroller-General (November 15, 1771) that the province has, for the most part, found its way out of its worst troubles, and he lays before his chief the *compte rendu* of 'operations relative to the Famine.' Never, assuredly, has a work of its magnitude—one which, in other hands, might so easily become a national disaster—been carried through by so moderate an expenditure of money.

We can do little more than glance at some of his many other reforms carried out in Limousin.

Disturbances at the militia-drawing

The periodical excitements and serious disturbances in the province at each drawing for the militia were among the early difficulties he had to encounter. Owing to bad management in the whole system, to the numerous and most invidious exemptions from service of the privileged classes and all their dependents, and to the very miserable pay of the men unfortunate enough to be drawn, the militia service in the provinces was thoroughly detested. The circumstances were alluded to afterwards by himself in his letter to the Minister of War, January 1773: 'The repugnance to service in the militia was so spread among the people, that each drawing was the signal for the greatest disorders throughout the country, and for a kind of civil war between the peasantry; the one party seeking to escape the drawing, taking refuge in the woods, the other, with arms in hand, pursuing the fugitives, in order to capture them and subject them to the same lot with themselves. Loss of life and minor outrages were common. Depopulation of many of the parishes, with cultivation abandoned, often followed. When the time came to assemble the battalions, it was necessary for the syndics of the parishes to lead on their militia-men escorted by the horse-police, and sometimes bound with cords.'[1]

With his characteristic good sense, he began his reform by forbidding the country people, under severe penalties, to pursue the fugitives, thereby at once checking a fruitful source of disorder. Before the next drawing he wrote to the *curés* to impress upon their parishioners that no fugitive whatever would be allowed to escape; that they would, by the authorities, be sought out in all the villages and towns of the province the same day; that they would be described and pursued into all the neighbouring provinces; that thus for those who dreaded belonging to the militia their greatest danger would be to flee, but that, if the lads would themselves come forward and with good grace, he would do everything in his power to mitigate their obligations. Consequently he took upon himself the responsibility of modifying the order by which those about to draw the ballot were forbidden to form a purse among them for him on whom the lot would fall; he allowed this voluntary contribution, and the attraction of the money reduced greatly the fear that the black billet inspired. It even often happened that lads volunteered to serve for the sake of the subscription. Turgot's firmness with the fugitives, and his accommodating disposition towards the others, revived the spirits of the young men, so that the position of a militia-man, which was at first the object of hatred, became in time a post gladly held.[2]

Billeting

Another improvement in the military system of the province he did something to advance. The practice of billeting the soldiers upon the inhabitants was, by its very nature, bad, both economically and morally.[3] He made head against the evil with what means he had. He rented several houses

[1] *Œuvres de Turgot*, ii. 128.

[2] Dupont, i. 105.

[3] A practice in use in Scotland down even to 1857!

and built others to serve as barracks in the principal halting-places in the country. The expense, being divided among all the ratepayers of the province, was much less felt, and the improvement in discipline was so evident that few felt a grudge in paying their share.

Agricultural improvement

No question had more interest for him as an economist, and none more occupied his mind and heart when intendant and minister, than that of agricultural improvement. He inaugurated the improvement in his own province by instituting the Royal Society of Agriculture of Limoges, of which he was naturally elected the president. 'The Society offered each year a prize on some subject relative to the practical utility of rural economy, and Turgot added to that a prize, from himself, on some subject of Political Economy, or on some function of the Administration, with which the success of agriculture was concerned.'

This was one of the earliest societies of the kind, and preceded the Bath and West of England Society by at least twelve years. One of his chief aims was to remedy, by the introduction of clover, lucern, and sainfoin, the natural deficiencies of Limousin in good pasture land; he procured considerable quantities of the seeds of these plants, distributed them to the three Bureaux of Agriculture, and through them to the most intelligent cultivators, with most excellent effect.[1]

He earned the distinction of making known to the peasantry the potato, and of establishing its culture in the province. But great difficulties had first to be overcome. There was the usual prejudice against a 'foreign' article. Buckwheat and chestnuts, uncertain as their harvest was, long kept their hold as the traditional food of the country. Condorcet tells us: 'The people at first regarded the potato with disdain and as beneath the dignity of the human species, and they were not reconciled to it till the intendant had caused it to be served at his own table, and to the first class of citizens, and had given it vogue

[1] Dupont, i. 126.

among the fashionable and rich.'[1] During the dearth of 1770 and 1771 he circulated widely among the people particular instructions upon the culture of the potato, we are told, 'according to the Irish method.'

Veterinary science

As an accompaniment to agricultural improvement he urged upon the farmers the importance to them of some knowledge of veterinary science—a matter, in those days, not so self-evident as it is now. He sent several pupils to the Veterinary School of Lyons, and afterwards established them as teachers in a similar school which he set up in Limoges.

Medical assistance for the poor

Medical assistance for the poor, and especially for married women at the most critical period of their life, was lamentably deficient in Limousin. He brought to Limoges Mme. de Coudray, an instructed and experienced *sage-femme*, guaranteed her a respectable position, enabled her to pass advanced courses at Limoges, at Tulle, and at Angoulême.

He encouraged other select women to join these classes of instruction, and arranged to settle in different parts of the province those who had gained most distinction. This was the origin of the 'Hospice de la Maternité.'[2]

Visits to Paris

§ 4. Although during the thirteen years of his intendancy he remained almost constantly at his post, it was necessary that he should visit Paris from time to time, if only to receive instructions from Government. On one of these visits, or more likely on a special one, he had the intense satisfaction of taking part, as a member of the High Court, in reversing the iniquitous sentence passed by the Court of Toulouse on the family of Calas, the Protestant martyr.

Meeting with Adam Smith

On another of his visits he made the acquaintance of Adam Smith, and this soon ripened into a real friendship. Professor Dugald Stewart gives us the date, and some particulars, of this interesting occurrence. Adam Smith, with the Duke of Buccleuch, had set out for the Continent in March 1764. After ten or twelve days in Paris, they proceeded to the South of France and to Switzerland. 'About

[1] Condorcet, *Life of Turgot* (Eng. trans.), p. 47.

[2] Dupont, i. 104.

Christmas 1765,' says Stewart, 'they returned to Paris and remained there till October following. The society in which Mr. Smith spent those ten months may be conceived from the advantages he enjoyed in consequence of the recommendations of Mr. Hume.' Then follows a list of distinguished men with whom Smith made acquaintance, Turgot being the first mentioned. Professor Stewart, speaking doubtless from knowledge derived from Smith himself, then relates: 'The satisfaction he enjoyed in the conversation of Turgot may be easily imagined. Their opinions on the most essential points of political economy were the same; and they were both animated by the same zeal for the best interests of mankind. The favourite studies too of both had directed their inquiries to subjects on which the understandings of the ablest and the best informed are liable to be warped to a great degree by prejudice and passion; and on which, in consequence, a coincidence of judgment is peculiarly gratifying.'[1]

Publication of the 'Réflexions'

The intercourse of Turgot with Adam Smith, and at the date mentioned, is of almost an historical importance, taken in connection with the fact that it was in 1766 that Turgot published his 'Réflexions sur la Formation et la Distribution des Richesses.' Smith was then forty-three; Turgot thirty-nine. Stewart informs us that Smith's thoughts 'appear to have been occasionally turned towards political economy from a very early period of life.' It was the same with Turgot. In 1752–53 Smith began delivering his course of Lectures on Moral Philosophy, into the last part of which, on the political institutions relating to commerce, he introduced many of the ideas he afterwards expanded in his celebrated work on the 'Wealth of Nations,' published in 1776. Turgot's first essay on Political Economy (on Paper-money) was written in 1749. Before 1755, at all events, he had joined the Economists, and was soon afterwards ranked among their leaders. 'His Éloge de Gournay' was published in 1759. Professor Stewart, speaking of this visit of Smith to France seven years later, remarks:—

[1] *Account of the Life and Writings of Adam Smith*, Sect. III.

Whatever were the lights that these travels afforded to him as a student of human nature, they were probably useful in a still greater degree in enabling him to perfect that system of political economy of which he had already delivered the principles in his lectures at Glasgow, and of which it was now the leading object of his studies to prepare for the public. The coincidence between some of these principles and the distinguishing tenets of the French economists, who were at that very time at the height of their reputation, and the intimacy in which he lived with some of the leaders of that sect, could not fail to assist him in methodising and digesting his speculations.

Pioneer in Political Economy

As Turgot's work on the 'Formation and Distribution of Wealth' first appeared in Dupont's 'Éphémérides du Citoyen,' in 1766, it was thus coincident, or nearly coincident, with the intercourse in Paris between Adam Smith and himself. At all events it, or the greater part of it, must have existed in manuscript about that time, and it is not unlikely that it formed the basis of discussion between the two economists.

The 'Réflexions' obtained some celebrity and passed through four editions. It was the most important work written by Turgot during his Limoges period. Our review of this period would not be complete without including some account of this, and of his other writings of interest that belonged to it.

A vanity natural to some of his admirers belonging to his own nation has led them to claim for Turgot the authorship of *the* original work on Economical Science, of which the 'Wealth of Nations' ten years later was, they say, an expansion. But this claim has no foundation, and no one would have discountenanced it more than Turgot himself. The 'Réflexions' was an unpretending essay of little more than eighty printed octavo pages, written for the instruction of two Chinese youths, then pursuing their studies in Paris. There was little in it of the character of a treatise; it consisted merely of a series of propositions embodying the main principles of Quesnay's system, presented in a very succinct form. Dr. J. K. Ingram, a very able writer on Political

Economy, and the latest biographer of Turgot in this country, makes this very just estimate of the work :—

> It gives, in brief compass, a luminous statement of some of the most important principles relating to the economic constitution of societies—the division of labour ; the origin and use of money ; the nature of capital and the different modes of its employment ; the necessary rise of capitalist chiefs of industry ; the legitimacy of interest and loans ; and the impossibility of arbitrarily fixing the rate of that interest. It unfortunately contains, along with many truths, the erroneous doctrines of the physiocrats on the exclusive productiveness of agriculture, and on the consequent propriety of imposing taxes only on the land of a country. . . . It is, in fact, not a work of research but of exposition, and, regarded in this light, has real originality, and may justly be pronounced a masterpiece.[1]

The 'physiocratic' system

The 'physiocratic' system, as the doctrine of the French economists was named by Dupont de Nemours, was a reaction against the 'mercantile' system, according to which the economic policy of the great European nations, in respect to foreign trade, had, for the preceding two centuries, been conducted, and particularly against that scheme of administration which might be styled Colbert's application of the 'mercantile' system to the interior of France. Accepting the doctrine that the wealth of a nation could only be increased by an excess of its exports over its imports, and the balance paid for in hard cash, it became the end of statesmanship to give every possible discouragement to the import of foreign goods, and every possible encouragement to the export of home goods. In the condition of France in Colbert's time this end could be reached only by centralising the industry of the kingdom within the large towns, for

[1] *Encyc. Brit.* (Turgot) xxiii. 629. 'It was no small proof of originality and enlightenment to precede Adam Smith by ten years in the doctrines of Free Trade, of free industry, of loans on interest, of the constitutive elements of price, of the effects of the division of labour, of the processes of the formation of capital.' (J. Morley, *Crit. Misc.* ii. 149.) The *Réflexions* was translated and published in London in 1793, and was subsequently reprinted (1859) in Lord Overstone's *Select Collection of scarce and valuable Economical Tracts.*

tne purpose of expanding their manufactures; and the long and vigorous administration of that statesman was specially applied to this object. A necessary consequence was that the best and the most energetic of the population in the provinces, taking their capital with them, resorted to Paris and the other towns. In order the better to sustain the manufacturing interests by the cheapening of provisions, Colbert prohibited the export of corn, &c., from the kingdom, thus depriving the agricultural classes of their natural markets. At the same time, to enable him to keep taxation moderate in the towns, he laid burdens on the agricultural classes, in proportion to their means, far beyond the rate contributed by the manufacturing classes. In short, in every way the country was sacrificed to the towns. The result of this policy in course of time manifested itself. The agriculture of France sank into that deplorable condition already described. Quesnay,[1] a native of the country, penetrated by the experience of its miseries and its wrongs, revolted at the economic policy which was greatly answerable for them. He devoted himself to teach a new doctrine the very antithesis of the old one; instead of despising agriculture as a source of national wealth, he placed it in the very centre

[1] Quesnay (François), born 1694 at Méray (Ile de France), brought up in the country, was ten years old before he could read; taught himself Latin and Greek. Often walked to Paris and back the same day, sixty miles, to buy a book. At sixteen became apprentice to a surgeon; was Master in Surgery 1718, commencing practice at Mantes. Came into relation with Marshal de Noailles, who spoke of him to the queen, an occasional visitor to the neighbourhood. Through her he came to the knowledge of the king, to whom he was shortly afterwards appointed first physician. The king (who called him his *thinker*) gave him great honour and respect. He was by no means a courtier, spoke his mind freely, and denounced more than one iniquity of the Government and intrigue of the Court. He spread his ideas through the *Encyclopédie* and other publications. Made it his special aim to cultivate the science of 'the useful,' to which he gave the name of 'Political Economy.' A collection of his writings was published by his disciple Dupont in 1768. Adam Smith, as Dugald Stewart tells us, if he had not been prevented by Quesnay's death, would have inscribed to him the *Wealth of Nations*. The misfortunes and privations of the poor occupied incessantly Quesnay's thoughts. For his principal book he took a very striking motto: 'Poor Peasants, Poor Kingdom; Poor Kingdom, Poor King.' Died 1774. (*Nouv. Biog. Gén.*)

of his system. The old theory of wealth was to his mind altogether artificial, without any foundation in the nature of things. Although his disciple chose a pedantic name to describe the new system—'physiocrate'—it indicated not inaptly the principle of the system which was to enforce obedience to the 'rule of Nature.' By setting his system on the facts of Nature and recognising in respect to social and economical phenomena the operation only of natural laws, Quesnay believed it to possess the character of a necessary truth. And what foundation of wealth could be more real than agriculture (in the broad sense of the word)—the produce of Nature, of the earth itself, our world? Much ridicule has been cast on Quesnay and his school for their holding agriculture (that is, farming) to be the only source of wealth, but here they have been greatly misunderstood. With them the source of wealth was, correctly speaking, industry applied to the earth (the globe) of which even the sea forms a part, and including everything upon the soil, and everything under it. What else is there that man's industry can be applied to? Let us look around. Every article of food, every necessary or luxury, that man consumes or enjoys, is derived from the land (either directly, as grown upon it, or indirectly from animals fed upon it) or from the sea. Every dwelling that he has built for himself, from the rudest hut up to the palace, is made of materials dug from the earth. Every article of his clothing, every article of furniture, in short, every form of matter on which the hand of the workman or the artist can be employed, or which chemistry can transform, or on which machinery can work, must first have proceeded from our own planet, the earth. Quesnay and his school, therefore, did not take so narrow a view of things as their critics imagined they did.

Of the soundness of their central principle that the original source of all wealth is on and in the earth we live on, there can be no doubt; it is only in some of the applications they made of the principle to a complicated state of society, by overlooking the necessity we are under of dealing not only with the primary source of wealth but with the secondary, tertiary, and all subsequent creations of it, by every addition of labour given by the hand of man directly or indirectly to the original materials, that the 'Economists' erred. The application they made of their principle in proposing a tax on the 'net product' of land—a single tax in place of all other taxes together—was justly condemned by general opinion. Their argument was that all the burden of taxation due upon all other interests, besides the landed, would be anticipated in the one burden on the landed. It was a legitimate deduction in pure science, the world being regarded as a single community, but it is evident that the division of the world into different nations, with different laws affecting trade with other countries, makes the unconcerted application of the single agricultural tax to any one nation impossible. It is one of the many instances common to all schools of economists, in which the special theorists have been carried away into fallacies by the apparently logical sequence of their ideas, when they omit to test these ideas, rigidly and constantly, by the touch of facts.

Services to the world by the French economists

But we must recollect that at the time of the physiocrats the science of political economy was almost in its infancy. We must acknowledge the immense services they, in spite of their doctrinal exaggerations, rendered to France. They were the means, at all events, by their intense earnestness and often by their moving eloquence, of bringing before the public mind the utterly miserable condition of agriculture and the agricultural classes, and of enlisting the strength of public opinion that demanded a better state of things, and it is not France only that owes to these economists a deep gratitude. They were the founders of social as well as political economy. Almost every social and every economical improvement in Europe and America, for the last hundred years or more, had its germ in the teaching of men who belonged to that early economists' school of France.

Before parting here from these French economists it may be remarked that there was one grand doctrine taught by them which has not yet been adopted by their own nation, nor indeed by any great nation except England—the doctrine of Free Trade. It is to the honour of Turgot and his companions that they were the very earliest to promulgate it. With them free trade was part of the 'rule of Nature.' They claimed for labour and for the productions of labour only liberty. They believed that if simply *let alone* the economical relations of things would adjust themselves to their true level. That a man has the natural right to sell the produce of his labour to anyone desiring to buy it, whether the buyer belongs to his own country or to another. That the locality or the country which can produce certain articles by the least expenditure of labour has the natural right to claim the preference for such articles in the market of the world. That governments which 'protect' their own producers or manufacturers by preventing free imports from other countries, and thus raise prices at home above their natural level, do this at the expense of their own people, who are thus deprived of their right to buy from those who are willing to sell. That the pernicious effect of such a policy is worldwide. Labour is diverted from its most profitable applications throughout all countries. All those *forced* products or manufactures of each country can be obtained only by a greater expenditure of labour than necessary in natural circumstances. This is a waste of labour, and therefore a *waste of the world's wealth.* A waste of the world's wealth cannot take place without the world, as a whole, being the poorer for it—without the world, as a whole, in some way suffering from it. Besides the interests of general society thus frustrated, there is the injustice done to the legitimate producer who has the right to the world's market on fair conditions; this is injustice between man and man. It cannot cease to be injustice because one of the parties belongs to a different nation from the other. It was evident to these economists, as it is to all reflecting persons at the present day, that it is useless to expect the world to emerge from its war-fever period until it has first found repose in a full international intercourse, free from all jealousies, the inhabitants of each separate country allowing the same rights of trade to foreigners as they allow to their own countrymen. When neighbouring *provinces* made laws against each other's commerce, they also made war against each other. When in course of time *interprovincial* life was developed, the different provinces became consolidated into a nation, and the same laws, commercial and political, ruling over all its provinces, interprovincial war necessarily came to an end. With separate nations, history will have to repeat the same lesson; a thorough free trade between them must exist before a permanent peace can prevail.

The principle of free trade, as it appeared to Turgot and the economists, was in its very essence humanitarian, and in the highest sense Christian, for it is in accordance with the Christian idea of the brotherhood of man, and in obedience to the Christian law, 'Do unto others,' &c. They would hold to the belief which their followers still hold, that the time must come when it shall be seen that whatever principle is right and best between one man and another is also right and best between one nation and another, and that the same common sense which in many places has abolished the toll-bar between parishes and between counties must, further applied, in time sweep away the abominable *douane* at the frontier of countries. Such were the 'visions' of Turgot and his brother economists. They may (who knows?) yet be realised.

§ 5. During his early years at Limoges, and before the publication of the 'Réflexions,' he had written the following minor works on taxation:—1. 'Plan d'un Mémoire sur les impositions en général'; 2. 'Comparaison de l'Impôt sur le Revenu des Propriétaires et de l'Impôt sur les Consommations'; 3. 'Observations sur un Projet d'Édit sur les Vingtièmes,' besides several papers in connection with the prize essays of the agricultural society already mentioned. Other works of this period

Throughout all these works it was his main design to enforce the advantages of direct over indirect taxation.

On the reform of the Militia

During the last year of his provincial government he addressed to the Minister of War, the Marquis de Monteynard, the letter on the Militia ('Sur la Milice,' 1773) to which we have already alluded. It was an elaborate discussion on the position of that force in relation to the regular army, and it pleaded for important improvements in its constitution and management.[1]

None of the suggestions made appear to have been carried out. It has been reserved for a quite recent writer to draw attention to the main proposal in this letter, so long overlooked. After describing the reforms recommended in it, M. Foncin, writing in 1877, concludes with these words: 'Thus a century before the grievous events which have taught us to know the value of the German *Landwehr*, Turgot proposed to create in France what we call the reserve of the active army and of the territorial army.[2]

The date of the unfinished essay on 'Valeurs et Monnaies,' and of the 'Mémoire sur les Mines et Carrières,' is uncertain, but both probably belong to the early part of the Limoges period.

Mine-working

The Council of State having requested his opinion on the concession desired of a lead-mine within his territory, his memorial in reply lays down those general principles in respect to proprietary rights and their practical application in the development of mines and quarries, which appear to him to be most conducive to the public good. He reasons out the whole subject in his usual thorough manner. The memorial may be said to be almost a code applicable to the

[1] M. Villey recently discovered, in the archives of Calvados, two letters of Turgot, while Minister, addressed to the Intendant of Caen (Nov. 27 and Dec. 11, 1775), instructing him to carry out a scheme for the assistance of young men, out of work, who would volunteer for a limited service in the army. In order to encourage the industrial employment of their free time, they were to receive (in addition to their pay) a *fifth part of the price* realised for the articles manufactured by them. (*Bulletin de la Participation aux Bénéfices*, 1888, pp. 65, 66.)

This is, perhaps, the earliest application known of the principle of *profit-sharing* between workmen and employer.

[2] Foncin, *Essai sur le Ministère de Turgot* (Paris, 1877), p. 143.

rights and duties of this species of property, from his peculiar point of view. At that time in France the Roman law still prevailed, by which the proprietary right of the landlord was limited to the soil, all under it being the property of the State. Sound as this law was in principle, it was in the circumstances not beneficial in its operation. The State lacked the energy to initiate and prosecute the search for minerals, being actuated by no immediate interest in the undertaking, and it had no official machinery for the purpose. Consequently the development of the mineral riches of the country was greatly neglected. On the other hand, Turgot saw the body of proprietors, great and small, destitute of commercial spirit and short of means, and that to make over to them the right to the minerals in their land would lead to little or no improvement in the production of mineral wealth. In his anxiety to enlist some enterprise, so greatly needed, he proposed to give the right of property in the minerals to the first occupant; he proposed even to give him the right (strange to our ideas) of extending his excavations under the soil of an adjacent proprietor who did not himself work the minerals in his estate.[1]

On the rate of interest

In 1769 he published his 'Mémoire sur les Prêts d'Argent,' and it had reached a second edition before Dupont included it in the collected works. This Memorial, addressed

[1] The progress of mineral industry in France continued to be slow. The Constituent Assembly, by the law of July 28, 1791, reaffirmed the principle that 'mines and quarries, metallic and non-metallic . . . are at the disposal of the nation'; and their 'exploitation' was still hampered by many troublesome regulations made necessary by a centralised Circumlocution Office. It was not till 1804, when Napoleon interested himself in this important question, that something like a new departure was made in it by the *Code*, Book II. ('De la Propriété'). By it, as M. Eugène Daire has observed, 'Napoleon drew much nearer to the ideas of Turgot than to those of all the jurisconsults.' The proprietor in France has still too large a property in a fund of wealth under his land which he has done nothing to create. It would have been most in accordance with Turgot's general principles of economy and of policy at the stage of advance made in mining industry in 1804, to have still provided for the greatest freedom in opening and in working mines and quarries, and at the same time to have preserved State rights by claiming the *royalties* for the National Exchequer instead of for the landlord.

to the Council of State, was occasioned by the existence of a monetary crisis in Angoulême, a part of his province. In his preface he alludes to the circumstances in which a higher than the ordinary rate of interest had become usual with the manufacturers and merchants of that town, and he mentions as one of the circumstances a trait of French character, unhappily still prevalent among that 'decoration'-loving people. 'The town of Angoulême,' he explains, 'by its situation on the Charente, at the very point of the river's course where it begins to be navigable, might be expected to be very commercial, but it is very little so. It is probable that one of the principal causes of this is the facility with which every family, moderately well off, is enabled to acquire a title of nobility on rising to the mayoralty. The consequence is, that as soon as a man has made some money, he hastens to quit commerce, in order to become noble. The capital he had acquired is soon dissipated in the idle life belonging to his new condition, or at least it is entirely lost for commerce. The little that remains, therefore, is all in the hands of men without adequate means, who can form only limited enterprises, who are almost always reduced to carry on their trade by borrowed money, and who cannot borrow except at high interest, on account of the actual scarcity of money, and of the limited security they have to offer to the lenders.' Two of the chief industries of Angoulême, the making of brandy and the manufacture of iron, had customs belonging to them which also contributed to the existence of a high rate of interest. 'The brandy trade is subject to excessive variations in price, thus giving rise to very uncertain speculations which may yield immense profits or entail ruinous losses. The undertakings of the iron-masters for the furnishing of the navy involve very large advances and with long credit; they are obliged to procure money at whatever price it may be.' Thus it came about that for nearly forty years back 'the most of the negotiations had been made on the footing of eight or nine per cent. per annum,' while six per cent. was regarded as the normal rate in other parts of France. In these circumstances it happened that what we now call a 'long firm' had entered upon some very extensive speculations and had supported themselves by a skilfully devised system of accommodation bills. The speculations failed. The debtors, in order to intimidate the creditors from pursuing them, threatened to denounce them to justice for having exacted usurious rates of interest.' Some timid creditors were frightened into making restitution. A panic arose. Almost the whole commerce of Angoulême became discredited—'the authority given to the bad faith of the borrowers shut all the purses of the lenders—no engagement expiring could be renewed—all new enterprises were stopped, solvent manufacturers were subjected to failure by the impossibility of finding any credit pending the return of their capital.' [1]

Turgot came to the rescue. Having laid before the Council of State, in full detail, the facts here sketched, he accompanied them by every argument proper to enforce the step he advised, which was for the Council to evoke to itself the hearing of the affair in Angoulême. This was done, and the procedures against the lenders were quashed.

His Memorial is, in fact, a treatise, developing the principle that interest being the price of money in commerce, this price ought to be left to the course of events and to the bargaining of commerce to adjust itself.[2]

Letters to Terray

During a tour of his province, towards the end of 1770, he wrote a series of letters to the Comptroller-General, M. Terray, on the interminable question, 'La Liberté du Commerce des Grains.' The letters were seven in number, each written from a different place on his journey. They

[1] *Œuvres de Turgot*, i. 106–52.

[2] 'Turgot's "Memorial" is the most complete and most perfect work that has ever been written on the question of lending at interest and of usury, and has raised its author at once to the rank of our first writers.'—Léon Say, *Turgot*, p. 72.

'The "Memorial" is as cogent an exposure of the mischief of usury laws to the public prosperity as the more renowned pages either of Bentham or J. B. Say on the same subject.'—J. Morley, *Crit. Misc.* ii. 138.

Jeremy Bentham's *Defence of Usury* was written in 1787, and published in 1816.

must have been in length equal to a printed volume of at least 200 octavo pages, and were written between October 30 and December 7, in less than six weeks, and in the margin of time left from his official duties.

As we have already seen, the liberty of the circulation of corn was established by the royal edict of July 1764. For six years this liberty continued, and then it was suppressed by ministers who had little faith in a great principle justifying itself in spite of adverse circumstances of a temporary nature. They reasoned that liberty was all very well in ordinary times, but that it was out of place in a time of scarcity—the very time when liberty would have proved itself to be the most beneficial corrective of the inequality of harvests. These seven letters (only four of which remain) were written with the object of converting the minister Terray to the wiser policy of maintaining freedom of trade inviolate, their argument being that the project of the Government must certainly be, in the long run, more injurious to the nation than the temporary and limited derangement it was meant to cure.

The letters were written with astonishing ability, and for completeness in the collection and statement of facts, for application of right dealing with these, and for the exhaustive anticipation of every possible argument on the opposite side, they form quite a model of controversial debate.

The conclusion of the last letter conveyed a warning of which many governments, in their time, have stood in need: 'To announce to the people that the dearness of food from which they suffer is the effect of artificial manœuvres, and not due to the derangement of the seasons; to tell them that they endure dearness in the midst of abundance, is to authorise all calumnies, past, present, and future, to which they too readily surrender themselves, encouraged by enemies of the Government; it is, at the same time, to render Government responsible for the inevitable scarcities that may exist or may again occur; it involves the ministry personally to procure abundance, whatever may happen, and they should be very sure of their ability before they undertake such an engagement. The people well know that Government is not the master of seasons, and they should be taught that they have no right to violate the property of the agricultural labourers or the dealers in corn. We stand firm, even before the people, when we say to them, "*What you ask is an injustice.*" Those who do not accept this reason will accept none, and will always calumniate the Government, whatever efforts are made to please them.'[1]

But Terray's decision had been already made; the policy of restriction was carried out. Some years later, however, three of the letters (those lost to us) were serviceable in enlightening Louis XVI. on this question, when it again came up in 1775.

His last work of importance while intendant was his letter to the Comptroller-General: 'Sur la Marque des Fers.' It is dated December 24, 1773.[2]

Free Trade and Protection

'La *Marque* des Fers' was the brand distinguishing the native iron of France from the foreign article. Since 1608, each Finance Minister in turn had proposed scheme after scheme of duties and regulations, with the view of encouraging the production of French iron and of discouraging the use of foreign metal and metal-work. This policy would have been less a failure had French iron been suitable for all sorts of manufacture; but not being so, the consequence was that French industry in iron *manufactures* and the interest of the public as consumers of them, were sacrificed in the attempt to promote French iron-*smelting*. Terray, in his turn, hoped to improve upon the attempts of his predecessors, and had repeatedly requested Turgot to assist him with information upon the state of the ironworks in his province. Turgot knew only too well the short-sighted economical views on this matter held by his chief, and did not hesitate to state with perfect frankness where the true remedy for industrial depression was to be found. 'I know,' he writes, 'no other means of quickening any commerce whatever than

[1] *Œuvres de Turgot*, i. 255. [2] See abridged, *infra*, pp. 249–55.

by granting to it the greatest liberty, and the freedom from all taxes, which the ill-understood interest of the Exchequer has multiplied to excess on all kinds of merchandise, and in particular on the fabrications of iron. . . . The opinion, founded on too many examples, that all the researches of Government have no other object than to find means of drawing from the people more money has given rise to universal distrust.' He then proceeds to the discussion of the matter in question, and to expose the evil results of a policy dictated by unenlightened national self-interest. He recapitulates his argument in this terse dictum: '*The truth is, that in aiming at injuring others, we injure only ourselves.*'[1]

It is astonishing in how deep an ignorance of moral and economical principles nations calling themselves the most enlightened still remain on these 'native industry' questions. In Turgot's letter, written 120 years ago, the reader will observe that its arguments and its illustrations are as literally true now against the miserable protectionist fallacies circulated by the Republican party in the United States as originally they were against the narrow views of M. Terray.

Appointment to the Ministry

The 'Marque des Fers' was the last treatise of an economical kind which he had the opportunity of composing. Within a few months after it was written, Louis XV. died. A new king and a new prime minister invited Turgot to a seat in the Cabinet.

It would be, perhaps, to attribute more honour and more wisdom to the king and to the Count de Maurepas than they deserve if we believed that Turgot was called to the Government solely by reason of his own merits. Promotion to high office in France was still brought about mainly by means of private pressure. It is said that his advancement to the Ministry might be traced by the following links:—M. de Maurepas, the chief minister, was greatly under the sway of his wife; Madame de Maurepas was under the influence of the Abbé de Véry, *prêtre-philosophe*, and the

[1] *Œuvres de Turgot*, i. 376–88.

abbé's influence with the lady was exerted, without stint, in favour of his old schoolfellow of the Sorbonne. Madame de Maurepas was well seconded by the Duchess d'Enville, a great admirer of Turgot.

We may partly imagine the feelings that actuated him in the unexpected circumstances. He had made Limousin his world, and he was justified in the satisfaction he felt that he was leaving it better than he found it. He had refused time after time promotion to more lucrative and more honoured intendancies, in order that the good work begun in this humbler one might not be endangered by the succession to it of a governor ignorant of the experience it had undergone, and perhaps less sympathetic than himself with the people he had grown to love. But the offer of a seat in the Government itself, at the capital, introduced new and important considerations, deserving of a fresh decision. Instead of being in a subordinate place, confined to making mere suggestions of reform, and on a limited area, and to have these suggestions often overruled, would it not be open to him, now, even to *initiate* wholesome laws, and these for administration throughout all France?

Unassuming as he was, by the whole tenor of his mind, and well as he knew the perils that would beset him as Minister—the intrigues that would surround him; the enmities of those interested in maintaining power only for selfish ends; the derision even with which his policy, dictated by nobler motives, would be received in certain quarters—he felt that he would be untrue to himself if he hesitated to make the attempt, at least, to reduce the burdens on the people, to introduce a sounder financial system, and to found some institutions for the political education of France. In the sequel we shall find how truly his fears were confirmed; but, on the other hand, we shall see how salutary it was, as a lesson to other nations, if not to France, that the attempt was made.

**Leave-taking of Limousin**

And now, after thirteen years of the best part of his life spent in a daily fight, not unsuccessful, against the vicious system that had oppressed his province, and in a daily work, in a great degree successful, of raising the condition, moral and physical, of its poor population, he had to bid farewell to Limoges.

M. Léon Say alludes to the opinions, by different classes, on the merits of Turgot's provincial government:—

> It was impossible for him to please everybody. We are told on one side that he made himself adored, while others maintain that he made himself detested. Both statements are, no doubt, correct. The Limousin nobles had been accustomed to make use of the intendancy to obtain favours, to get the *tailles* and *capitations* of their *protégés* reduced, and to get their own *vingtièmes* reduced. They could not forgive Turgot for having broken with traditions which had hitherto been favourable to them. . . . But if the nobility were hostile to him it was not the same with the peasantry. His departure was announced publicly from the pulpit by all the *curés* of the province, who celebrated mass everywhere on his account. The countrymen suspended their work in order to be present, and all cried: 'It is wisely done by the king to have taken M. Turgot, but it is very sad for us that we have lost him.'[1]

These two very different estimates made in Limousin of Turgot's character and work need not surprise us. In our own time we had a similar instance, on a much larger field. In 1884 a viceroy, taking leave of India, was, with almost unparalleled demonstrations of love and of grief, accompanied to the coast by countless multitudes, grateful to the ruler who had made their welfare the single purpose of his reign. But, on the other hand, what were the feelings expressed on the same occasion by the 'well-informed classes,' the British residents, towards this viceroy, who dared to think that *they* were made for India, and not India for them? Turgot was 'unpopular' in Limousin, as Lord Ripon was 'unpopular' in India.

[1] Léon Say, *Turgot*, p. 64. 'The intendance had been a good house of entertainment for certain persons when they found there a sumptuous table, ladies, and gambling. Turgot, laborious youth, who dines almost by himself and soberly, and never plays, was not their man.' (Abbé Bandeau, *Chron. sec.*

# CHAPTER III

1774—1776

## COMPTROLLER-GENERAL OF FINANCES

### Introduction

*Sketch of French Government*, 1723–1774

THE majority of Louis XV., in his fourteenth year, was pronounced in the Parliament January 22. The Regent, the Duke of Orleans, had, shortly before, nominated Cardinal Dubois as first Minister, but, as such, under his own direction. The Cardinal died within seven months after, and Orleans followed him four months later. The king naturally turned for advice to his preceptor Fleury, Bishop of Fréjus, who recommended as Minister the Duke de Bourbon. The two, along with the Marshal de Villars and a fourth—not the least in importance—the Marquise de Prie, Bourbon's mistress, constituted the Government. The currency was tampered with, and every possible misrule prevailed. 1723

Bourbon, with sinister objects, married the young king to Mary Leczinska, daughter of Stanislaus, formerly King of Poland. Bourbon grew jealous of the influence of Fleury with the king and intrigued against him. 1725

Fleury, in self-defence, took advantage of the unpopularity of Bourbon to urge his dismissal from the king's council. The duke was ordered to his country seat at Chantilly; the Marquise de Prie was exiled. The king declared that henceforth he would be his own prime minister; but Fleury, now created cardinal, retained great power over him. 1726

All the energies of the cardinal were devoted to the maintenance of peace, and his policy was uniformly successful, until the death, in 1733, of Frederick Augustus I., King of Poland. Louis XV. became involved in the scheme of restoring his father-in-law to 1727–33

Introduction that throne. This was frustrated by Russia and the Emperor of Germany.

1734 In reprisal, Louis XV. seized upon Lorraine and allied himself with Spain and Savoy. France was fortunate in her Generals Villars, Coigny, and Broglie, who achieved several successes.

1735 By the peace of Vienna (October 3), Stanislaus, renouncing Poland, obtained Lorraine (to revert to France), and France agreed to accept the 'Pragmatic Sanction' of Charles VI., which settled his dominions on his daughter Maria Theresa.

1741–48 On the death of Charles VI. (October 20, 1740) Cardinal Fleury, now grown old, weakly permitted the Count de Belle-Isle to indulge his ambitious schemes against Austria. France shamefully broke off from the treaty, solemnly sworn to five years before, and allied herself with Bavaria, Spain, Prussia, Sardinia, and Poland, in order to rob Maria Theresa of the greater part of her possessions, to be divided among Charles of Bavaria and the other allies. Maria Theresa (now married to Francis of Lorraine, Duke of Tuscany), by an act of sublime daring, in personally appealing before the States of Hungary, roused the enthusiasm of her people in her defence. An army was raised which speedily gained signal victories, in different quarters, over the forces of Spain, France, and Bavaria. The King of Sardinia forsook the alliance; Prussia followed, being induced by the cession of Silesia. The French army was left helpless in Bohemia, Belle-Isle evacuated Prague, and the campaign, in which there were many other events, ended by Charles of Bavaria renouncing his claims upon Austria. Cardinal Fleury meanwhile died (January 29, 1743). Charles of Bavaria (Emperor of Germany as Charles VII.) died January 20, 1745. Maximilian Joseph, his son, surprised the world by siding with Maria Theresa and supporting her husband as candidate for the imperial throne. He was elected emperor (September 15, 1745). France was furious at the course events had taken, and continued to make war. The following campaigns, although successful for France in Flanders, were elsewhere unfortunate for her and for her allies. Louis XV. signed (October 18, 1748) the preliminaries of the Peace of Aix-la-Chapelle. 'France restored Savoy to the King of Sardinia, the Low Countries to the Empress Maria Theresa, and to the Dutch all the places conquered from them; the only result to France of this sanguinary and unjust war, which had lasted so many years, was the enormous charge of 1,200 millions which it had added to its debt.'[1]

[1] Bonnechose, *History of France* (Eng. ed.), p. 454.

*Coup d'État against the Parliament of Paris.*—In 1713 the Pope, influenced by the Jesuits, promulgated his bull *Unigenitus* against certain doctrines of the Jansenists. During the fifty years to follow, the identification of the Jesuits with the militant power of the Church exercised against the State gave to the Parliament of Paris, the State's defender, great popularity. In 1746, the fanaticism of De Beaumont, the new Archbishop of Paris, revived the conflicts. He issued orders to all priests within his province to refuse the Sacrament to anyone, even at the point of death, who had not accepted the Pope's bull. The Parliament retaliated by prosecuting those priests who obeyed these orders. The Government was induced to protect the priests. The Parliament refused to yield. It increased its popularity by opposing new taxes. At last the Government made its *Coup d'État* of the night of May 8–9, 1753, when the members of the Parliament were ordered to leave Paris within twenty-four hours. A Royal Chamber was created to take its place. **Introduction** **1753**

In honour of the birth (August 23, 1754) of the Dauphin (afterwards Louis XVI.), an amnesty was granted and the Parliament recalled. It abuses its power and endeavours to form a league of all the parliaments of France against the Government. On December 13, 1756, the Parliament was again suppressed. The people took up its cause under great excitement. The great body of the magistrates sent in their resignation. Paris was on the eve of an insurrection against the Government, when the act of a madman drove events into the very opposite channel. The king was stabbed by Damiens on January 5, 1757. A sentimental reaction in favour of the king and Government at once set in, and flowed onwards to the most irrational extreme. The magistrates withdrew their resignation and tendered to the king the most abject submission. The king, in return, recalled most of the magistrates who had been disgraced, and the Parliament was restored. The Marquise de Pompadour, who had been forced to efface herself, in order that the odour of sanctity should be perfect around the king's death-bed, returned as soon as the danger was over, to give an odour of another kind to the king's life. Machault was dismissed, along with D'Argenson, and the Marquise became more powerful than ever before. **1754–56**

In 1756 began the war between Great Britain and France, in consequence of disputes as to the demarcation of their possessions in North America. It extended itself to Europe and became the 'Seven Years' War' (1756–1763). Maria Theresa allied herself **1756–63**

Introduction

with Elizabeth of Russia and the Kings of Poland and of Sweden, with the object of regaining from Prussia her lost provinces of Silesia. Frederick II. having dropped some words disrespectful of Madame de Pompadour, Maria Theresa took advantage of the opportunity, treated her with very marked courtesy, and, through her, won the alliance of France. Thus, on one side were ranged all the great powers of Europe, on the other the King of Prussia. Great Britain assisted him with a limited number of Hanoverian troops, but her part in the war was vigorously played in other quarters of the world—in Canada and the East Indies, where she shattered the Colonial Empire of France. The extraordinary successes on the battlefields of Europe, achieved over all his enemies in turn, by the daring military genius of Frederick, are known to all readers. During the war, the Duke de Choiseul, a statesman who was for a long period to exercise power in France in and out of office, entered the Council as Foreign Minister, afterwards becoming Minister of War, owing his promotion to Madame de Pompadour. The finances were in the hands of M. de Silhouette. He began by making some important savings in the collection of the Revenue. 'Although praised by everybody for these judicious proceedings, he as quickly became the subject of obloquy, when, in 1760, his reforms attacked the rights of the higher classes.'[1]

Choiseul, in desperation at the ill fortune of France in the war, concocts, in secret, the 'Family Compact,' which was signed August 16, 1761. This was a secret treaty with Charles III. of Spain, by which the members of the House of Bourbon constituted themselves one and indivisible for purposes either of offence or defence. The Empress of Russia died January 2, 1762. Her nephew and successor, Peter III., reigned a few months, and was dethroned by his wife Catherine II. The new empress stood neutral towards the belligerents. This event, together with some successes on both sides, occurring during the campaign, disposed the different powers to conclude a peace, on February 10, 1763, known as the Treaty of Paris. It was altogether disastrous to France; 'the English, who a century before possessed little beyond the Britannic Isles but Jersey and Guernsey, were at the conclusion of the Treaty of Paris masters, in all the seas, of a multitude of islands and the strongest naval stations; the French marine was almost annihilated, and from that time the empire of the ocean was acquired by England. The peace was equally signed by the

[1] Bonnechose, p. 461.

Empress-Queen Maria Theresa, the Elector of Saxony, and the King of Prussia, and, after seven sanguinary campaigns, everything was re-established among these three powers upon the same footing as before the war. Frederick retained Silesia and promised his vote to the son of Maria Theresa, the Archduke Joseph, who was elected King of the Romans, and succeeded to the empire on August 18, 1765. Intro-duction

In 1762–64 the order of the Jesuits was abolished in France, a step which was followed by all the other Catholic powers of Europe.

On the death of Stanislaus, Lorraine became incorporated with France. 1766

The Seven Years' War (1756-63) had entailed enormous financial burdens on the Government. The Parliament of Paris, which in nearly every preceding instance had made itself the instrument of political tyranny and religious bigotry, at this time gained considerable popular sympathy by protesting against some arbitrary measures of taxation. In this it was supported by the Parliament of Rennes. This parliament had denounced the Duke d'Aiguillon, the governor of its province (Brittany), for extortions. The Government imagined they could enforce a lesson upon the provincial parliament which they were not bold enough to dictate to the Parliament of Paris. The foremost members of the Parliament of Rennes were imprisoned and afterwards exiled. The Duke d'Aiguillon, thus encouraged, carried his high-handed dealing to still greater excess until he provoked a general reprobation. The king had to recall him. The parliament in Brittany, re-established, made it its first duty to impeach the duke, and the Parliament of Paris made common cause with it. D'Aiguillon was cited before the Parliament of Paris. At this conjuncture, through the intrigues of Madame du Barri, managed by the Richelieu faction, was projected that 'triumvirate' of Maupeou, Terray, and D'Aiguillon which shortly afterwards entered upon its career of misgovernment, which lasted to the death of Louis XV. Acting upon the advice of the triumvirate, the king annulled the proceedings of the Parliament of Paris against d'Aiguillon, and 'in a bed of justice' required the Parliament to give in its own resignation. The Duke de Choiseul was dismissed and exiled (December 24, 1770). Maupeou had shortly before been made Chancellor, D'Aiguillon was made Foreign Minister, and the Abbé Terray Comptroller-General of the Finances. A *coup d'état* was then struck against the magistracy (January 19, 1771). By the 1767–74

Introduction

authority of *lettres de cachet* they were apprehended, and were scattered in exile through France. A Commission was created of notables, drawn from different bodies, which formally abolished the old parliament and nominated a new one. These despotic proceedings provoked the opposition of many of the better classes and of almost the whole magistracy throughout France. But Maupeou skilfully made a handle of the past misdeeds of the old parliament, such as in the cases of Calas and the Chevalier de la Barre, and by reversing those unjust decisions he gave a colour of reform to the new order of magistrates, which in less than a year he succeeded in establishing. But these 'Maupeou parliaments,' as they were called, failed to gain the respect of the nation. Terray was equally arbitrary as Minister of Finance. One of his many imprudent acts was the abrogation of the law permitting the free circulation of corn through the kingdom. Expenditure was unchecked, and the most reckless expedients were adopted to find resources. France had sunk so low in the opinion of the other powers of Europe that she was taken no account of by Russia, Prussia, and Austria, who effected in 1772 the Treaty for the dismemberment of Poland. Louis XV., bitterly regretting his loss of Choiseul, drowned his mortification in a course of increased debaucheries, and died May 10, 1774.

§ 1. Louis XVI., on succeeding to his grandfather, was under twenty years old; his queen was under nineteen. Amongst all classes a feeling prevailed that France was about to enter upon a new era. The king shared the same feeling, and was earnestly ambitious to make his reign a contrast, in every respect, to the preceding one. The old ministry fell as a matter of course. The field of choice of a new premier was very limited. It was necessary to select one with some experience in State affairs, and the ministers of the late long reign were mostly discredited.

Count de Maurepas Premier

Deliberations on the part of the king's best advisers and intrigues on the part of some interested courtiers seemed to point in the same direction, and the appointment was given to the Count de Maurepas. Maurepas was as old as the century. Bred from his youth to official life, he was Minister of Marine at four-and-twenty. During more than twenty years following he filled several offices in succession, until his banishment, April 24, 1749, on suspicion of being the author of an epigram pointed at Madame de Pompadour. He was kept in disgrace for the remainder of the reign. To recall a victim of the immorality of the past period, in order to mark the contemplated morality of the new, seemed an act of dramatic justice. Maurepas had many Court connections, and was quite the man to extend them. He was not disturbed by any serious ideas of public duty. Marmontel draws his portrait: 'He supplied in council, by skill and dexterity, what he wanted in study and meditation. Insinuating and mild in manners, flexible and fertile in resources, alike for attack and in defence, . . . he possessed a lynx-eye to seize upon the weak or ridiculous in men, and an imperceptible art to draw them to his purposes; . . . he made sport of everything, even of merit itself.'[1] A man of this character was not unwilling to attach some reputation of liberalism to his ministry, by including in it one or two members who took higher views of public life than he himself held, and who had distinguished themselves in other fields than the Court. Accordingly, when Madame de Maurepas urged strongly the claims of Turgot for office, her husband readily admitted them, and recommended him to the king.

**Turgot Minister of Marine**

Turgot was nominated to the Ministry of Marine July 20, 1774. The other members of the Cabinet were:—Hue de Miroménil, Chancellor; Count du Muy, Minister of War; Count du Vergennes, of Foreign Affairs; the Duke de la Vrillière, of the King's Household; and (in the meantime) the Abbé Terray, Comptroller-General.

Turgot's brief tenure of the Ministry of Marine was barely sufficient for him even to take measure of the disorganised state of the naval administration. Among the reforms he contemplated was one which marked his freedom from official routine, and from the national prejudices of the time. He projected the building of vessels in Sweden, instead of in France, calculating that an economy of two-fifths would be thereby effected. 'He did not grudge to a friendly and allied

[1] Marmontel, *Mémoires*, ii. 196.

nation the profit she would make from this industry, believing that in the end it would not result in less employment in France, knowing that the Swedes drank the wines of France, consumed the coffee and sugar of her colonies, and wore the stuffs of French manufacture.' Dupont mentions another scheme Turgot had: 'He counted upon adding much to the instruction of the Navy, and to the still imperfect knowledge we have of the world, by a permanent employment of a number of light vessels drawing little water, to conduct *savants* over all parts of the globe, and, above all, into the least known parts of it. He would have realised the project of a "Voyaging Academy," an academy not less useful than the academies that are sedentary, and which would have greatly enlightened the others.'

Comptroller-General, August 24

But he was soon called upon to serve France in the most important work which at that time lay before her, and the prosecution of which has, much more than any other event in his career, made his name illustrious. On August 24, 1774, he was appointed Comptroller-General of the Finances. By this time, no doubt, Maurepas had learned something of Turgot's administration of Limoges, in which financial matters formed a large element, and he resolved at last to sacrifice Terray, who, as Comptroller, had long been condemned by public opinion. The choice for this office of a Minister as famed for his probity as Terray was for his rascality, gained for Maurepas much applause.

Turgot had now attained to really the most responsible position in France. 'The Comptroller-General,' says De Tocqueville, 'gradually took upon himself all the affairs that had to do with money, that is to say, almost the whole administration; he thus performed successively the duties of Minister of Finance, Minister of the Interior, Minister of Public Works, and Minister of Trade.'[1]

The few weeks Turgot had already passed amidst the rival interests of ministers and courtiers, and of king and queen, were sufficient to fill him with the gravest anxiety.

[1] De Tocqueville, *Ancient Régime, &c.*, Eng. trans., p. 43.

Terray had kept his position as Comptroller for nearly five years by his ever-ready facility in supplying the late king's demands for money. His yearly deficits were met by loans, and each year's deficit exceeded that of the year before. Turgot knew that those reforms, necessary to save France, which his duty would compel him to propose, would inevitably meet with the most determined opposition from all the self-interests attacked. With this feeling upon him he sought an interview, and laid before the king his whole mind, his hopes and his fears. 'The king found himself in the presence of a man of more than common height, with eyes and mouth expressive both of winning amiability and of firmness ; an abundance of brown hair falling on his shoulders with a natural and careless grace ; his features strongly accented, his forehead elevated, his pale complexion taking colour from each emotion of his soul.' [1]

Interview with the king

The king was deeply impressed by Turgot's earnest nature, and by the prospects raised before him of a reign devoted only to the public welfare and to be recompensed by his people's love. With a full heart, he assured Turgot that, as Minister, he might count with confidence on the king's as well as the man's full sympathy and steadfast support. Turgot was so elated by this favourable interview, that he asked the king's permission to make a memorandum of it, and, on this being granted, he addressed a letter to the king, which, when read in the light of after events, became one of the documents of French history.

His memorable letter

Compiègne, August 24, 1774.

SIRE,—Having just come from the private interview with which your Majesty has honoured me, still full of the anxiety produced by the immensity of the duties now imposed upon me, agitated by all the feelings excited by the touching kindness with which you have encouraged me, I hasten to convey to you my respectful gratitude and the devotion of my whole life.

Your Majesty has been good enough to permit me to place on

[1] Alph. Jobez, *La France sous Louis XVI.* Paris, 1877, p. 144. 'Turgot's countenance was fine and majestic, it had something of the dignity remarkable in antique statuary.' (Montyon.)

record the engagement you have taken upon you to sustain me in the execution of those plans of economy which are at all times, and to-day more than ever, of an indispensable necessity. I would have desired the opportunity of developing to you the reflections suggested to me by the present position of the finances; but time does not permit of that, and I reserve myself to explain that position more fully when I shall have taken more exact measure of it. At this moment, Sire, I confine myself to recall to you these three words:—

No Bankruptcy.

No Increase of Taxes.

No Loans.

No *bankruptcy*, either avowed or disguised by illegal reductions.

No *increase of taxes*; the reason for this being in the condition of your people, and, still more, in that of your Majesty's own generous heart.

No *loans*; because every loan diminishes always the free revenue and necessitates, at the end of a certain time, either bankruptcy or the increase of taxes. In times of peace it is permissible to borrow only in order to liquidate old debts, or in order to redeem other loans contracted on less advantageous terms.

To meet these three points there is but one means. It is to reduce expenditure below revenue, and sufficiently below it to insure each year a saving of twenty millions,[1] to be applied in redemption of the old debts. Without that, the first gunshot will force the State to bankruptcy.

The question will be asked incredulously, 'On what can we retrench?' and each one, speaking for his own department, will maintain that nearly every particular item of expense is indispensable. They will be able to allege very good reasons, but these must all yield to the absolute necessity of economy.

It is, then, of absolute necessity for your Majesty to require that the heads of all the departments should concert with the Minister of Finance. It is indispensable that he should discuss with them, in presence of your Majesty, the degree of necessity for all your proposed expenses. It is above all necessary, as soon as you, Sire, shall have decided upon the strictly necessary scale of maintenance of each department, that you prohibit the official in charge of it to order any new expenditure without having first arranged with the Treasury the means of providing for it.

[1] *Livres*, equal potentially to 100 million francs of our time.

Without this, each department will charge itself with debts, which will become your Majesty's debts, and your Minister of Finance will be unable to answer for the balance between expenditure and income.

Your Majesty is aware that one of the greatest obstacles to economy is the multitude of demands by which you are constantly besieged, and which have been unfortunately sanctioned by the too great facility of your predecessors to entertain them. It is necessary, Sire, to arm yourself against your kindheartedness by your own increased sense of the same virtue; to consider whence comes to you this money which you are able to distribute among your courtiers, and to compare the misery of those from whom it has to be extracted (sometimes by the most rigorous methods) with the situation of the class of persons who push their claims on your liberality.

There are certain favours which, it is thought, you can more easily grant, because they do not bear immediately on the royal Treasury. Of this kind are the interests, the *croupes* (covert-partnerships) and privileges; they are of all concessions the most dangerous and the most subject to abuse. Every profit made on the taxes which is not absolutely necessary for their collection is in reality a debt due to the taxpayers or to the needs of the State. Besides, these participations in the profits of the farmers of the revenue are a source of corruption for the nobility and of vexation for the people, by giving to all such abuses powerful and secret protectors.

It may reasonably be hoped by the improvement of cultivation, by the suppression of abuses in the collection of the taxes, and by their more equitable assessment, that a substantial relief of the people can be attained without diminishing greatly the public revenue; but without economy being the first step all reforms are impossible. So long as finance shall be continually subject to the old expedients in order to provide for State services, your Majesty will always be dependent upon financiers, and they will ever be the *masters*, and by the manœuvres belonging to their office they will frustrate the most important operations. Thus the Government can never feel itself at ease, it can never be acknowledged as able to sustain itself, because the discontents and impatience of the people are always the means made use of by intriguing and ill-disposed men in order to excite disturbance. It is, then, upon economy that, above all, the prosperity of your reign depends; that the tranquillity of your kingdom, the respect held for it by other powers, the happiness of the nation and your own happiness, depend.

I must impress on your Majesty that I take office at a conjuncture beset by great difficulties, by serious disquietude prevalent respecting the sustenance of the people ; a disquietude aggravated by the fermentation that has been active in the public mind for some years, by the want of uniformity in the principles of the administrators, and by some really imprudent operations on their part, and more than all aggravated by the occurrence of a harvest below the average. On this subject, as on others, I do not expect your Majesty to adopt my principles without first having them thoroughly examined and discussed, as well by yourself as by persons in your Council in whose judgment you have confidence. But when you shall have once recognised the justice and necessity of these principles, I implore you to maintain with firmness their execution, without allowing yourself to be dismayed by the clamours which are absolutely certain to arise on such matters, whatever system we adopt, whatever line of conduct we pursue.

These are the matters which I have been permitted to recall to your Majesty. You will not forget that in accepting the place of Comptroller-General I have felt the full value of the confidence with which you honour me; I have felt that you entrust to me the happiness of your people, and, if it be permitted to me to say so, the care of promoting among your people the love of your person and of your authority.

At the same time, I feel all the danger to which I expose myself. I foresee that I shall be alone in fighting against abuses of every kind, against the power of those who profit by these abuses, against the crowd of prejudiced people who oppose themselves to all reform, and who are such powerful instruments in the hands of interested parties for perpetuating the disorder. I shall have to struggle even against the natural goodness and generosity of your Majesty, and of the persons who are most dear to you.[1] I shall be feared, hated even, by nearly all the Court, by all who solicit favours. They will impute to me all the refusals; they will describe me as a hard man because I shall have advised your

[1] 'It is evident that Turgot dreaded the influence of the queen. I have read the original draft itself of this document. After having written the words "*contre la générosité de votre Majesté*," Turgot had traced the words "*et de la*," when he checked himself, and covered the "*de la*" by "*des personnes*."' Léon Say, p. 93.)

Majesty that you ought not to enrich even those you love at the expense of your people's subsistence. And this people, for whom I shall sacrifice myself, are so easily deceived that perhaps I shall encounter their hatred by the very measures I take to defend them against exactions. I shall be calumniated (having, perhaps, appearances against me) in order to deprive me of your Majesty's confidence. I shall not regret losing a place which I never solicited. I am ready to resign it to your Majesty as soon as I can no longer hope to be useful in it. . . .

Your Majesty will remember that it is upon the faith of your promises made to me that I charge myself with a burden perhaps beyond my strength, and it is to yourself personally, to the honest man, the just and good man, rather than to the king, that I give myself.

I venture to repeat here what you have already been kind enough to hear and approve of. The affecting kindness with which you condescended to press my hands within your own, as if sealing my devotion, will never be effaced from my memory. It will sustain my courage. It has for ever united my personal happiness with the interest, the glory, and the happiness of your Majesty. It is with these sentiments that

I am, Sire, &c.[1]

This very remarkable letter displays the pure and high motives that actuated Turgot in accepting the comptrollership; the uncompromising principles that would guide him in its administration; his pledged self-devotion to the king's service and the public welfare. These were his engagements with the king. We shall see in what measure he was able to fulfil them; and on the other hand, in what degree the king was faithful to his own engagement with Turgot.

Recall of the parliaments

§ 2. The first important event in the reign of Louis XVI. was the recall of the parliaments. Since the *coup d'état* of January 19, 1771, the new courts of Judicature, although subjected to much public criticism, had fulfilled the judicial functions of the old parliaments with tolerable success. Some dislocation in procedure must necessarily have occurred. Cases in progress before the change would either have to be argued afresh before the new magistrates, or would run the

[1] *Œuvres de Turgot*, ii. 165.

risk of being imperfectly dealt with. All unsuccessful litigants would naturally attribute their unsuccess to the want of wisdom in the judges, and would believe that in the old order of things justice would have been done to them. The new magistrates were unpopular because they were upstarts, and time had not been given for this prejudice against them being overcome. The old magistrates had connections with the privileged classes throughout the kingdom, and particularly with leading men and women at Court. In the mind of the general public they still held some prestige, derived from certain incidents in their history, in which their self-interested opposition to the Government of the time was gratifying to the popular feeling, just because of the opposition being to the Government and to the Court.

Maurepas was eagerly solicited by all the friends of the late magistrates, and he lent a willing ear to their arguments. He saw in their restoration the opportunity given him of inaugurating his ministry by an act which would gain for him the support of many powerful families. In the Cabinet the project was at first opposed by Vergennes, but Maurepas succeeded in winning him over; the only ministers who opposed it to the last were Du Muy and Turgot. His standpoint on this question has been already indicated. He objected on principle to men whose office was acquired by the power of the purse being entrusted with the grave responsibility of sharing in making the laws of the kingdom. If even the venal character of their office might be tolerated, their function should simply be a judicial one. He had, as we have seen, given practical proof of these convictions, at an earlier stage of his career, by accepting a judicial office on the nomination of Louis XV., when the members of the old Parliament were temporarily suppressed. Above all he dreaded the revival of the Parliament, because he felt certain that it would lay serious, perhaps insurmountable obstacles in the way of the financial and political reforms he contemplated. The members of the Parliament, by their antecedents, by the constitution of their office, by their position as a privileged order, would mostly sympathise with those class interests and class prejudices which would necessarily be attacked by almost every measure designed for the public good. It is said that he pressed these considerations earnestly on the king, who replied to him: 'Fear nothing; I will always sustain you.' Although the Parliament was not summoned till some months afterwards, its recall was virtually decided on August 24, when its enemy, Chancellor Maupeou, was dismissed. It was peculiarly unfortunate that the, in itself, wise act of suppressing the parliaments had been due to such men as Maupeou and Terray.

He re-establishes the freedom of the corn trade

Within twenty days from his accession to the comptrollership Turgot had to decide now for the whole kingdom the question that occupied him so much, on a smaller scale, during his intendancy of Limoges—the free commerce in corn. On September 13, 1774, he had the satisfaction of issuing the decree of the Council of State, which re-established the declaration of May 1763, suspended by Terray. By the new decree, Art. I. declares that 'it shall be free to all persons whatever to carry on, as it may seem best to them, their trade in corn and flour, to sell and to buy it, in whatever places they choose throughout the kingdom,' and by Art. II. the king reserves the right to enact the freedom of export when circumstances shall have become more favourable.[1] He accompanied this decree with a preamble, setting forth its justification. This practice he continued in all the published decrees, edicts, &c., during his ministry. He believed that unless laws rested on a necessity for their existence, in order to remedy certain evils felt and acknowledged by the people, and unless, in their application, they were really understood by the people, their efficacy would be greatly impaired. The preambles to his several acts of administration thus constituted so many lessons in a public education. Voltaire playfully alluded to the new tone taken in the king's edicts from the point of view of a peasant: 'I learned that a Minister of State who was neither lawyer nor

[1] *Œuvres de Turgot*, ii. 177.

priest had just published an edict by which, in spite of the most sacred prejudices, it was permitted to every Perigourdin to sell and to buy wheat in Auvergne. . . . I saw in my canton a dozen of labourers, my brethren, who read this edict. "How then ?" said an old man ; 'for sixty years I have been reading these edicts which, in unintelligible language, have always stripped us of natural liberty ; now here is one that restores us our liberty, and I can understand every word without difficulty. This is the first time a king reasons with his people.'[1]

While the decree for freedom of the corn trade was being published, he had, in the financial department of his office, to deal with the interests of a powerful body in the State known as the Farmers-General. They were contractors for the collection of a considerable portion of the taxes, who, by furnishing an always needy Government with some ready money, acquired rights to remunerate themselves, by a most undue amount, at the public expense. An idea may be formed of the system of jobbery belonging to the institution, by mentioning the case of the 'pot-de-vin,' of which Turgot had now to dispose.

Declines the gifts of the financiers

The 'pot-de-vin' was a gift of 100,000 crowns (= 300,000 livres) made by the Farmers-General to the Comptroller-General on the signature of a new contract. The evil tendency of this custom need scarcely be commented upon. Turgot at once declined the gift and abolished it.[2] In respect to recent contracts in which it had already formed an element of calculation, but had not been paid to the late comptroller, he ordered that the money should be entrusted to the *curés* of Paris, to be spent in the purchase of wool and cotton yarn for knitting work for the use of the poor of their several parishes.

Of a similar nature was the practice of the Farmers-

[1] Voltaire, *Œuvres*, Diatribe, &c., May 10, 1775.

[2] 'This splendid deed won Turgot public admiration and private enmity; the majority of men in secret ever hate a generosity which they feel themselves unable to imitate.' (Sir A. Alison, *History*, i. chap. 3.)

General, on obtaining a contract, of giving gratuities to influential persons at Court, or to their family connections. These gifts amounted in the last contract, passed by Terray, to 1,980,000 livres.[1] Turgot writes to the Farmers-General September 14, 1774 :— Abolishes their gratuities to courtiers, &c.

> . . . His Majesty has observed with pain that a considerable part of the profits resulting from your contract has been applied in acquitting engagements made by several of your body with certain persons useless to your administration. H.M. directs me to inform you that he is determined no longer to permit such private gratuities being given, regarding them [as dangerous and injurious in all their operations]. . . . It is also the intention of the king in future to grant no place of Farmer-General except to persons who shall have been employed for some years in the higher offices of the Farm-General, and who shall be vouched for as competent by several members of your body. H.M., in the nomination for places, will have no regard to any *bonuses* which may have been given.[2]

On September 28 he issues a circular-letter to the intendants of the provinces, on the *octrois municipaux*, (town dues). He had, for many years, been painfully impressed by the abuses in the assessment and the collection of the *octrois*, particularly in the country towns. He had, November 9, 1772, endeavoured, without success it may be presumed, to induce the Abbé Terray to remedy some of these abuses. Turgot now, by his own authority, directs the attention of the intendants to the main defects of this system of local taxation, and suggests the spirit that should guide them in undertaking its reform. Among the defects he mentions: 'Another vice to be swept away is the injustice with which nearly all the large shopkeepers of the towns have freed themselves from contributing to the common expenditure, in order to shift the burden on the humbler citizens, the small merchants, and the peasants and poor of the country. The duties of *octrois* were established in order Reforms the town dues

[1] Jobez, *La France sous Louis XVI.*
[2] *Œuvres de Turgot*, ii. 432.

to provide for the expenses of the towns; it is therefore just that the citizens for whose benefit the expenses are made should bear the cost. . . . It has happened nearly everywhere that the burden has been placed on the commodities mainly consumed by the poor. If, for example, duties have been placed on wine, care has been taken to exempt the better kinds, consumed by the well-to-do citizens. In the same way have been exempted all products which these citizens derive from their own farms in the country; thus, those who profit most by the expenses of the municipality are precisely those who contribute to these expenses almost nothing.'[1] The rest of the circular is occupied with instructions for carrying out, in careful detail, certain reforms mentioned.

Removes disabilities of foreigners

During the last three months of this year he was chiefly engaged in informing himself upon the past records of his department, and in maturing those larger plans of reform which were to make the following year so memorable. Of the minor acts of his administration in these remaining months of 1774 we may mention two. In November letters-patent were issued to twenty-three imperial cities removing disabilities of foreigners residing in them, and abrogating the law which escheated the property of a deceased alien to the Crown. 'M. Turgot and M. de Vergennes,' says Dupont, 'thought alike that it would be very advantageous to the State and to the finances to abolish the *droit d'aubaine*, which debarred the settling in France of a great number of clever men and industrious artists, of capitalists, and useful merchants, who would have desired nothing more than to make France the centre of their affairs, and which debarred even retired foreigners of wealth attracted by the pleasures of society and the agreeableness of the climate. Turgot held that it was necessary to abolish this *droit d'aubaine*, towards all nations, by a general law, and without concerning ourselves with reciprocity, since the good of its operation would be certain for

[1] *Œuvres de Turgot*, ii. 434.

France, and the evil would be but for those countries which did not imitate her. M. de Vergennes, on the other hand, thought it was right to suppress the *droit* only provisionally, and to make use of this suppression as a bait, in order to obtain from other nations some commercial advantages. The two ministers, however, at length came to an understanding, and the letters-patent were issued.' The last act of the year took the form of a Declaration of the king 'concerning the trade in butcher-meat during Lent in Paris.' The sale of poultry, game, and meat during Lent had been subjected to great restriction, being a monopoly of the chief Hospital of Paris. Many abuses were the consequence. The Declaration established the same freedom of trade in such provisions in Lent as at other times.

The year 1775 had just begun, when, amidst the efforts he was making so earnestly, so laboriously, and so unflinchingly, to fulfil the duties that lay before him, he was struck down by a serious illness. Gout had been for long hereditary in his family. In ordinary circumstances, the present attack might have been overcome, but most unfortunately at this very time there occurred in the southern provinces of France a calamity, demanding his immediate and unceasing vigilance, and the anxiety thus produced so aggravated his illness as to bring the gout into his chest. For nearly four months he was unable to leave his room. Is stricken with serious illness

The calamity was an outbreak of cattle-plague (*épizootie*) early in January 1775, which soon spread to a most alarming extent. The bulk of correspondence, and of relative documents, of this year, belonging to Turgot's administration, preserved in the national archives, has reference to this distressing malady. The heaviest part of the correspondence and of decrees, &c., &c., was dictated by him during these four months of protracted sufferings. The cattle-plague

But amidst these troubles he never missed an opportunity of remedying abuses of administration. While intendant at Limoges, seeing close at hand all the machinery connected with the *taille*, he felt deeply the injustice of the law of Mitigates the pressure of the *taille contraintes solidaires,* which made a select number of the inhabitants of each parish, and these necessarily the most industrious, responsible for any deficiency that might occur in the yield of the tax, or in its collection. A certain sum was assessed upon the locality, and, in the event of adverse circumstances, disabling the poor inhabitants from paying their portion, or in the event of their gaining the collector to this belief, the deficiency was still held as due by the parish, and the collector now fell back on those inhabitants from whom the money could be most readily got.

On January 3, 1775, he addressed a memorial to the king, fully describing this inequitable practice. Guided by his own experience, he makes a forcible appeal in favour of the class of small farmers who suffered from this law—'the best-off, generally the most intelligent and the most profitably industrious of their parish. We should not conclude, because they are well-to-do, that they have consequently much money in their chests. They would employ it to increase the number of their beasts, or to have them of a better breed, fit for more work. Or they might use it in other ways, for the improvement of their farm, as favourable opportunities presented themselves. Sometimes it would be spent in drainage, at other times in irrigation or in fencing. These men find their own prosperity in making it that of their canton and of the kingdom. If these valuable men are put in prison on account of a deficit in the revenue of the parish, which they could not have foreseen or prevented, all their labours are suspended, and all the profit that the nation would derive from them ceases to exist. If, in order not to be separated from their family, they make efforts to pay, this course is possible for them only by the forced sale, and consequently at much loss, of a portion of their stock. . . .'[1] This memorial was marked *approved* by the king, and a Declaration in accordance with it was issued the same day.

Written in the same spirit of consideration for the cir-

[1] *Œuvres de Turgot,* ii. 372–78.

cumstances of another class, often roughly dealt with, was his 'letter to the Inspectors of Manufactures regarding the carrying out of the regulations concerning industry,' issued a few months later (April 26, 1775). The letter contains advice pertinent, even in our own day, to the system of framing regulations and to the conduct of officials in executing them. He writes: 'Those who have studied with fairness and with reflection the theory and practice of a system of "regulations," must confess that where there is a multiplicity of these, the execution of them is rendered almost impossible. . . . People complain also of the embarrassments they are thrown into by the extreme severity of the penalties, often for the slightest faults. It is indispensable to remedy this, as well as the inconveniences manufacturers suffer from the *contradictions* in the regulations, and to shield them from the abuse of the authority by the Bureaux of Inspection.' He gives a hint to the inspectors as to their treatment of a class of workers, then very numerous in France, the very small manufacturers: 'Above all, nothing is more urgent than to provide for the protection of the labouring and often indigent class, by not encroaching upon the means left to them of alleviating their misery by their activity and their feeling of security. Consequently, I would wish you to turn your attention to the instructions which that class of manufacturers and workers appear to you to stand in need of. You should neglect nothing that can encourage, or even console them, when their own efforts are not sufficient to improve their situation. You are not to seize anything belonging to them, any stuff or merchandise, on the pretext of its faultiness. You will confine yourselves to exhorting these poor artificers to make the things better, and to indicate to them the means of doing so.'[1]

**Relieves the small manufacturers**

§ 3. The gout had just somewhat abated when he forced himself, in spite of medical advice, to return to active superintendence of his bureau, which had now a new difficulty as serious as the *épizootie* to encounter. This was the series

**The corn riots**

[1] Foncin, *Essai sur . . . Turgot*, pp. 194, 590.

of corn riots that were taking place in different parts of the kingdom. The origin and progress of these riots were a puzzle to historians of their own time, and remain still a puzzle to this day. It is possible that the law passed by Turgot for the free circulation of corn may have had something to do with them. A district with natural agricultural advantages over others would have in its principal town an exceptionally large stock of corn, and generally the price in the adjacent country places would be low. The inhabitants would feel a claim to these natural advantages, and would grudge to see the stock in the local granaries being reduced to supply other parts of the kingdom. A rise in price would be taking place, and as the stock became further reduced popular anxiety and discontent would be excited. The spirit of discontent might easily spread to quarters where the conditions were different. It might then become an instrument in the hands of a political faction to be used for political purposes.

The first appearance of popular disturbance was at Dijon, April 20. The harvest of 1774 had been only middling, but there had been harvests even worse without leading to any public disorder. Dijon, however, was the scene of a serious outbreak. 'The peasants, after having demolished the mill of a proprietor whom they accused of monopoly, ransacked the house and smashed the furniture of a councillor of the ex-Parliament, whom they believed to be a forestaller. . . . Quelled in Burgundy, the tumult reappeared suddenly at the gates of the capital, and assumed a graver character. Now its march became disciplined, and its acts were of a nature that implied a plan to starve the city. From Pontoise, the centre of the insurrection, on May 1, brigands departed who spread themselves over all the surrounding country. They roused the people with the cries of "Famine!" and "Monopoly!" they led them to an attack on the markets, exciting them to demand corn and flour below their value, and issuing forged decrees of Council reducing the price. They were kept supplied with gold and silver, and they sometimes bought and sometimes stole provisions, but always in order to *destroy* them. They burned barns, set fire to whole farms, sank boats laden with corn, and intercepted the arrivals by the Lower Seine and the Oise. Next day, May 2, the insurgents arrived at Versailles, pillaged the flour stores, and demanded a reduction in the price of bread. The king, alarmed, was weak enough to direct the police to make a reduction. The agitators during the night marched on Paris. Next morning they pillaged the bakers' shops everywhere. Amidst these extraordinary riots, in which were heard the cries of poor wretches for cheaper bread, while corn, flour, and bread were thrown into the gutter, the authorities were culpably negligent; the disturbances did not seem to displease the Parliament, the Lieutenant of Police, and other great personages.'[1] Turgot did not view these matters with a like equanimity; he believed himself to have reliable information (the sources of which were never rightly known) that these commotions were directed by certain persons of high position and of great wealth, for some sinister purposes of their own, and that the riots would soon become more prevalent and even wilder in their character unless they were at once put down with a strong hand.

He had meanwhile been successful in convincing the king in favour of a firm maintenance of public order. Louis, almost immediately after his concession to the mob at Versailles on May 2, began to suspect he had committed an error. Turgot that day was at Paris. The king wrote to him a letter, reiterating his confidence in him and desiring his presence, ending in these words: 'I fear I have made an error in policy, which I am anxious to repair.'[2] Turgot hastened to Versailles, and carried the king with him in the vigorous action now adopted.

On the day of the riot the Parliament had stuck up in public places a decree which, while forbidding mobs to assemble, suggested that the king should be petitioned to 'reduce the price of bread to a rate proportionate to the

[1] Daire, in *Œuvres de Turgot*, i. xcv. [2] Foncin, *Essai*, liv. ii. chap. v.

needs of the people.' Turgot at once directed the military authority to placard over this decree, with a royal ordinance which interdicted the demanding of bread below the market price. All the bakers' shops were protected by sentinels. A merchant named Planter received at once 50,000 livres as value of a boatful of wheat which the insurgents had cast into the river. Lenoir, the Lieutenant of Police, who had compounded with the insurrection, was dismissed the same night, May 3. Next day the economist Albert was appointed to the place. The Parliament desired to have explanations on these transactions. Turgot had them summoned to Versailles, and obliged them at a bed of justice held on the 5th to register a proclamation of the king, ordering the pillagers to be tried at the courts of the Provost-Marshal. At the same time, sustained in the ministry by Malesherbes [1] and the old Marshal de Muy, Turgot obtained from Louis XVI. a *blanc-seing* (mandate, *carte-blanche*) which placed the military authority under his direct orders, and enabled him to strike the final blow to the *émeute*. An army of 25,000, at the head of which was the Marshal de Biron, pursued the fugitives in all directions and remained encamped along the Seine, the Oise, the Marne, and the Aisne, until the arrivals of grain had taken their ordinary course and public tranquillity was entirely established.' [2]

His vigorous action successful

There is indeed much reason to suspect that an important element in these commotions was the design to discredit Turgot's ministry by a party closely attached by self-interest and convictions to existing privileges which were menaced by his well-known reforming aims. He had, in the meantime, signally triumphed over his enemies; there was left to them the mortification of defeat, and the desire to be revenged. Condorcet had probably good reason for his opinion, afterwards expressed to Voltaire, as to the real feelings of the Prime Minister respecting the Comptroller.

[1] Malesherbes had, some months before the termination of the riots, taken the place of La Vrillière in the Cabinet.

[2] Daire, *Œuvres de Turgot*, i. xcvii.

You know (he writes) the Count de Maurepas, his feebleness, his frivolity, his jealousy of all superior talents. . . . The character, the virtue, the wide views of Turgot oppressed him and humiliated him. Everything, however, went on very well between them until the time of the riots. . . . Maurepas was at the Opera that night; Turgot had been up three nights running. M. Lenoir, a kind of valet at the service of all the Ministers, pleased Maurepas very well; but Turgot got him dismissed for some reason without consulting Maurepas. The Parliament, which wished to increase the disturbances, while making appearance to quiet them, was reduced to silence. The necessity for this was not seen until eleven o'clock at night. Turgot posted to Versailles; he awoke the king, the Council was assembled during the night, the bed of justice resolved upon, the placards of the seditious decree effaced before day. Maurepas, astonished, afraid, allowed this to pass, but there remained in him a settled jealousy against Turgot, whom he now regarded as a dangerous rival. The Keeper of the Seals (Miroménil) perceived this feeling, and took care to nourish it.[1]

During this period of the corn riots a name of some eminence came into conflict with Turgot's. Shortly before the riots had broken out appeared M. Necker's work 'Sur la Législation et le Commerce des Grains,' which was little else than an apology for the popular prejudices against the free circulation of corn, and was evidently intended to check the rising influence of Turgot in the Government. It was within Turgot's power to suppress the work, and he was strongly advised by some to do so, but he was too true a friend of free discussion to listen to such advice. The unpractical, superficial, and almost puerile character of Necker's ideas may be seen from the leading proposal made in his work. Necker

So long, he says, as corn has not reached the price to which it can be raised without causing great inconvenience, there should be the most complete liberty of sale or purchase. . . . But as soon as it shall have advanced to a high price, I would prevent all advances in price derived from the intervention of the merchants. I would bring the sellers direct to the consumers by

[1] Condorcet to Voltaire, June 12, 1776 (quoted by Mastier in *Turgot, sa Vie et sa Doctrine*, p. 435).

ordaining that, beyond a certain price, corn was not to be sold in the market.[1]

Monopolies suppressed

He now found himself free to complete his scheme for establishing the perfect freedom of the corn trade, throughout the whole kingdom, by removing several antiquated legal trammels, and by abolishing oppressive *octroi* duties at Dijon, Beaune, Pontoise, Bordeaux, and other places by several edicts, issued during June, July, and August. One of the edicts applied to a state of things at Rouen which was so illustrative of the corrupt fiscal condition of many parts of France at the time, that it deserves to be specially mentioned. It will be best described in his words of the preamble to the edict itself of June 1775.

The millers of Rouen

In the city of Rouen the trade in corn and flour is permitted exclusively to a Company of privileged merchants, numbering 112, created by the edicts of November 1692 and July 1693. Their privileges extend not only to the right of being the sole sellers of grains in the market of the city and at their shops, but of being the sole purchasers of grains brought from the interior of the kingdom or from abroad. . . . In this same city the buyers of corn are not free to choose their own porters, at wages agreed upon between them, but the sole right of handling is confined to ninety porters, whose offices, very anciently created, then abolished, were established and confirmed by letters-patent of September 28th, 1675, and August 1677. . . . In this same city of Rouen there exists a right of thirlage (*banalité*) attached to the five mills belonging to the town, which is as hurtful as the privileges already stated to the means of freely provisioning the public and to a moderate price of bread; for this right forbids the bakers of the town to buy or use any other flour than that ground by these mills. Moreover, these mills not being sufficient to meet consumption, the bakers can only obtain extra supply of flour from outside by paying to the farmer (lessee) of the *banalité* an equivalent for the charge for grinding held to be lost to

[1] Necker, *Sur la Législation, etc., des Grains*, part iv. chap. v. 'Necker's book,' observes M. Gustave de Molinari, 'shows superabundantly that he was but a poor economist; his conduct at the *début* of the French Revolution, although honourable, proves, with not less evidence, that there was not in him the stuff of a great minister. He was only a clever financier of the second rank, and an honest philanthropist—nothing more.' (*Mélanges d'Économie politique*, ii. 209.)

the mills of the town. If institutions, as injurious to the sustenance of the people as they are contrary to every right principle, require a revision wherever they exist, they demand it more particularly in our city of Rouen, which Nature has designed by the advantages of its fortunate position to become the metropolis of a large commerce, the most convenient depôt for the importation of foreign grain, and for the circulation of home-grown, the centre from which abundance, in the city itself and secured to its inhabitants, ought to spread itself by the Seine towards our good city of Paris, and to the interior provinces of the kingdom.[1]

Without injustice

It was consistent with his just manner of dealing with every place of privilege, that while declaring that, for the public good, these privileges in Rouen must be immediately abolished, the edict concludes with an assurance that equitable compensation would be made to all who would suffer loss of office, or of income, by the suppression of the old system.

The consecration of the king

In the meantime the arrangements for the consecration and coronation of the king engrossed public attention. Turgot was anxious that the ceremony should take place in Paris, as marking a departure from mediæval associations, and that it should be purged from its old leaven of superstition, and from the sanction of intolerance, given by the king's vows to exterminate heretics. But the clergy were furious against any change, and their power, supported by the time-serving Maurepas, was decisive. The ceremony was conducted on the old lines, and at Rheims (June 15, 1775). It is said that when the king came to the exterminating passages ('I swear . . . to exterminate, &c., entirely from my States all heretics . . . condemned by the Church') he delivered it very indistinctly—almost inaudibly. Very shortly afterwards Turgot made this occasion a text for addressing to the king a memorial 'Sur la Tolérance,' the object of which was to encourage the king to treat the formula as a dead letter.[2] His memorial was not unnecessary, for only three months after this the clergy (September 24, 1775),

[1] *Œuvres de Turgot*, ii. 200–203.

[2] Abridged, *infra*, pp. 256–64.

hoping to overawe the young monarch by a published remonstrance, implored him to remember his oath. 'It is reserved for you,' they said, 'to deal the last blow to Calvinism in your kingdom. Order the schismatic assemblies of the Protestants to be dispersed; exclude the sectaries without distinction from all the branches of public administration. Your Majesty will thus assure among your subjects the unity of the Catholic worship.' This had been answered by anticipation in Turgot's memorial, to the effect that 'The Church has the right to judge in matters of religion—yes, without doubt; it has the right to exclude from its body, to anathematise, those who refuse to submit to its decisions. . . . But the Church is not a temporal power. . . . The prince who orders his subject to profess a religion he does not believe, or to renounce the one he does believe, commands a crime; the subject who obeys acts a lie, he betrays his conscience, he does an act which, he believes, God forbids. The Protestant who through self-interest or fear makes himself a Catholic, and the Catholic who by the same motives makes himself a Protestant, are both guilty of the same sin.'[1]

Malesherbes in the Cabinet

La Vrillière, old minister of the late king, at this time retired. Great efforts were made by a clique of courtiers, countenanced by the queen herself, to procure the appointment for a creature of the Duke de Choiseul. But Maurepas, for some personal reasons, disliking the man proposed, listened favourably to Turgot's earnest recommendation of Malesherbes for the office. The character of Malesherbes standing so high, and his abilities being so unquestionable, Maurepas knew that his appointment could not, at least, be openly opposed by the intriguers. But there was great difficulty in obtaining Malesherbes' acceptance of the office. His position as president of the 'Cour des Aides' was one that in every way suited his character and his inclinations. It gave him great dignity without any political responsibility. In these respects no rank in the State is more enviable than that of a judge whose eminence is universally acknowledged.

[1] *Œuvres de Turgot*, ii. 496.

No man was more conscious than Malesherbes of the necessity of reform in all departments of State, no man could be more eloquent in denouncing the evils existing, and, as the author of the remonstrance of his Court to the king, proposing the summoning of the States-General, he gave evidence of his constitutional leanings and of his courage in speech. But it is easier to see the evil, and to give the best advice for curing it, than to take an active hand in the cure itself, and to be personally responsible for the result. When the seat in the Cabinet was offered to Malesherbes he declined it; after repeated pressing he still declined it. Turgot and Malesherbes had for years been of one mind on nearly all practical public questions; they admired, they loved each other; each believed the other to be the destined means of regenerating France. Turgot, by a wonderful good fortune, was now in power, but his work was scarcely begun; he was single-handed in the Ministry; he knew what opposition he would meet with from his colleagues to almost every measure dealing boldly with finance. But, with Malesherbes at his side, in the Council, all might be right. Feeling Malesherbes' accession to the Government to be almost a matter of life or death for the cause of reform, Turgot made such earnest appeals to his sense of public duty and to his friendship that at last he was gained over. He accepted the portfolio of the *Maison du Roi* (July 19, 1775), and was gratified by receiving the following letter from the king: 'I have charged M. Turgot to express to you the high estimation in which I hold your fidelity to my service and your love for the public good, and that I wish to see you both beside me, acquiring in concert new claims to my esteem and my warm friendship.'

The importance of this step was very hopefully felt by many who were closely watching the course of events. Mlle. de Lespinasse, for example, writes with enthusiasm to Guibert as soon as she hears the news: 'Never, yes, never, have two men more enlightened, more virtuous, more disinterested, more active, been joined together and animated more strongly by the highest motives. . . . You will see it, their Ministry will leave a deep impression on the minds of men.'

Count St. Germain

The only other official change that occurred in the Ministry while Turgot belonged to it was brought about by the death (October 10) of Du Muy, the Minister of War, who was succeeded (October 21) by the Count St. Germain. This appointment was due mainly to the influence of Turgot and Malesherbes, who believed St. Germain to be actuated by a public spirit kindred to their own. St. Germain had been popular while an officer in the army, and been noted for advocating radical improvements in military administration. This had prejudiced Turgot in his favour. Before committing himself with St. Germain, however, interviews had been held in which the Count expressed unreservedly his acquiescence in Turgot's schemes and general policy. But St. Germain, too eager to gratify his ambition, was willing enough to give pledges, the importance of which, and their obligation upon him, did not deeply impress him. This high promotion was so completely unexpected by him, that it may be truly said to have turned his head. After introducing a few salutary minor reforms in the army, his schemes of a larger comprehension were ill-considered and deservedly unsuccessful. He forgot his engagements with Turgot to keep the military expenditure in accordance with the financial scheme of the Comptroller-General, and claimed independence for his own office. The majority in the Council profited by this disposition of St. Germain to make use of him against Turgot, who by this time was in public opinion beginning to be acknowledged as the really important man of the Ministry. Thus, it was left to the minority of two, Turgot and Malesherbes, to struggle on for the ten months that remained for them. They were able to accomplish much, owing to the prudence with which Turgot selected for his attack abuses which were really flagrant, and to his directing his attack on them with great skill, justifying each act by reasons convincing to all fair minds, and at the same time disarming those interested

Turgot and Malesherbes only

in the existing systems by admitting all claims they could justly urge; and last, but not least, owing to the fact that Turgot had been successful in prepossessing the king in favour of the reforms proposed.

§ 4. The time had now come for him to apply himself to the chief duty of a finance minister—the construction of his Budget. Any attempt here to present a view of his financial operations in detail to the English general reader, at a distance of more than a century after the event, would be positively tedious. It will be sufficient to give a brief summary of these operations, taken from writers who have made them a special study. The Budget.

At the 1st of January, 1775, this was the situation of the Treasury: the revenue of the State amounted to 337,000,000 livres [francs]; but after deduction made for interest on the debt, funded and floating, the expenses of the king's and princes' households, and of sundry other charges, there remained free only the sum of 213,000,000 for the public services. As the expenditure on these came to 235,000,000, there was thus a deficit of 22,000,000. Besides this, the *anticipations*, that is to say, the advances made by the financiers on the produce of taxes yet to be collected, formed an uncovered balance of 78,000,000, and another, which amounted to 235,000,000, was represented by the *dette exigible*, which we now term the floating debt. Such was the heritage which, after a series of infamous financial dishonesties, Abbé Terray left to his successor. . . . To respect the legitimate engagements contracted by the State, to repay them to the extent the resources of the Treasury allowed, to increase these resources by a better system of administration, to limit the expenses of the Court and of the Government to a scale of the strictest economy, to extinguish the *anticipations* and the *dette exigible* in order to escape from the ruinous dependence upon the financiers, finally, to deliver industry from a burden of taxes, most vexatious in character and yielding little revenue—such was the plan of the new Comptroller-General. The application of it allowed him to raise the extraordinary receipts of the current year to nearly 67,000,000, to pay off 15,000,000 *dette exigible*, 28,000,000 *anticipations*, and to leave for the balance-sheet of 1776 a deficit now under 15,000,000.[1]

[1] Daire, *Œuvres de Turgot*, i. p. lxxxviii.

Taking the actual results of Turgot's whole financial period, and their bearing upon the balance-sheet of his successor, he succeeded in recovering for the Treasury more than he had estimated, and as the expenditure had been maintained within the estimate, and there remained at his disposal 12½ million livres not expended in 1775, the minister who succeeded to Turgot had to find, to balance the deficit of receipts, only 4½ million livres.[1] Turgot had, by skilful operations in finance, restored public confidence in the Government. At the time of his leaving office, in order to pay off a loan more burdensome, he had negotiated in Holland a loan at 4 per cent.; his predecessor had paid in some cases 12 per cent. and more.[2]

Reform of Governmen contracts

Probably the most arduous work of all to which he applied himself was the reform of the Government contracts. His predecessors in office had involved the State in engagements with the Farmers-General and other syndicates of financiers, and with syndicates managing different monopolies, the results of which were vast gains for the contractors, with a comparatively trifling benefit to the Government.

The *domaine réel* (Crown lands) had, by Terray just the previous year, been let to the Farmers-General on a lease of *thirty* years, in consideration of their giving a moderate advance upon the rents previously payable by different tenants on short tenures. One provision in the lease was that the farmers, besides the cultivated lands formerly let, should, without further payment, have the use of all the domain lands not yet cultivated. Another provision gave them the right to all lands to which the Crown might yet lay claim. Worse considered conditions than these for the State could scarcely be conceived. The farmers were able, under them, to effect in the very first year of their lease sub-leases for six or ten years, the rents of which nearly covered their own whole rent due to the Government. Turgot cancelled this thirty years' lease of the *domaine*, organised a fresh

[1] Jobez; *La France sous Louis XVI*, i. 450–51.

[2] Batbie, *Turgot, Philosophe, Économiste et Administrateur.* Paris, 1861.

administration of it, from which the Government drew a rent of six instead of one and a half millions, and limited its duration to nine years.

The contract to supply the Government with gunpowder and saltpetre rested on terms as disadvantageous to the State as those of the lease just mentioned. The monopoly of the manufacture and sale of these articles had been granted to a company on condition of a certain quantity of powder being supplied for the arsenals and the Navy at a price considerably lower, indeed, than the cost of production. But during a time of peace, the Government requirements coming far short of the stipulated quantity, the burden on the company was comparatively slight; on the other hand, during a time of war, the company not being required to supply any more than the stipulated quantity, and this being greatly insufficient, the Government had to obtain further supplies from other sources. The company was under the obligation to take their saltpetre from the incorporated saltpetre makers at seven sous per pound; but as the price of the article fixed forty years before had risen, the Government had to indemnify the saltpetre makers for the loss they sustained.[1]

Thus any saving to the Government in the cost of powder was neutralised by the cost of saltpetre. As it was, the Powder Company were able to enjoy a dividend of 30 per cent. He revoked the contract, arranging for the company's capital being reimbursed within four years, and meanwhile paying them 10 per cent. interest. He established, in their stead, a Government *régie* (Board), and placed at its head Lavoisier, the greatest chemist of the time. A great economy was the result. At the same time he appointed a commission of scientific men to report upon the supply of saltpetre and on the methods of manufacture, and authorised the Academy of Sciences to offer a prize for the best essay on the subject.

[1] The manufacture of saltpetre was then conducted in France according to very primitive principles, unimproved upon since the time of Francis I. It was obtained by demolishing old buildings and excavating foundations, and then lixiviating the rubbish.

Abolition of sinecures

The Revenue of the State being insufficient even for the necessary expenditure, he felt himself compelled to abolish, as far as he could, the sinecures which, under a succession of corrupt administrations, had grown up.

The Court banker was an intermediary, whose reason of existence was to levy a commission on a large amount of Government transactions, which could more satisfactorily have been managed directly. This official was typical of a class, and we may be sure that in suppressing the office Turgot must have made for himself enemies of all those who considered it to be the principal duty of the Government to find for them places with the least possible work to do, and with the highest possible pay to them for doing it. He did not, however, indulge his passion for economy to the injury of any having a fair claim upon the generosity of the State. After overtaking the arrears in the payment of interest on the public debt, he proceeded to pay up the State pensions which had been suspended for three and four years: with his usual consideration for the necessitous, he ordered two years' arrears at once to be paid to the pensioners of the humblest rank.

Superintendence of the Posts

In July 1775 the Superintendence of the Posts was included in the Comptroller's department; Turgot giving an example to other officials, by undertaking the new duties, while declining to accept their usual emoluments.

Conveniences for travelling in France at that time were far behind those in other countries. He reformed the contracts for the stage-coaching on the great roads, and introduced a service of new diligences of lighter build and better arranged, and plying at reduced fares; these became popularly known as *turgotines*.[1]

Freedom of the wine trade

The wine trade of France was then (as it still is) one of her most important sources of wealth, but production, transport, sale, and purchase were all hampered by a multiplicity of local monopolies, iniquitous restrictions, and absurd and vexatious regulations, the mere description of which, in the

[1] 'Thanks to Turgot, five and a half days were now taken between Paris and Bordeaux instead of fourteen.' (H. Martin, *History*, xvi. 362.)

edict abolishing them, occupies about twenty pages. For examples, at Bordeaux it was forbidden to sell and to consume any other wine than that produced from the vineyards within that seneschal's district. A maker could not sell his own wine by retail without being a burgess of Bordeaux and unless he lived in the town with his family for six months in the year. The wines of Languedoc were not permitted to descend the Garonne before St. Martin's Day; those of Perigord, &c., not before Christmas. A curious instance is given of the extreme to which rules suggested by self-interest may be carried in connection with Marseilles, whose local authorities, by an edict of March 1717, had forbidden all captains of ships touching at the port to buy any other wine for the ship's provision than that of the territory of the town; 'and in order,' it is stated, 'to prevent infractions of this article, the magistrates shall *not sign any bill of health* for the said vessels without having first had the certificate of the two intendants that they have searched the said vessels and found that the wine on board had been bought in the town of Marseilles.'

It took some time for him to prepare the way for the extensive reform he contemplated, which was nothing less than the establishment of complete freedom in the wine trade over France; but this he at last accomplished by the edict of April 1776. The justification for it was stated in these words:—

> It is the interest of the whole kingdom we have to consider, the interests and the rights of all our subjects, who, as buyers or as sellers, have an equal right to find a market for their goods and to procure the object of their needs on the terms most advantageous to themselves; and it is the interest of the State itself, because its wealth depends upon the most extensive demand being obtained for the produce of its land and its industry, and upon the increase of revenue, which is the consequence of that national development.[1]

These words appear commonplace to us when read at the present day, but at that time and for long afterwards in

[1] *Œuvres de Turgot*, ii. 344–57.

France such ideas were considered by the majority of people to be quite sufficiently condemned in being called Quixotic and *doctrinaire*.

Minor fiscal reforms

We have dwelt only on the most important reforms effected by him in his short administration of twenty months, during nearly a fourth part of which he was kept from active work by his severe illness of the winter 1774–75, and by repeated attacks of gout at other times. A list of the minor fiscal reforms made, on which we have not touched, would itself have been enough to signalise the career of an ordinary Comptroller-General. We are tempted to mention just one of these as displaying his singular freedom from the red-tape spirit of officialism. In any case of obscurity in the meaning of fiscal regulations, it had been the practice invariably to interpret the law in favour of the Treasury ; Turgot reversed this, giving the benefit of the doubt to the public.

Science

In his short ministry the claims of science were not neglected. Two chairs were established in the College of France, one for Law, the other for French Literature. Medicine received an effective impulse by the foundation of a school for Clinical studies and another for Comparative Anatomy, March 1776, and by the foundation of the Royal Society of Medicine—the origin of the existing Academy. Hydro-dynamics was the object of a special teaching, entrusted to Bossut (September 1775). Three illustrious savants, D'Alembert, Bossut, and Condorcet, were charged with the preparation of a large scheme for the construction of canals. To Turgot belongs the first idea of a unitary metrical system. He wrote to the Marine Astronomer, Messier, that he had 'the project to get ascertained, by exact experiments, the precise length of oscillation of the pendulum, which should serve as a common standard and as a term of comparison to all the measures, which could easily be reduced from it.' [1]

[1] Eugène Asse, in *Biog. gén.* xlv. 726. This idea of a philosophical and natural standard for all weights and measures was sanctioned by the French National Assembly March 17, 1791, but the system adopted was reduced from the Quadrant of the Meridian.

The *Caisse d'Escompte* (Discount Bank) was founded by Turgot by an order of Council March 24, 1776. Its capital was fixed at fifteen millions divided into five thousand shares of three thousand livres. 'This capital,' says Gomel, 'which would be thought small to-day, appeared very considerable at the beginning of the reign of Louis XVI. The creation of the *Caisse d'Escompte*, which afterwards the Consulate was to imitate in founding the Bank of France, is for Turgot a very high mark of honour.' [1]

Banking

Never neglectful of the claims of the provinces, he projected the establishment also of country banks, which would have advanced money to proprietors on the security of the heritages; thus, as Tissot observes, 'anticipating by three-quarters of a century the functions of the Crédit Foncier.'

Scheme of local government

§ 5. In 1775, Turgot (assisted by his devoted friend and secretary, Dupont de Nemours), during the intervals of more urgent affairs, had laid down the lines of a scheme of 'municipalities.' Circumstances did not permit of the scheme being ever submitted to the king and the Council. It deserves our notice, however, as indicating the direction in which his policy would have advanced, had he retained power. To describe the scheme briefly, it was one for establishing local government in the provinces of France by a series of local councils, beginning at the parish [2] and the village, rising to the arrondissement and to the district, thence to the provincial assembly, and thence to the General Assembly. The qualification for the parish and village council, and the foundation of the whole 'hierarchy' of municipalities, was the possession of real property, of any amount, however small. All having 600 or more livres

[1] Gomel, *Les Causes financières de la Rév. fr.* (1892), p. 435.

[2] The first step in France to place local government on a representative basis was taken by the decree of December 14, 1789. In the United Kingdom, municipal reform (we may almost say municipal life) dates from 1835. But no attempt was made to deal with Turgot's chosen unit—the *parish*—in the modern spirit till the much-debated Parish Councils Bill for England and Wales was passed in March 1894.

income were to be members of the council and to have equal votes, but those under 600 livres to have only a 'fractional' vote; three of 200 or six of 100 livres, clubbing together, could elect one member of the council. Those thus qualified for the parish or village councils would not exceed a convenient number for voting, in person, at the council, but for the council of the arrondissement, a much larger district, representation would be necessary by a deputy from each parish or village council within the district; the provincial assembly would be composed of deputies from the arrondissement councils, within the boundaries of the province; a member from each provincial assembly would be elected to the General Assembly in Paris. The series of municipalities was elaborated in considerable detail.[1] The property qualification is one of which modern democratic opinion would scarcely approve. In fairness to Turgot, however, we should recollect that the scheme was designed for the country districts, not for the towns (which had some government of their own), and that peasant proprietors in France formed a very large body even in his time, although not so numerous as they became after the Revolution. It may be stated that he afterwards saw reason to broaden his views in respect to the electoral basis. There were other features in the scheme that experience in working would no doubt have greatly modified. But had some such scheme as this been carried at the time, it would have done much to check the tendency to centralisation, excess of which has been the constant bane of the French political system to this day.

National education

The memorial on municipalities is admirable if for nothing else than the prominence given in it to 'the first and most important of all the institutions necessary, and the one most fit to immortalise your Majesty's reign,' the organisation by the State of a system of national education, an organisation not attempted by the French Government (nor even, adequately, by any other) for nearly another hundred

[1] *Œuvres de Turgot*, ii. 502–50.

years. From the earnestness of his language when dwelling upon this topic, we may reasonably conclude that, had he been allowed to remain in power, a plan of national education would have formed his principal work.

**His views on representative government**

The mention of Turgot's scheme of local government naturally suggests the inquiry, what were his views on the larger question of representative government in the form of a really National Parliament? It must be candidly admitted that we have no evidence before us that he rightly appreciated the immense educational advantages to the people of thoroughly representative institutions. He regarded the French people of his time as not sufficiently instructed to be trusted with much political power. As Mr. Morley has said, 'everything for the people, nothing by the people, was the maxim of the Economists, and Turgot held it in all its rigour.' But it may be said for Turgot that, seeing the condition of the people to be so utterly miserable, he felt himself impelled, in the circumstances, to seize upon the *readiest* means of raising their condition, and he found this means in the existing ample power of the monarchy. As minister, he availed himself of that authority to the full extent permissible. It is possible he did not sufficiently realise that all permanent improvement in the people's character and condition must be mainly accomplished by themselves. Possibly he did not perceive that even the errors committed by the people, in the exercise of their political rights, are a true education to them, and that to withhold liberty from the people, from fear of the wrong use they might make of it, is just as wise as the dictum that no man must go into the water before he has learned to swim. Although a plea for a representative legislature, as a practical measure, is not clearly advocated in his writings, we may be unjust in accusing him of underrating its advantages. We may venture to believe that he looked forward to the time for such a legislature to be established in France, and considered that it would be fortunate for her if the first direct efforts of her people's political life had not to encounter arrears of misgovernment too vast for them to deal with patiently. Hence his anxiety to clear away, in the meantime, by such power as the king possessed, all the grosser abuses in the State, in order to prepare for a time when the people could take upon themselves a larger share in the government, and when the political atmosphere would be charged with the least possible danger. This is indeed only a conjecture upon Turgot's views, but it is one, at least, not inconsistent with the tenor of his political doctrine and of his writings.

Turgot's opponents: § 6. It is now time that we bring within our view the reception given to his measures by certain classes, and persons influential with the Government and at the Court.

The two great classes, who had long held in their hands the control of all public affairs, were the Nobles and the Clergy. While Intendant of Limoges, in his dealings with the *taille*, the *corvée*, and other public grievances, he had never concealed his opinion that there could be no real improvement for France while the unjust and absurd 'privileges' of the Nobles were maintained. As far as an intendant had power, he did not hesitate to restrain these privileges when necessary for the protection of the oppressed peasantry. Thus, he had already one of the great classes in opposition to him. The Clergy felt they had a common interest with the Nobles, in having also privileges of their own to defend, and Turgot was specially an object of their dislike. He was known for holding liberal views on religion—not indeed those of a shallow sceptic, careless of truth or error, but those of an earnest believer in religious principles of action, who had the audacity to desire that 'Christian' principles should guide *public* as well as private life. We need not be surprised, then, at the Clergy calling Turgot 'a dangerous man.' He had besides offended them notably by the efforts he had made to modernise the king's consecration, and by his eloquent plea for toleration.

Mainly recruited from the families of these two great privileged classes were two bodies—limited in numbers, but, by the nature of their functions, having a direct and strong influence on the course of affairs—the Parliament and the financiers. The Parliament, as restored, was Turgot's declared enemy. When, during the late reign, it was suspended, Turgot, as we have seen, had accepted one of the vacant judicial offices, in order that the administration of justice should not be hindered. By these unionists of the legal profession he would, no doubt, be looked upon as a 'blackleg.' He was well known, besides, to have always regarded the Parliament as responsible only to itself, quasi-hereditary and venal in constitution, as a dangerous *imperium in imperio*, and to have opposed its recall at the beginning of the present reign. It is not surprising, then, that the Parliament was Turgot's declared enemy.

Again, by his reform of contracts injurious to the State, by the strictness of his financial economy, and his determination to save the Government as much as possible from anticipating the revenue, he necessarily displeased the men who profited, and profited enormously, by the old system of finance.

Thus it was that all the great 'classes' found themselves at one in disliking Turgot; and, as they had reason to believe that he contemplated still further reforms in the State—what they would call invasions upon their privileges—they prepared themselves to make use of their first opportunity of effecting his overthrow.

This main body of his opponents was augmented by all the smaller classes, whose self-interests had been attacked by the carrying out of his many administrative improvements and by his abolition of useless offices, and it was further augmented by other persons, still in office, who, conscious of performing there no public service, feared that their own time would come for being similarly dealt with.

No 'public opinion'

Against all these foes, what were the forces on his side that he could count upon? His beneficent policy as Minister had as yet had no time to bear the fruits which would have justified it in public opinion and gained for him a popularity that would have strengthened his position. There was, indeed, little of what could be called 'public opinion' in France in those days. The tittle-tattle of the Court, carried into the several coteries of society, constituted nearly all the discussion and criticism to which affairs of State were subjected. The general public had little or no information to guide them on political questions. The newspaper press, as a means of disseminating such information and of directing opinion, was quite insignificant. Thus, there was no educated or organised public opinion to which Turgot could immediately have appealed. Could he, then, like other statesmen in similar cases, have fallen back upon the passive or active strength of a time-honoured political constitution? But France had no constitution. It was Turgot's dream that the efforts he was making for her redemption would in time assist in building up a constitution, to be crowned afterwards by other hands than his. The only substitute she had for a constitution was the power resting in the king. This, although ill-defined and certainly not indefeasible, was a real power. 'The divinity that doth hedge a king' was still reverently recognised, and by use and wont for many centuries the kings of France had been allowed to exercise, unchallenged, considerable personal power in the Government.

The monarchy

At this critical time of Turgot's ministry, Louis XVI. had reached his twenty-second year. He was still animated with the sincere desire to do all that a king could do for the good of France, but he was sadly at a loss to know what would make, and what would not make, for the good of France. With only average mental endowments, he had not much improved these by any proper education. Aware of his deficiencies, he was ready enough to be guided by others. Himself well-meaning, he believed others to be the same, and was too easily a convert to his last adviser. He had been deeply impressed by Turgot's earnest character and by the importance of the financial and other measures laid before him. These were always patiently explained to him, and thus, in Turgot's hands, he was gradually receiving some good training in political science and political government. Turgot and the king, indeed, had become fast friends. Turgot's edicts, decrees, ordinances, &c., in the king's name, made up the greater part of the public acts of the ministry. People were beginning to talk of Turgot as the principal man in the Government. This, and especially the king's favour for him, gave rise to a feeling of jealousy in old Maurepas and the personal friends of Maurepas in the Ministry. They had little sympathy with Turgot's reforming spirit, and, in the Council, gave little support to his policy; their programme would rather have been 'how *not* to do it.' This puzzled the king, and he often gave expression to the feeling that it was 'only Turgot and himself who really loved the people.'

**The Court**

Maurepas and his personal *entourage* might have been named a committee of the Court, and their ideas on Turgot were soon communicated to, and accepted by, the larger body.

That his policy should meet with no favour at the Court was quite to be expected. A reforming minister is ever the *bête noire* of a court. The French Court hated Turgot for daring to think that the weight of taxation bore too heavily upon the poorer, and too lightly upon the richer classes. They hated him because he had abolished sinecures, the very object of a courtier's most sacred respect. They hated him because he was preaching economy—was pressing the king, in the interests of the State, to reduce the extravagant expenses connected with the Court and to revise the lavish list of pensions, which had grown to an extraordinary number and amount. Every one at Court was more or less a place-hunter, if not for himself at least for his friends. Turgot reduced the salary of several offices that had been overpaid, and instead of accepting, for any vacancy, an incompetent courtier, or a courtier's incompetent friend, he bestowed the office on the man most fit for it, and, where possible, on one connected with the particular department concerned, deserving a promotion. The magnitude of this offence, as measured by the Court mind, can be easily conceived. They hated him for his independence of character in actually taking part against persons of rank and title when found guilty of evading the law. He had not been in office more than three months when he had to refuse to the Prince de Condé permission to acquire land compulsorily in the town of Stenay for the erection of an ironwork. He wrote to the Prince (November 29, 1774), politely but firmly:—

> His Majesty is persuaded of the utility which would follow from such an establishment; he, on the other hand, thinks that the case is not the same with an ironwork as with a public building or a highway. These last objects belong eventually to the general welfare, and there is an indispensable necessity to take possession of property required for them; but if, for a private work, we subject proprietors to the compulsory sale of their patrimony, it would be a kind of spoliation, for it could not be reconciled with the principles of justice and security which form the basis of all rights existing in the State.

The Duke of Orleans had applied for authority to establish a market at Livry, on his own property, with the right of levying dues on the merchandise brought to it. Turgot replied that there could be no objection to the market, but that the dues could not be allowed. 'With an establishment of this kind,' he said, 'existing only for the advantage of the public, it would be against this principle to allow those private individuals who founded it to impose duties which could only tend to raise the price of the commodities and of the cattle sold there.'

A sample of the overbearing character often displayed by the nobles was furnished by a practice many of them had of driving at a furious rate through the barriers of Paris, in order to prevent their carriages being inspected by the collectors of the *octroi*. The examination of every basket and bundle carried by the poor was rigidly enforced; it was not in Turgot's nature to permit the regulation to be treated with such contempt by the rich. He published an ordinance of the king (February 15, 1775) that 'all postilions, coachmen, or conductors of carriages, even of the equipage of the king, of the queen, and of the princes of the blood, must stop at the gates and barriers of Paris at the first request of the clerks stationed there. The trunks, boxes, valises, &c., must be examined, if necessary, even in the bureau,' and that any persons evading this regulation would be punished 'by the confiscation of the merchandise, with five hundred livres of fine and imprisonment.'[1] Law, administered without respect to persons, was quite a new experience of the nobles; a minister so enforcing it would deserve from them the name he now got, 'Monster.'

It was every day made more and more clear to him that only by his having the king resolutely on his side could he cope with his united enemies. To have kept the king steady in his favour, there was needed only the support, or at least the neutrality, of the queen.

It was not in the queen's nature to remain neutral when she had an opportunity of asserting herself. Supercilious, self-willed, conscious of possessing greater ability than her husband, she seemed to expect that the prerogatives of royalty should fall mainly to herself. Not content with being the leading personage at the Court, she was never happy unless interfering with State appointments and State affairs, and, unfortunately, this interference was, in nearly every case, ill judged and misdirected. Her conduct in this respect caused deep anxiety to her mother, the Empress Maria Theresa, who was kept regularly informed ef events at Versailles and at Paris by her ambassador, M. de Mercy. The queen

It was at his mother's suggestion, no doubt, that the Emperor Joseph II.[2] wrote to Marie Antoinette, his sister, a letter of advice and warning. The letter actually sent has not been preserved, but it was a modification of the following, its first draft, which is in itself peculiarly interesting:—

[1] *Œuvres de Turgot*, ii. 489.

[2] Joseph II., the reforming emperor, was naturally an admirer of a reforming minister, and during his tour through France he had made it a point to have an interview with Turgot on at least two occasions.

> As far as I can understand [writes the emperor], you meddle with an infinity of things that, first of all, do not concern you, which you know nothing about. . . . What business have you, my dear sister, to interfere with the placing of ministers, to get such a department given to this one, and such to that, in order to influence in favour of a particular law-suit, and to create a new and extravagant charge at your Court?[1] What studies have you made fitting you to mix yourself with the affairs of Government of the French monarchy?—you, an endearing young person, whose thoughts centre in frivolity, in your toilet, in your whole day's amusements, who never read or listen to reason a quarter of an hour in a month, who never reflect, never meditate, I am sure of it—never. Only the impression of the moment concerns you; your only guides are the words and arguments of your protégés.[2]

Maria Theresa clearly foresaw the troubles her daughter was preparing for the monarchy and for herself. In reply to a letter from De Mercy with the latest news of the queen's political intrigues, and those of her favourite advisers, the empress writes: 'My inquietudes are only confirmed; she is going with rapid strides to her ruin.'[3]

The opposition made by the queen to the appointment of Malesherbes, and the mortification she felt at her schemes being overturned by the influence of Turgot with the king, have been already mentioned. A few months after the nomination of Malesherbes, the opportunity occurred for the re-arrangement of the Post administration, which Turgot, as we have seen, made use of to effect a saving to the State. The queen had intended that the lucrative and easy office of Superintendent of Posts should be conferred upon the Chevalier de Montmorency. The king sided with his minister. She could not conceal her annoyance, and, as Mercy states, 'when the Comptroller-General presented himself before her, the queen did not address him.'[4]

She was still more incensed at the opposition Turgot felt

[1] Alluding to the De Guines affair and to the Lamballe appointment.

[2] Marie-Antoinette, *Correspondance secrète entre Marie-Thérèse et le Comte de Mercy*. Par D'Arneth et Geffroy (Paris, 1874), ii. 363.

[3] Jobez. (But I have not found these words in the *Corresp. sec.*)

[4] *Corresp. sec.* ii. 366.

himself constrained to make to her reviving the old dignity and emoluments of Superintendent of the Queen's Household for her favourite the Princess de Lamballe. The normal salary had been 15,000 livres, with 30,000 to keep table at Court. But Mademoiselle de Bourbon, the last superintendent, got hers increased to 50,000 crowns (150,000 livres). The Princess de Lamballe, who was very self-interested, desired to have the same, and was supported in this by the queen.[1]

There was [says Foncin] no harmony possible between the severe Comptroller-General and a queen who considered it her chief duty to demand places and money for her friends. Not content to have obtained 50,000 crowns for the Princess de Lamballe, she must grant 600 louis to the Count d'Esterhazy in order to pay some of his debts; she must grant a widow's pension to the Countess de la Marche, who was only separated from her husband; she must solicit for the Viscount de Polignac (father-in-law of her favourite) the embassy in Switzerland.[2]

Some time before this, the Baron de Besenval, a clever intriguer, and devoted to the queen, had brought about an understanding between her and the Prime Minister:— The queen gains over Maurepas

The Count de Maurepas has seized upon this circumstance [of the Princess de Lamballe] to place himself in favour with the queen, and has undertaken to get the king's consent to expedients to gratify her wishes. The result is that now the old minister is much in the queen's favour, and she is equally pleased with M. de Malesherbes, who, in his capacity as Master of the King's Household, has entered into the arrangements proposed. There is only the Comptroller-General who is still treated coldly by the queen.[3]

We have here a picture of the Court at this conjuncture of the 'weakness of the king, the imperious requirements of the queen, the duplicity of Maurepas who hastens to her side, and, as soon as he scents for himself the least danger, abandons the Comptroller-General; the leaning of Malesherbes

[1] Foncin, liv. ii. chap. xiv.

[2] *Ibid.* chap. xix. and *Corresp. sec.* ii. 398–400.

[3] *Corresp. sec.* ii. 387.

to make concessions and compromises, and the indomitable firmness of Turgot in his love for economy.'[1]

The fatal six edicts

§ 7. Such was the situation of affairs when Turgot, in January 1776, addressed his memorial to the king on the fatal 'six projects of edicts.' These were, 1, for the suppression of the *corvée*; 2, 3, 5, and 6 for the suppression of several regulations, duties, and offices interfering with the provisioning of Paris; and 4, for the suppression of the *jurandes* (the government of privileged corporations). As it was upon numbers 1 and 4 of the edicts, the suppression of the *corvée* and of the *jurandes*, that the battle, the last battle between Turgot and his enemies, was mainly fought, we confine ourselves to the consideration of these two. They were certainly the most important reforms he had yet attempted. It is possible, nay, probable, that fearing it would be beyond his power to carry them into effect, he had advisedly confined his first efforts to the framing of measures that could provoke least controversy, that he might at all events accomplish some of the needed financial improvements. But it was not possible for him to shirk the more perilous duties that lay before him. Until the *corvées* and the *jurandes* were abolished, neither the peasants in the provinces nor the artisans in the towns were free to make the best of their labour, and thus a spirit of discontent was nourished, in town and country, that must some day explode.

The *corvée* edict

The nature of the *corvée* was described while reviewing the Limoges period.[2] His suppression of it within his own province had been a marked success; he could point to that as an encouragement for extending the same benefits to those parts of the kingdom where it still existed. In his memorial to the king of January 1776 he refers to having, more than a year before, drawn up a paper on the subject, which had so forcibly convinced the king of the impolicy and injustice of the *corvée*, that he at once consented to its complete suppression. Turgot could only abolish it in Limoges by finding means to pay for making and repairing of the roads, and

[1] Foncin, p. 310. [2] See *supra*, p. 41.

the only means that lay within his reach, as intendant, was by an addition there to the *taille*. But this burden was already heavy enough upon the common people, and the addition to it could only be justified by the necessity of the case. Turgot, as minister, now proposed to suppress the *corvée* in all the provinces, and to provide the necessary funds by a tax, on the basis of the *vingtièmes*, paid by landed proprietors, great and small.

Probably Malesherbes was the only member of the Council who sincerely supported him in pressing on the proposed edict. His opponents in the Council, while ostensibly falling in with the leanings of the king, suggested at the same time that a measure so important should be remitted for the examination of the Keeper of the Seals, M. Hue de Miroménil, and he, acting with the approval of Maurepas and others in the Council, prepared an elaborate report against the proposed edict. As it may be interesting to some, to know what could possibly be pleaded in defence of so iniquitous a burden as the *corvée*, we make a few brief extracts from the report, adding Turgot's replies:—

*Miroménil:* The proprietors are not the only class benefited by good roads. . . . The simple peasant goes on foot on a good road more easily than on a bad one, and loses less time.

*Turgot:* The Keeper of the Seals must permit me to believe that the pleasure of walking on a well-made road can scarcely compensate the peasant for making it without being paid.

*Miroménil:* A man with nothing but his hands contributes scarcely anything to the taxes.

*Turgot:* Here we are concerned only with the *corvée*, but certainly the man who has only his hands contributes to the taxes in the most exorbitant proportion. A man who has nothing to live upon for himself and his family but what he gains by his labour, and from whom we extort fifteen days of his time, giving him hard work, no wages, and no food, contributes really too much by the making of the roads.

But the Keeper of the Seals soon reveals that the real opposition to Turgot's project is due to its being in principle an attack on a 'privileged' class—the nobility.

*Miroménil :* I cannot hesitate to say that in France the privilege of the nobility ought to be respected, and that it is the interest of the king to maintain it.

*Turgot :* The expenses of the Government having for their object the interest of all, all ought to contribute to them ; and the more any class enjoys advantages of social order, the more should it feel bound in honour to share the State's necessary charges. If one considers the question from the side of humanity, it is difficult to congratulate oneself on being exempt from a tax by being a gentleman, while it is exacted from the peasant even by the distraining of his cooking-pot (*marmite*). If we examine the question from the side of political advantage and of a nation's strength, we see at once that if the privileged persons are of great number, and possess the bulk of the nation's wealth, while the expenses of the State require a considerable sum, this sum may be beyond the ability of the non-privileged people to furnish. Then it follows, either that the Government must be deprived of the means of support and of defence it has need of, or the non-privileged people must be burdened beyond their strength ; and this certainly will soon impoverish and enfeeble the State. A large number of rich privileged persons is thus a real diminution of strength for the kingdom.

Some have hastily formed the notion that Turgot was rash and regardless of circumstances in pushing on his reforms, but the next paragraph is one of the many proofs that might be adduced of his wise moderation. He continues :—

Does it follow from this that we must destroy all privileges? No ; I know as well as others that it is not necessary to accomplish all at once the *best possible*, and that, while we ought not to neglect to correct by degrees the defects of an ancient constitution, we can only work slowly and as public opinion and the course of events make such changes possible.

He next reminds the Keeper of the Seals of the origin of 'privilege' :—

Privilege was founded at a time when the nobles, as a class, were under special obligations to render military service, which they fulfilled in person at their own expense. Now, on the one side, this personal service having become more inconvenient than useful, is fallen entirely into desuetude; on the other side, all the military power of the State consists in a numerous army, kept up at all times, and maintained by the State. The nobles who may serve in this army are paid by the State, and not only are they under no obligation to serve, but, on the contrary, it is the common people (*roturiers*) alone who are compelled to serve, since the establishment of the militia, from which the nobles, and even their valets, are specially exempt. . . . Another reason operates to render privilege most unjust and at the same time less respectable. It is that by means of the facility existing to acquire nobility, by a payment in money, there is no rich man that does not speedily become noble, so that the body of the noble comprehends the body of the rich, and the cause of the privileged is no longer the cause of distinguished families against the *roturiers*, but the cause of the rich against the poor. The reasons we might have had to respect this privilege when it was confined to the ancient defenders of the State certainly cannot be entertained when the privilege has become common even to the race of revenue-farmers and contractors who have plundered the State.

*Miroménil:* To reduce the nobility to the common condition of the *roturiers* is to stifle emulation and to deprive the State of one of its principal forces.

*Turgot:* No one has ever spoken of reducing the nobility to the *roturiers*; so that the Keeper of the Seals may be tranquil in this respect.

*Miroménil:* In fact, the officers in time of peace cannot well live on what the king gives them, and when we are at war they make astonishing efforts to meet their expenses.

*Turgot:* The *roturiers*, who serve in very great numbers, make the same efforts. Moreover, what the Keeper of the Seals has just observed is one of the causes of the ruin of the State. We underpay the officers because so many wish to serve, and we create useless places to provide for them. They spend much beyond their small pay, because those officers who are somewhat richer force the others by their example to adopt a style of luxury which they cannot maintain. In the superior ranks their aim is to make a display. Every one *then* makes of his ruin a title to compensation by the State, and the State is ruined in its turn, in order to maintain an army whose strength does not correspond to what it costs.

*Miroménil:* Deprive the nobility of its distinction, and you destroy the national character; and the nation, ceasing to be martial, will soon become the prey of stronger neighbouring nations.

*Turgot :* The nations in which the nobility pay the taxes along with the people are not less martial than our own nation. In our own the *roturiers* are not poltroons, and in the provinces where the *taille* [instead of being personal and limited to the *roturiers*] is on real property, as in Languedoc, Provence, &c., although the nobles and the *roturiers* are treated in the same manner as far as this tax is concerned, the nobility in these provinces are not less brave nor less attached to the king, nor are they less distinguished in virtue of their rank.

*Miroménil :* There are in France three great Orders—the Clergy, the Nobility, and the *Tiers-État.* Each of these Orders has its rights, its privileges, perhaps its prejudices, but, at all events, it is necessary to preserve them such as they are.

*Turgot :* . . . The Keeper of the Seals speaks of the privileges of the *Tiers-État.* We know that the Nobility and the Clergy have privileges, and that some privileges are attached to certain towns and certain corporations. But the *Tiers-État* in body, that is to say, the people, are very far from having privileges ; the case is inverted, for the burden which those now exempt from it would formerly have borne is now borne by those who were formerly exempt.

*Miroménil* [playing his last card] : Besides, I believe the better course is (instead of making an edict) to do in all the generalities of the kingdom what M. Turgot did at Limoges, M. de la Corée at Montauban, &c.

This, of course, was plainly a suggestion of 'how not to do it.' He knew there could not be a Turgot in all the generalities, and he knew that although ten years had elapsed since Turgot's act, few intendants had been bold enough to imitate it. Turgot, knowing the insincerity of the suggestion, deals with it very briefly, alluding to the plan as being 'very embarrassing in the details, very slow in its establishment, and as keeping up the unjust extra charge on the *taillable* poor.'

In a previous paragraph he had said : 'The *corvée* ought to be abolished for the very reason that it involves an unjust and exorbitant privilege. In abolishing it we should return to the true principles of justice.' [1]

[1] *Œuvres de Turgot*, ii. 251–87

The king read this discussion between the two ministers and took side with Turgot. The edict was signed at the Council on January 6, 1776.

The edict on *jurandes* and the other four were signed February 5 and 6. The *jurandes* edict

A knowledge of the question of the *jurandes* will be best gathered from Turgot's own statement of it in his comprehensive preamble to the edict. Here we have space only for a condensation, necessarily very imperfect.

As an indirect consequence of the Reformation, some breaking up of the system of trade corporations had been more or less general in almost all countries. But in France, at the period we are touching, the old trade customs and laws still held almost unmitigated rule.

In almost all the towns the exercise of the different arts and trades is concentrated in the hands of a small number of *maîtres*, united in corporations, who alone can, to the exclusion of all other citizens, make or sell the articles belonging to their particular industry. Any person who, by inclination or necessity, intends following an art or trade, can only do so by acquiring the *maîtrise* (freedom of the corporation) after a probation as long and as vexatious as it is superfluous. By having to satisfy repeated exactions, the money he had so much need of in order to start his trade or open his workshop has been consumed in mere waste. . . . Citizens of all classes are deprived of the right to choose the workmen they would employ, and deprived of the advantages they would enjoy from competition operating towards improvements of manufacture and reduction in price. Often one cannot get done the simplest work without its having to go through the hands of several workmen of different corporations, without enduring the delays, the tricks, and the exactions which the pretensions of the different corporations necessitate or favour, and the caprices of their arbitrary and mercenary government. Thus the effects of these establishments are, in regard to the State, a vast tyranny over trade and industrial work; in regard to a large body of the people, a loss of wages and the means of subsistence; in regard to the inhabitants of towns in general, a slavery to exclusive privileges equivalent to a real monopoly—a monopoly of which those who exercise it against the public are themselves the victims whenever, in their turn, they have need of the articles or the work of any other corporation. . . . Among the infinite number of unreasonable regulations, we find in some corporations that all are excluded from them except the sons of *maîtres*, or those who marry the widows of *maîtres*. Others reject all those whom they call 'strangers,' that is, those born in another town. In many of them for a young man to be married is enough to exclude him from the apprenticeship, and consequently from the *maîtrise*. The spirit of monopoly which has dictated the making of these statutes has been carried out to the excluding of women even from the trades the most suitable to their sex, such as embroidery, which they are forbidden to exercise on their own account.

He then proceeds to make a declaration of the 'rights of industry,' worthy of being placed alongside of the best declarations of political independence: 'God, by giving to man wants, and making his recourse to work necessary to supply them, has made the right to work the property of every man, and this property is the first, the most sacred, the most imprescriptible of all.'[1]

The edict abrogating so complicated a system as the *jurandes* was necessarily of considerable length, and consisted of twenty-four clauses. Clause I. declares:—

It shall be free to all persons, of whatever quality or condition they may be, even to all foreigners, to undertake and to exercise in all our kingdom, and particularly in our good city of Paris, whatever kind of trade and whatever profession of art or industry may seem good to them, for which purpose we now extinguish and suppress all corporations and communities of merchants and artisans, such as the *maîtres* and the *jurandes*. We abrogate all privileges, statutes, and regulations of the said corporations, so that none of our subjects shall be troubled in the exercise of his trade or profession by any cause or under any pretext whatever.

In our days of Trades Unions and combinations of employers, Clause XIV. must appear strange to us, for by it 'it is forbidden to all masters and all journeymen, workmen, and apprentices to form among themselves any association or assembly.' So rare is it for a mind, however enlightened, to accept at once the full consequences of a principle.

[1] *Œuvres de Turgot*, ii. 302–16.

Such words [says Foncin] are regrettable, above all in the mouth of a Turgot, but we may suppose some excuses for them. If he had authorised the masters or the workmen to associate themselves, there was a danger that in this liberty might be found an indirect means to re-establish under other names the corporations just destroyed, and Clause XIV. has an important corrective in Clause X., that 'there shall be formed in the different quarters of the towns . . . a syndic and two assistants, to be elected annually by the merchants and artisans of the said arrondissement in an assembly held for that purpose, the said syndic and assistants to be sworn to watch over the interests as well of the merchants as of the artisans in their district.'

The importance of this order [continues Foncin] will be mistaken by nobody. It authorises the artisans to unite with themselves, and to elect annually chiefs who will become their natural representatives before the public authority. Here was the germ at once of chambers of industry and of commerce, of which the syndics and assistants would have been the members. Clauses XI. and XII. are not less worthy of attention. They establish a kind of justice of peace to decide technical disputes between artisans themselves. Clause XII. provides for the settlement (free of expense) of disputes which might arise in the execution of time-engagements, contracts of apprenticeship, and other agreements made between the masters and the workmen in their service.[1]

These, certainly, were mitigations of the severity of Clause XIV. But experience proves more and more that in every sphere liberty of discussion is the best policy, and that liberty of action, even though committing mistakes, is after all the shortest road to a durable settlement.

After passing the Council, the six edicts, in order to acquire legal force, had to be registered by the Parliament. To that court we must now follow them. They were presented on February 9. To give an appearance of conciliation to their proceedings, the Parliament registered the least important of the six (that on the *Caisse de Poissy*, with which we are not concerned), and named a Commission to consider the other five. On February 17 the Parliament again met. Taking first into consideration the edict on the

[1] Foncin, liv. iii. chap. ii.

Remonstrance of the Parliament

*corvée*, the president intimated that the report of the Commission was adverse to this edict. The report was then read, and, after deliberation, it was resolved that the Parliament should present a remonstrance to the king, 'supplicating H.M. to withdraw the said edict as inadmissible, in its principle as well as in its provisions.' Commissioners were appointed to prepare the text of the remonstrance. At the next meeting, March 2, of the Parliament 'the president stated that the Commissioners had finished their work. The remonstrance was read and approved of. It was resolved that a deputation of Parliament be sent to Versailles to present the remonstrance to the king.' This deputation attended Versailles on the 4th and handed in the text of the remonstrance.

Bearing in mind that the edict against the *corvée* was simply to relieve the poor peasantry from making and repairing the roads *without being paid for their work*, some parts of the remonstrance are peculiarly interesting, as expressing the sentiments of the educated classes only twelve years before the Revolution.

The Parliament [says the document] has not registered the edict for the suppression of the *corvée*, because this suppression would be against justice. The first rule of justice is to preserve to every one what belongs to him: this rule consists, not only in preserving the rights of property, but still more in preserving those belonging to the person, which arise from the prerogative of birth and of position. . . . From this rule of law and equity it follows that every system which, under an appearance of humanity and beneficence, would tend to establish between men an equality of duties, and to destroy necessary distinctions, would soon lead to disorder (the inevitable result of equality), and would bring about the overturn of civil society. The French monarchy, by its constitution, is composed of several distinct estates. The personal service of the clergy is to fulfil all the functions relative to instruction and worship. The nobles consecrate their blood to the defence of the State, and assist the sovereign with their advice. The lowest class of the nation, which cannot render to the king services so distinguished, acquits itself towards him by its tributes, its industry, and bodily service. To abolish these distinctions is to overthrow the whole French Constitution.[1]

The king supports Turgot

Three days later, March 7, the deputation attended at Versailles for the king's reply, which was simply this: 'I have examined the remonstrances of my Parliament; they contain nothing which was not foreseen and maturely reflected upon.' About this time was written the following letter of the king to Turgot:—

I have read with care all the memorials which you have submitted to the Council, and the six projects of edicts, of which I have already approved. The want of unanimity in my Council upon these proposals, and the opposition they have met with outside, have given me much to think of, but the projects appear to me too useful and conformable to the public welfare not to be published and maintained by my whole authority. To take, in spite of him, the time of a workman, even in paying him, would be equivalent to a tax; it is all the greater injustice to take his time without paying for it. You say wisely that the man who works unwillingly and without remuneration works ill. These considerations are self-evident, and I am grieved that an edict so well founded in reason and in equity has raised up so much opposition. But there are so many private interests opposed to the general interest. The more I think of it, my dear Turgot, the more I repeat to myself that there are only you and myself who really love the people.[2]

The *lit de justice*

The king thus remaining firm, it was necessary, in order to give the edicts the force of law, to have them compulsorily registered by the Parliament at a *lit de justice*. This took place at Versailles March 12. The defence of the Parliament was conducted by the eminent Séguier, Advocate-General. The old arguments against the abolition of the *corvée* were restated: the substitute for it would 'confound the Nobility, who are the strongest support to the throne, and the Clergy, the sacred ministry of the altars, with the people, who have no right to complain of the *corvée*,' &c. The edict on the *jurandes* was condemned in the same temper that

[1] Jobez, *La France sous Louis XVI*, i. 329–31. [2] *Ibid.* i. 337.

animated the remonstrance. Séguier boldly challenged the main principle of the edict in these words :—

The object proposed to your Majesty is to extend and multiply commerce by freeing it from the inconveniences, the trammels, the prohibitions surrounding it. We venture, Sire, to advance to your Majesty the proposition, diametrically opposite, that it is these inconveniences, these trammels, these prohibitions, which make the glory, the safety, the immensity of the commerce of France. . . . To give to all your subjects indiscriminately the right to hold a store or to open a shop is to violate the property of the *masters*, who compose the communities.

The result of emancipating industry would be that—

every manufacturer, every artist, every workman would regard himself as an isolated being, depending upon himself alone. . . . All subordination would be destroyed. . . . There would be no longer any weights or measures, the greed of gain would pervade all workshops. . . . Indefinite liberty would evaporate that perfection of our products which is the sole cause of the preference they have obtained. . . . Commerce would languish, and France would lose that source of riches which her rivals have long sought to divert from her . . . the best workmen would soon leave the capital, this indefinite liberty would tend to confound all talents, and to extinguish them by the mediocrity of wages. . . . Loss of profits would cause a multitude of bankruptcies, want of confidence would arrest all operations of credit, &c.[1]

**The revenge of the 'classes'**

§ 8. Nevertheless, by the exercise of the king's prerogative, all the edicts were duly registered by the unwilling Parliament. Turgot had gained a victory, but by the victory he lost his ministry. The Parliament was exasperated by its defeat. His enemies drew reinforcements, from all sides, in order to crush the man who, because he suppressed some flagrant abuses, was accused, as usual in such circumstances, of 'unsettling everything.' A *grande dame* of the Court is said to have expressed the general feeling of 'everybody' when she exclaimed: 'Why these innovations?—are we not well enough as we are?'

[1] *Œuvres de Turgot*, ii. 334–37, and Foncin, liv. iii. chap. ix.

By a coalition of the several 'classes' he was devoted to destruction. In the condition of France at that time he could obtain no support from the 'masses,' in whose cause he had so courageously fought.

A more fatal step for France was never taken than by the recall of the Parliament in 1774. Had there been no Parliament to overcome, the spirit of retaliation from a large and influential body would not have been evoked, the opposition to Turgot's liberal measures could not have been so effectively organised, and it is possible he might have remained some years longer in office, during which the good results from his financial and other operations having been seen, this success would have strengthened him for effecting those larger schemes of improvement through which France would have gradually developed into the condition of a constitutional monarchy.

A section of the Parliament took an early occasion of indulging the spiteful antipathy of their order to the statesman who had overpowered it. Boncerf, a clerk in the Comptroller's office, and known as Turgot's friend, had published a work exposing some of the abuses of the feudal laws. According to M. Droz, the historian, nothing could be more conformable to public interest and to reason than the principles of this work. But the *esprit de corps* of the judges was deeply wounded; the Advocate-General not only fulminated a violent speech against the book, but it needed even the intervention of the king to save Boncerf from imprisonment.[1] The Court ordered the book to be burned by the hands of the executioner, and passed a decree petitioning the king to 'put an end to economical outrages.'

A prince of the blood, the king's own brother, 'Monsieur,' Count de Provence (afterwards Louis XVIII.), joined the *cohue* by circulating a pamphlet in which attempts at wit

[1] Daire, in *Œuvre de Turgot*, i. cix. Boncerf afterwards became secretary to the Duke of Orleans, and had his revenge upon the Parliament of 1774 in the Constituent Assembly of 1789, on their great day of renunciation of privileges, August 4, when the whole feudal system was completely abolished.

are much overstrained, attacking Turgot and Maurepas as well. 'He described the genius of England wishing to degrade the French by altering their established system of laws, leading astray M. de Maurepas in the choice of Minister of Finances.' The count thus portrays Turgot: 'There was then in France a man, awkward, thick-set, heavy, endued with more uncouthness than character, with more obstinacy than firmness, more impetuosity than tact, a charlatan of administration as well as of virtue,' and so on. The appearance of this pamphlet served as the signal for a deluge of writings of the same kind, with which the Court and Paris were inundated.[1] The attacks became more violent and malicious every day.

The Count de Creutz (Swedish Ambassador at Paris) writes to Gustavus III.:—

> M. Turgot finds himself threatened by the most formidable league, composed of all the great people of the kingdom, of all the parliaments, of all the financiers, of all the ladies of the Court, and of all the *dévots*. . . . It is not surprising that the Prince de Conti opposes with such violence the suppression of the *jurandes*, for he loses by that the benefice of the *franchise du Temple* and fifty thousand livres of income. The Parliament loses the very large procedure business connected with the old system. You may see in this the motives of their resistance.[2]

**The queen's influence**

During all this time the queen had never ceased to make use of every opportunity of weakening Turgot's influence with the king. Her feeling of ill-will had been recently rekindled by the proceedings of the ministry in the case of her protégé the Count de Guines, for which, however, Turgot was not solely responsible. The count, a man of handsome appearance, accomplished and of insinuating manners, was a special favourite with the Court ladies. He was French Ambassador in London, and by some diplomatic indiscretions had compromised the foreign policy of France in his dealings with the English Cabinet. Vergennes, acting with

[1] Foncin, liv. iii. chap. xv.

[2] Introduction to the *Corresp. sec.* p. lii.

the king's approval, recalled De Guines. The personal friends of the ambassador, forming the intimate coterie of Marie Antoinette, resented this disgrace to one of their set. The queen pledged her word to them that De Guines should be maintained. She brought every possible pressure to bear upon the king to dismiss Vergennes and Turgot. Vergennes was too able a foreign minister for Louis XVI. to sacrifice, especially in the now critical position of affairs between Great Britain and her American colonies. A treaty of peace was brought about between the king and the queen, by one article of which he agreed to create De Guines a duke, and by another, it was said, he gave the queen reason to hope that his support of Turgot would be withdrawn.

Against Turgot intrigue followed upon intrigue. His reputation even as a minister of finance, which a year ago was so undisputed, was now to be assailed, in order that the king's confidence in this also should be shaken. There is reason to believe that Maurepas lent himself to this plot. He was every inch a courtier, and seeing the tide now turning against Turgot, he threw his own influence into it. A M. Pezai ventured to tackle the operations in the Budget of 1776, and, with the assistance of Necker, discovered what appeared to be serious errors in the Comptroller's calculations. Every one knows how easily these financial criticisms are made. It is not ascertained whether the criticisms were ever shown to Turgot—probably they were not. But Maurepas laid them before the king. It is not surprising that the poor king, never strong-minded at his best, found it difficult to withstand all these persistent attacks upon the minister whom he had really loved and esteemed. Turgot, soon, could not but feel conscious, in his interviews with the king, that there was less of the old frank cordiality between them, and he saw what was coming. About the end of April he read a report to the king on a matter in dispute between the Chamber of Commerce of Lille and the Customs officers at Lyons (which is memorable for containing an eloquent plea for Free Trade). This was the last report he

The king gives up Turgot

wrote. Different accounts are given of some expressions that came from the king on its being read. It has been said that while Turgot read it, the king listened with impatience, and when it was ended he asked Turgot dryly: 'Is that all?' 'Yes, Sire.' 'So much the better,' the king replied, turning his back on Turgot.[1]

Males-herbes' resignation

Just at this time there was impending an event which more than any other deprived him of all hope that he could retain power and exercise it for any great purpose. Malesherbes, for some months, had been contemplating his resignation, and was now more than ever desirous to be free from the responsibilities of public life. In vain did Turgot use every argument with Malesherbes to induce him to remain; in vain did Turgot beseech him by every appeal to his sense of duty at a great crisis, and by every appeal to his sense of friendship. Malesherbes was obdurate. He believed that the forces enlisted against Turgot and himself were stronger than they could possibly overcome, and he longed for a quiet life.[2] Turgot himself was full of despair, but he felt that it would be cowardly to relinquish his post by his own act while there remained to him the possibility of still using his official authority to some good account. The responsibility for ending his life of public service must rest on others, not upon himself. Of an indirect responsibility for Turgot's fall it is impossible to acquit Malesherbes. In a Cabinet Council of six ministers two voices in accord cannot fail to get themselves listened to, and to exert some influence, but when it comes to one against five, the dissentient becomes almost extinguished. Malesherbes' responsibility was increased by another circumstance. The king

[1] Foncin, liv. iii. chap. xiv.

[2] Want of decision of character and tenacity of purpose were Malesherbes' main defects. 'He found in his head,' says Condorcet, 'reasons without number to defend the *pro* and the *contra*, and found not one to make him decide. As a private individual, he had employed his eloquence to prove to the king and the ministers that it was necessary to concern themselves for the good of the nation; having become a minister, he employed it to prove that it was impossible to effect the good.' (Condorcet to Voltaire, June 12, 1776.)

entertained the very highest respect for his judgment, and when Turgot was about to be deserted by his own friend this fact greatly helped in inducing the king to believe that Turgot's cause was now discountenanced on every side.[1]

Males-herbes' successor

Arrangements were made for the choice of Malesherbes' successor. Maurepas proposed for the office M. Amelot, his relative, a creature devoted entirely to himself, a sworn opponent of all 'innovations,' and closely allied with Miroménil and the enemies of Turgot. That Malesherbes should be succeeded by a man of this stamp was galling to every one who had hoped for better things under the new reign. It was going back to the corrupt times of Louis XV. Malesherbes and Turgot in the Council fought zealously against Maurepas' intention. 'The nomination of Amelot,' writes Mercy to Maria Theresa, 'was the adjournment of all reform of the *Maison du Roi*. Turgot understood this as soon as he was warned of it. At once he wrote to the king, making strong reclamations against the appointment. Malesherbes took the same course, but the queen declared herself for Amelot.'[2]

The crisis reached

The 'strong reclamations' to which Mercy alludes were conveyed in a series of four private letters by Turgot to the king, written in the passionate earnestness of his desire to

[1] Malesherbes (C. D. de Lamoignon de). Born December 6, 1721; died (guillotined) April 22, 1794. Son of the Chancellor G. de Lamoignon, to whom he succeeded December 14, 1750, as first President of the *Cour des Aides*. We owe to his tolerance while Censor of the Press the publication of the great *Encyclopédie*. For persistent opposition to the illegal acts of the Government he was, in 1771, exiled to one of his estates. On the accession of Louis XVI. he was recalled and restored to his presidentship. He resigned that on joining the Ministry, July 19, 1775. Retired May 12, 1776; after this he took no conspicuous action in public affairs. But in December, 1792, in a spirit of chivalrous loyalty, he left his retreat and volunteered to defend the king, now on his trial before the Convention. Louis accepted his services. At that solemn juncture the minds of the two must have recurred to their last brief intercourse during 1775–76, and perhaps they may have confessed that had Turgot's wise efforts for reform been more vigorously supported, it would have been better for France. In little more than a year after the execution of the king, Malesherbes, with all the members of his family, accused of 'conspiring against the unity of the Republic,' shared the same fate as his master.

[2] *Corresp. sec.* ii. 442.

enlighten him upon the serious crisis, for himself and for France, in which he was now called upon to act. A crisis it certainly was. When we retrace these events, we now see in the question of this ministerial appointment one of the fatal turning-points of French history. These four private letters were expressed in the most unreserved language. We may judge of the boldness of the writer by his daring to give to Louis XVI. the ominous warning that it was the instability of the character of Charles I. of England, and his neglect to deal wisely for his kingdom when he had the power, that eventually 'placed his head upon the block.' The letters were marked as strictly confidential, for they dealt with the character of others in the Ministry. What became of the originals we do not know. Turgot's own drafts of them were after his death saved by Malesherbes, and made over to Turgot's executors, with a recommendation that they should be destroyed: this advice seems to have been taken. A copy of one of the four, however (the last), remains to us. It came into the possession of the Abbé de Véry, with whom Turgot was in close relationship, and whom he had designed to be Malesherbes' successor. It is dated April 30. He begins by referring to his previous letters, and to the king's neglect to acknowledge them.

Private letters to the king

SIRE,—I cannot conceal from your Majesty the deep pain I have suffered by your cruel silence towards me on Sunday last, after I had in my preceding letters described to you so distinctly my position, your Majesty's own position, the danger that your authority and the glory of your reign were incurring, and the impossibility of my continuing to serve you unless you give me your firm and steady support. Your Majesty has not deigned to reply to me. . . . I have braved the hatred of all those who profit by certain abuses. So long as I had the hope of holding your Majesty's esteem and of doing good, nothing disturbed me. What is now my reward? Your Majesty sees how impossible it is for me to resist those who injure me, not only by the ill they directly do me, but by the good which they hinder me from doing. Your Majesty gives me neither assistance nor consolation. How can I believe that you any longer esteem me? Sire, I have not deserved this. . . .

I owe to M. de Maurepas the place which your Majesty has entrusted to me. I shall never forget this, I shall never fail in the respect due to him; but I owe a thousand times more to the State and to your Majesty, and I cannot without guilt sacrifice their interest. It costs me much pain to have to say to you that M. de Maurepas, if he proposes to you M. Amelot [to succeed to Malesherbes], is really culpable; or, at least, that his pliancy in the hands of others would be as fatal to your Majesty as a wilful crime. . . . I do not wish to undermine the confidence you have in M. de Maurepas. He merits that confidence in many respects by his experience, his enlightenment, his great capacity for affairs. . . . But, Sire, you must know his weakness of character, and how easily he is influenced by those around him. . . . During a bed of justice I have seen him ten times changing his opinions, according as he observed what was thought by the Keeper of the Seals, or the Lieutenant of Police, or myself. . . . It is this that has made him listen so readily to the cries of the Court against me, the effect of which has been to deprive me of all power in my department. . . . Do not forget, Sire, that it was weakness that brought the head of Charles I. to the block. . . . You, Sire, have been sometimes believed to be weak, but I have seen you in trying circumstances show real courage. You have said it yourself, Sire, that you want experience, that you have need of a guide. For such a guide, intelligence and energy of character are both required. M. de Maurepas has the former of these, but he has not the latter without being spurred on by others. He feels that himself. I see it by the choice of Minister he has in view, and by the very slight effort he has made to influence you in favour of the Abbé de Véry. He dreads precisely what would give to him real strength. He does not see that, after having isolated me, after having prejudiced your Majesty against me, and having compelled me to leave you, the whole storm, directed now against me, will come in time to burst upon himself, that he will end in failure, dragging with him in his fall your authority. . . . See, Sire, how you stand: with a ministry weak and disunited; outside, all minds in fermentation, the parliaments leagued with all the discontented parties, the revenue short of the expenditure, the greatest resistance made to an indispensable economy, no harmony in your Council, no fixedness in its plans, no secrecy kept with its resolutions; and it is in these circumstances that there is proposed to your Majesty for office a man without talents, who has no other merit but his subservience—and to whom? Not to one of your ministers who shows ability and strength in office, but to the Keeper of the Seals. . . . I implore you yet to reflect before deciding upon a choice which will be bad in itself and fatal in its consequences. . . .

If, after all, I am so unfortunate as to have brought upon me by this letter your Majesty's condemnation, I beg you will inform me of it yourself; at all events I depend upon your holding the letter as secret.

I am, Sire, &c., &c.[1]

The king sent no reply.

At a meeting of the Council, Malesherbes took offence at some expressions by Maurepas—perhaps designedly uttered, and at once intimated his resignation. At the interview with the king when it was formally given in, Louis, beginning at last to feel the anxieties of his position, used these impressive words, which time has made still more impressive: 'You are a happy man who can resign; I wish I could.'[2]

Turgot does not resign

It was expected that Turgot would resign along with Malesherbes, but he allowed events to take their course. Before having cut off from him every opportunity of further serving France, he desired once more to impress the king with the grave difficulties in which the nation was involved. He sought an interview; the king was at the chase. He called again; the king was changing his dress. He would call again next day. But, in the interim, Louis XVI. sent his old minister, Bertin, to announce to Turgot that he was no longer Comptroller-General.

His dismissal, May 12, 1776

The same day, May 12, 1776, Maurepas sent to him a polite formal note of regret: 'I beg of you,' he wrote, 'to believe in the full share I hold with you in your situation.' The note was acknowledged by Turgot in the letter following:—

Paris, May 13, 1776.

Letter to Maurepas

I received, Monsieur, the letter which you have done me the honour of writing to me. I do not doubt of the share you have taken in the event of the day, and I have for it the gratitude which I owe.

[1] Léon Say, *Turgot*, pp. 165–74. [2] Bachaumont, *Mém. sec.* ix. 149.

The obstacles which I met with in dealing with the most urgent matters had for some time convinced me of the impossibility of my usefully serving the king, and I had resolved to ask from him my release. But my attachment to his person rendered this step a painful one. I feared I might some day reproach myself for having left him. The king has now relieved me of this pain, and the only one I suffer from is through his not having had the kindness himself to inform me of his intentions.

As for my present situation, with which you are kind enough to concern yourself, that can only affect me by the loss of the hopes I had of seconding the king in his desires for the good of the people. I trust that some one else will realise these. But when one carries with him neither shame nor remorse, when one has pursued no interest but the good of the State, when he has neither disguised the truth to his master nor concealed it from him, he cannot be unhappy. I beg of you, &c., &c.[1]

Next day the queen wrote to her mother: 'M. Malesherbes quitted the ministry the day before yesterday; he has been succeeded by M. Amelot. M. Turgot was dismissed the same day, and M. de Clugny will succeed him. I confess to my dear mother that I am not ill-pleased at these departures, but I have not meddled with them.'[2] Mercy, however, in a letter to the empress (May 16), gives a very different account of the queen's conduct:—

The queen to her mother

I cannot [he writes] and ought not to hide from your Majesty that for some weeks things have been taking a turn here, as unfortunate for the queen as it is disheartening for me. The consequence will some day bring upon her the just reproaches of the king, and even of the whole nation. The king is compromised in the sight of the public, who are ignorant of none of the circumstances, and are well aware that the responsible cause of them is the will of the queen, exercised by her almost in a violent manner on the mind of the king. The Comptroller-General, aware of the dislike held of him by the queen, decided mainly by that cause to resign; the queen's design was to have him turned out (*chassé*) by the king—even sent to the Bastille the same day

[1] *Œuvres de Turgot*, i. cxii. [2] *Corresp. sec.* ii. 441.

De Guines was to be declared a duke. . . . This Comptroller-General enjoyed a high reputation for integrity, and was loved by the people.[1]

**Triumph of the Court party**

The Court party was intoxicated at its triumph. The old Marquise du Deffand writes (May 14) : 'What gratifies me most, I confess, is the triumph of M. de Guines. What joy M. Necker will feel!' The Duchess de Choiseul replies: 'I am, like yourself, transported with joy at the victory of M. de Guines. The disgrace of the two members which accompanies it I feel to be like the Roman triumphs, draggng their captives in their train.'

**Despair of the reformers**

There were, however, some minds which judged of these events very differently, whose vision extended beyond the narrow and petty interests of a Court. Those who had been earnestly longing to see France, by the adoption of timely political reforms, entering upon a new course, to save her from the rocks to which, otherwise, she was rapidly drifting, felt, by the resignation of Malesherbes and the dismissal of Turgot, all their hopes to be cruelly blasted.

The greatest Frenchman of the time, to whom, irreverent as he was in some respects, the cause of humanity was always dear, felt, in his old age, the disaster to his country in all its seriousness. Voltaire writes (May 15) to Devaines: 'Ah, mon Dieu, what sad news I hear! France would have been too fortunate. . . . I am overwhelmed in despair.' And for weeks and months after his emotion is not yet calmed. He writes (June 10) to La Harpe: 'I see only death before me since Turgot is out of place. I cannot conceive how he could have been dismissed. A thunderbolt has fallen on my head and on my heart.' And (August 5) he writes to D'Argental: 'You believe that I am not dead, because I write to you by my own feeble hand, but I am really dead since Turgot has been deprived of power.' It was at this time that, to console himself in consoling Turgot, Voltaire addressed to him the fine 'Épître à un Homme.'

[1] *Corresp. sec.* ii. 447.

Condorcet had written to Voltaire (May 15) a pathetic letter on the subject, ending with the words: 'Adieu! we have had a beautiful dream.'

Turgot obtained permission to write to the king a farewell letter. As this letter, which we are about to give, contains a passage of covert meaning, explained by some as alluding to what was called the 'incident of the Treasury order,' we may first briefly narrate this alleged incident.

**Behind the scenes**

The queen was notoriously extravagant. For example, Mercy, writing to her mother (June 19, 1776), mentions that her daughter had 'received from the king, by several instalments, more than one hundred thousand *écus* of diamonds, but still she had a great desire to buy some girandoles of a jeweller who offered them for six hundred thousand livres. She dared not ask this money from the king; she bought the girandoles with four hundred and fifty thousand, all the money she had left, engaging to pay the balance in four years.'[1]

'Turgot,' says Bailly, 'had obtained from Louis XVI. the promise that no cash order (*ordonnance de comptant*) should be presented within a certain period. A few days afterwards, an order for five hundred thousand livres, in the name of a person of the Court, was presented at the Treasury. Turgot went to get the king's instruction in respect to it, and reminded him of the promise given. 'I am surprised,' said the king. 'Sire, what ought I to do?' 'Do not pay it.' The Minister obeyed: his dismissal followed three days after.[2]

According to the credited tradition, observes Foncin, 'the person who had claimed payment of the draft was the queen; she would be revenged for Turgot's refusal by exacting from the king his dismissal.' While there is no documentary evidence for the truth of this story, there is much reasonable probability in support of it. Henri Martin, the classical historian of France, whose painstaking impartiality is ac-

[1] Foncin, liv. iii. chap. xvi., and *Corresp. sec.* ii. 418.
[2] Bailly, *Hist. financ.* ii. 214, *note.*

knowledged, believes it to be 'implicitly confirmed by the farewell letter of Turgot to the king.'[1]

His farewell letter to the king

The farewell letter was dated May 18, 1776, six days after his dismissal. It commences by thanking the king for the permission to write to him, and for his kindness in offering to make whatever pecuniary arrangements should be desired by the ex-Minister.

You know, Sire, what I think of pecuniary objects. Your kindness has always been dearer to me than your benefactions. I will accept the salary of Minister, because without that I should find myself with an income about a third less than I should have had as Intendant at Limoges. I have no need to be richer, and I ought not to give the example of being so at the charge of the State. I would beg of your Majesty to reserve the favours you design for me, in order to recompense with them some persons who, after having made the sacrifice of their estate to assist me in my work, will lose in consequence of my retirement what I had procured for them, and who will find themselves without resources if they do not meet with your Majesty's kind assistance. . . .

As for myself, Sire, I cannot but regret the loss of your confidence, and of the hope that gave me of being useful to the State. The step that I took, which appeared to have displeased you, has proved to you that no other motive could have attached me to my place, for I could not be ignorant of the risk I ran, to which I would never have exposed myself had I preferred my fortune to my duty. You have also seen in my letters how it became impossible for me to serve usefully in that place and to remain in it, if you left me to stand alone and without support.

He next feelingly alludes to the manner in which his retirement had been brought about:—

I trusted that you would graciously have informed me of your intentions; I will not hide from you that the form in which you at last notified them to me has caused me very acute pain. Your Majesty will not misapprehend the nature of this impression if you have been conscious of the truth and depth of the attachment I held to you. If I regarded only the interests of my reputation, I ought, perhaps, to consider my dismissal as better for me than a voluntary resignation, because many people might have re-

[1] *Hist. de France*, xvi. 379.

garded the resignation as a mere impulse of temper. Others might have said that, after having opened imprudent operations and having embarrassed affairs, I retired at the moment when I no longer saw ready resources; others would have blamed me with good reason, believing that an honest man ought never to abandon his place while he is able to effect some good there, or to prevent some evil, and while not knowing, like myself, how the possibility of being useful was taken from me. Besides, I myself might have been haunted by the fear of having too soon despaired, and of having merited the very reproach that I made to M. de Malesherbes. At all events, being dismissed, I have the satisfaction of having no remorse to suffer, no reproach to endure. I have done, Sire, what I believe to be my duty in laying before you with a frankness without reserve, and one without example, the difficulties of the position I was placed in, and what I thought to be your own true position.

My whole desire, Sire, is that you may find that I have seen things erroneously; that I have warned you of imaginary dangers. I hope that time will never justify me, and that your reign will be as happy, as tranquil, for you and for your people, as you, from your own qualities of justice and benevolence, deserve it should be.

I have, Sire, one last favour to beg of you. The most precious possession that will remain to me is to preserve your esteem. I would desire ever to have a right to that. Persons will certainly work with you to make me lose it. They will endeavour to bespatter both my administration and myself. . . . Your Majesty will perhaps disdain them at first, but by dint of their being continually pressed on you, calumny may succeed in fulfilling its object while I have been unable to ward off the slanders of which I was ignorant. I can have no other defender with your Majesty than yourself. . . . I have not the conceit to believe that I have never committed blunders; but of this I am sure, they have been neither serious ones nor voluntary. Permit me, Sire, &c., &c.[1]

When Louis XVI. read this letter he could scarcely fail to be reminded of a former 'letter to the king' of August 24, 1774, written by Turgot on his accession to the Comptrollership. In that letter, if he referred to it, the king would have read Turgot's prophetic words with more meaning in them than he saw at first:—

[1] *Œuvres de Turgot*, i. cxiii.–cxiv.

I feel all the danger to which I expose myself. I foresee that I shall be alone in fighting against abuses of every kind; against the power of those who profit by these abuses; against the crowd of prejudiced people who oppose themselves to all reforms. . . . I shall have to struggle even against the natural goodness and generosity of your Majesty and of persons the most dear to you. I shall be feared, hated even, by nearly all the Court, by all who solicit favours. . . . Your Majesty will remember that it is in the faith of your promises to sustain me that I undertake a burden beyond my strength.[1]

Reaction complete

His enemies were now enabled to take their own way without hindrance. As far as they could they undid the beneficent work he had begun. His solicitation of the king—his one farewell request to protect the friends who had sacrificed their position to assist him, does not seem to have been heeded. Dupont, his private secretary, was exiled. The Abbé Baudeau (whose 'Nouvelles Éphémérides' was suppressed) was also exiled.

Clugny became Comptroller-General. The Dutch refused now to carry out the loan of sixty millions at four per cent. The shareholders of the *Caisse d'Escompte* (founded by Turgot) would not pay up the ten millions subscribed. 'It was necessary, June 30, to establish a Royal Lottery to meet the deficit! To such expedients was the State driven a month after the departure of Turgot.'[2]

The *corvées* were re-established on August 11. It is said that Turgot shed tears on hearing of this.

The *jurandes* were re-established August 19.

The freedom of the corn trade was suppressed in September.

Thirteen years afterwards, in very different circumstances, on August 4, 1789, among the mass of privileges abolished were the *jurandes*.

The National Assembly, by the law of March 2, 1791, established complete liberty of all industry, enforcing Turgot's decree, and in his own words.

[1] See *supra*, p. 88.

[2] H. Martin, *History*, xvi. 383.

The complete suppression of the *corvées* formed part of the immense legislative work of the National Convention. But another of its acts was the abolition of the monarchy; and, in its executive capacity, it directed the 'Reign of Terror.'

Turgot's dismissal closed for ever his public life.

The Turgot period has been reviewed, in our own day, from the standpoint of a French historian, and has had pronounced on it, by him, the following verdict:— **Verdict on the Turgot period**

> This minister, so superior to his age, wished to accomplish without shock, by the power of a legislative king, the changes which could alone safeguard us from revolutions. His contemporaries, selfish and superficial, could not comprehend him; and we have expiated by long calamities their disdain of his virtues and of his enlightenment.[1]

To say that if Turgot's reforms had been carried out and followed up the great Revolution would have been altogether averted might be saying too much. But, if they had been, their natural effect would have been to remove many of the worst evils that afflicted France; the passions of the people, roused against the rule of injustice, would have been less deeply excited, would have become less pent up, and when they broke out, they would, at all events, have spent themselves in less fury, and been guiltless of those excesses which have disgraced a Grand Era.

[1] Droz, *Hist. du règne de Louis XVI*, i. 210.

# CHAPTER IV

1776—1781

## IN RETIREMENT

'Turgot carried to his retreat,' says his attached friend, 'a mind of undisturbed serenity. Although his health was shattered, that bore no influence on his temper; never had he been more amiable or dearer to those who had the advantage to live in his society. Literature and science, and the care to relieve the unfortunate, filled all the time which his malady left him to enjoy. He applied himself to advanced geometry with the Abbé Bossut, chemistry with Lavoisier, optics and astronomy with the Abbé Rochon —the latest of his friends but not the least dear.' [1]

**Returns to science and literature**

On May 31, within two weeks of his transmitting his farewell letter to the king, he is corresponding with Condorcet on telescopes and the stars. On June 22 he writes to his friend Caillard, with a jocular allusion to his economical doctrine: 'I am now in full liberty to make use of the book you have sent me and of all the rest of my library. Leisure and complete liberty will form the principal *produit net* of the two years I have spent in the Ministry. I shall endeavour to employ them agreeably and usefully.'

Condorcet writes to Voltaire, some months afterwards: 'Turgot is reading Aristotle, is making experiments in physics and mechanics, and would have forgotten all that has passed during the last two years if the sight of the evils that he wished to remove did not compel him to remember.' [2]

[1] Dupont, *Vie de Turgot*, i. 412. [2] Condorcet, *Œuv.* i. 129.

He attended as often as was possible to him at the Académie des Inscriptions, of which he had been elected honorary member (March 1776), and of which he was Vice-Director in 1777.

He returned with renewed zest to the favourite literary work of his youth, that of assimilating to his mind the classic masterpieces, by the process of translating them into verse.

He kept up a studied correspondence with many distinguished men of the time, notably with Adam Smith on economical questions, with Dr. Richard Price on the Constitution of the United States, and with Benjamin Franklin,[1] his esteemed friend, to whom he addressed a treatise on the 'true principles of taxation.' His more frequent, more general, and more spontaneous correspondence was with Condorcet.

**An international act**

His life at this period necessarily presents few points of historical importance. On one occasion only did the retired statesman return, in one sense, to public life by a brief act, his part in which was kept secret at the time from fear that it might prejudice the matter in the eyes of the Government. Owing to the support given by France to the American colonies, war with England became imminent. Turgot got transmitted to the Minister, M. de Sartine, through another hand, a memorial proposing to declare exempt from hostilities Captain Cook and his vessel; the memorial was favourably received at the Council and due effect given to it. The authorship was not known until the record of it was found among Turgot's papers after his death. It may fittingly find a place here as a typical illustration of the high purposes to which, to the last, he devoted his thoughts and his actions.

*Note on the Voyage of Captain Cook.*

Captain Cook, one of the ablest officers of the English Royal Navy, after having twice sailed round the world, after having in the course of these two voyages given for the first time to Europe an

[1] Turgot is known as the author of the epigrammatic inscription on Franklin's portrait: *Eripuit cælo fulmen sceptrumque tyrannis.*

exact knowledge of the southern hemisphere, perfected navigation, enriched geography and natural history with a vast number of useful discoveries, has undertaken to make a third voyage, the object of which is to reconnoitre and to describe the coasts, islands, and seas situated to the north of Japan and of California.

He embarked from Plymouth in July 1776, in the vessel the 'Resolution,' the same he had commanded on his second voyage. This ship, of from four hundred to five hundred tons burden, and with about a hundred of a crew, is not a vessel fitted for military operations; it was constructed originally for trading in coal.

Captain Cook is probably on his way returning to Europe. His expedition having for its only object man's increase of knowledge of the globe he inhabits, and being consequently one interesting to all nations, it would well accord with the king's magnanimity that the success of the expedition should not be compromised by the hazards of war. In the event of rupture between the two crowns it is proposed to his Majesty to issue orders to all the officers of his navy and to all owners of privateers, who might meet with Captain Cook, to abstain from hostility towards him and his ship, to allow him freely to continue his navigation, and to treat him in every respect as it is customary to treat the officers and the vessels of nations neutral and friendly, and, in leading him to recognise this mark of the king's esteem for his person, prepossess him that his Majesty expects that he, on his side, shall abstain from all hostile acts. It is advisable that knowledge of this order should be communicated to the ministers of his Britannic Majesty.[1]

Personal appearance

Some of our readers may have a natural desire to form some image in their mind of Turgot's personal appearance. Dupont has portrayed him with remarkable minuteness:

He was tall and well-proportioned; his face was beautiful. Owing to his dislike of self-assertion, he did not hold his head pretentiously high. His eyes were of a clear brown, and expressed perfectly the blending of firmness and suavity which made up his character. His forehead was dome-shaped, lofty, noble, and serene; his features well pronounced. . . . He had a peculiar smile

[1] *Œuvres de Turgot*, i. cxvii. 'To my mind there is something truly noble and deeply affecting in this spectacle of a great statesman, though disgraced and worn by disease, turning his thoughts in mingled wisdom and kindliness to the promotion, by the same act, of human knowledge and international courtesy.' (Hodgson, *Turgot, his Life, Times, and Opinions*, pp. 33–34.)

difficult to describe, which by persons who did not know him was thought to express disdain, although it was really the effect of simplicity and of the habit of embarrassment formed in youth, from which he had never been able entirely to free himself. He blushed with a too great facility and at every kind of emotion, either of impatience or of sensibility. His hair was brown, abundant, and very fine, he retained it completely to the last; clad as magistrate, his locks scattered on his shoulders with a natural and negligent grace, he formed a striking picture.

Private character

Perhaps [continues Dupont] no man was ever dearer to his friends, for no man ever loved his friends more, no man ever counselled them with so much reason and so much charm in his words, ever pardoned their faults with so much indulgence, enlightened their minds with so little pretension, relieved and consoled them with so much sweetness and sensibility, or partook of their pleasures or their sufferings with a truthfulness and simplicity more touching. . . . Although he never married, he loved the society of women, and had as many friends among them as among men, but he was never carried away by the fashionable gallantry of the time.[1]

One trait in his character may be noted as being in striking contrast to the manners of his day. Bachaumont mentions that 'he carried his benevolence so far in the late years of his life as to arrange for his servants being lodged as comfortably as himself.'[2] Many may smile at this as an eccentricity, but it is, we think, a touching proof of an earnest desire to make his own practice accord with the great principle of his public life, the recognition of the claims of the lower orders of society upon their superiors.

His religious views

We have no definite knowledge of his religious views. Although he took a keen interest in the great work of the 'Encyclopédie' and was on friendly terms with some of its principal supporters, and had himself contributed some important articles to the earlier volumes, we know that he severed his connection with it afterwards. He cannot be said to have 'belonged' to that party. While he could not be insensible of the ardent feeling entertained for him by Voltaire, he was certainly not a Voltairian. Alluding to a

[1] *Vie de Turgot*, i. 418–19. [2] *Mém. sec.* ix. 273.

reported commentary on the Bible by Madame du Châtelet, the friend of Voltaire, written no doubt from a very 'free-thinking' point of view, Turgot in his letter to Condorcet, June 21, 1772, deprecates all unscholarly criticisms of the Scriptures. 'Such a commentary,' he writes, 'will be an interesting work, but I would wish it made dispassionately, and with a design to gather from the text all that it contains of what is useful, in many respects, as a precious historical monument. The desire to discover absurdities and things to ridicule (which sometimes are not there) diminishes the effect on the mind of the incongruities which really are there.' [1]

He desired to see a separation between Church and State, and above all to see education freed from clerical management and from the teaching of dogmas. From these and other opinions he expressed, we may conclude that he made no claim to be considered orthodox. It would indeed be surprising if a man of his character of mind were not 'heterodox.' A man in advance of his time in other respects must, if he consistently applies his reason in that direction, necessarily be in advance of his time in his views of religion, 'orthodoxy' being the mere *status quo* in a realm of thought which is subject, like every other sphere of humanity, to progressive enlightenment.

Taking all we know of Turgot's opinions into account, along with the known moderation of his mental temper and the truly religious spirit so evident throughout his life and his writings, we are inclined to believe that he may be regarded as standing in close relationship to that class of independent thinkers which in our own day is receiving more and more accessions, the short statement of whose creed is 'the Christianity of Christ,' meaning that pure and simple religion, true for all time, enunciated in the Sermon on the Mount, uncorrupted by the since invented theologies and formalisms of the Catholic and the Protestant Churches.

Death

Towards the end of 1780 he had an attack of gout, more

[1] *Corresp. inédite de Condorcet et de Turgot.* Par G. Henry. Paris, 1887.

prolonged and more painful than he had previously experienced. In January 1781 he applied himself to literary composition for the last time by translating into verse Horace's Ode 'Æquam memento,' into which he felt might be read much of himself and his situation. In little more than two months, on March 18, 1781, he died, in his fifty-fourth year. He had never expected to survive the period of middle life. 'You blame me for attempting too much,' he said to his friends, 'but you know in my family we die of gout at fifty.'

We may finish this imperfect sketch of the life of a man who was as unselfish as he was just, far-seeing, and courageous, with the words of Malesherbes, which may fitly serve for his epitaph :—

He had the Mind of Bacon
And the Heart of L'Hôpital.

## L'ENVOI

The reader will find in the selections made from Turgot's writings one taken from his first discourse at the Sorbonne, when two and twenty: 'Well-timed reform to avert revolution.' This was the keynote of his public life. That life was a failure in itself, but it has taught a lesson for all time. There is no finality in dealing with political (or with social) problems. Each generation has for itself to solve new problems, to combat new difficulties, more complicated, perhaps more dangerous. It will be fortunate for the world when these difficulties are approached in good time, and dealt with by statesmen actuated by the spirit of Turgot. Their position will be stronger than his was, for it will be strengthened by an educated public opinion now able fully to assert itself. But public opinion has its duties as well as its rights. We must never forget another of his great sayings: 'It is not error which opposes so much the progress of truth; it is indolence, obstinacy, the spirit of routine, everything that favours inaction.'

# SELECTED WRITINGS OF TURGOT

(TRANSLATED)

WITH NOTES BY THE EDITOR

'There are hardly any works which can yield to the journalist and to the statesman an ampler harvest of facts and of instruction than may be found in the writings of Turgot.'

J. B. Say (*Traité d'Économie politique*, ii. 555).

# DISCOURSE AT THE SORBONNE, DECEMBER 11, 1750.

## *On the Successive Advances of the Human Mind.*[1]

THE phenomena of Nature, subjected to constant laws, are confined in a circle of ever the same revolutions. All perishes and all revives; in these successive generations, by which vegetables and animals reproduce themselves, time only gathers back in each case the image of what it had made disappear.

The succession of man, on the contrary, offers from age to age a spectacle ever varied. Reason, the passions, liberty, incessantly produce new events. All the ages are linked together by a sequence of causes and effects which connect the existing state of the world with all that has preceded it. The multiform signs of language and of writing, by giving to men the means of insuring the possession of their ideas and of communicating them to others, have made of all the individual funds of knowledge a common treasure, which one generation transmits to the next, along with an inheritance always increased by the discoveries of each age; thus the human race seen from its origin appears to the eye of a philosopher as one vast whole which itself, like each individual composing it, has had its infancy and its development.

We see societies establishing themselves, nations forming themselves, which in turn dominate over other nations or become subject to them. Empires rise and fall; laws, forms of government, one succeeding another; the arts, the sciences, are discovered and are cultivated, sometimes retarded and

[1] See *supra* pp. 8, 9.

sometimes accelerated in their progress, they pass from one region to another. Self-interest, ambition, vainglory, perpetually change the scene of the world, inundate the earth with blood. Yet in the midst of their ravages manners are gradually softened, the human mind takes enlightenment, separate nations draw nearer to each other, commerce and policy connect at last all parts of the globe, and the total mass of the human race, by the alternations of calm and agitation, of good conditions and of bad, marches always, although slowly, towards still higher perfection.[1]

. . . . . . .

The most sublime mental attainments are only, and can be only, founded upon our ideas of sensation, developed and combined; just as the edifice, whose towering height most excites our admiration, necessarily [has its materials derived from and] is supported by the earth we tread on. The same senses, the same organs, the spectacle of the same universe, have everywhere given to men the same ideas, as the same needs and the same inclinations have everywhere taught them the same arts.

A faint brightness commences to penetrate the long night that rested on all nations, and spreads itself from one place to another. The inhabitants of Chaldæa, nearest neighbours to the source of the first traditions, the Egyptians, the Chinese, appear to surpass the rest of the peoples; others follow them far off; progress leads to further progress. The inequality of nations increases: here the arts commence to rise, there they advance at a rapid rate towards perfection. Some nations further back are arrested in their mediocrity, elsewhere the original darkness is not dissipated. By this infinitely varied inequality the actual state of the universe, in presenting at the same time all the shades of barbarism and of civilisation, shows us in some sort under one view the

[1] 'The opening lines are among the most pregnant, as they are among the most original, in the history of literature, and reveal in an outline standing clear against the light a thought which revolutionised old methods of viewing and describing the course of human affairs, and contained the germs of a new and most fruitful philosophy of society.' (J. Morley, *Crit. Misc.* ii. 26.)

monuments and vestiges, and all the steps of the human mind, the reflection of all the degrees through which it has passed—in short, the history of all the ages.

Is not Nature, then, everywhere the same?—and if she conducts all men to the same truths, if even their errors are alike, how is it that they do not march at an equal pace on the road which is traced for them? Doubtless the human mind everywhere contains the germ of the same progress, but Nature, unequal in her benefits, has given to certain minds an abundance of talents which she has refused to others; circumstances develope these talents, or leave them buried in obscurity, and to the infinite variety of these circumstances is due the inequality in the progress of nations.

Barbarism makes all men equal. In the early times those born with genius find always the same obstacles. Meanwhile societies form themselves and expand, national hatreds, ambition, or rather greed, the only ambition of barbarous peoples, multiply ravages and war. Conquests, revolutions, mix in a thousand ways peoples, languages, manners. Chains of mountains, great rivers and seas, by confining within certain limits the arenas of peoples, and consequently of their intermingling, produce independent languages. These become a tie between nations, and eventually gather into certain great divisions the nations of the world. Tillage causes dwellings to be less temporary, it is able to feed more men than are employed in it, and hence imposes on those left idle the necessity of rendering themselves either useful or formidable to the cultivators. Hence towns, commerce, trades, the lesser arts, the separation of employments, the difference of education, the increased inequality of conditions, hence that leisure by which genius, relieved of the weight of the first necessities, emerges from the narrow sphere in which they retained it, and directs all its strength to the culture of the sciences. Hence that more vigorous and more rapid movement of the human mind, which carries with it all sections of society, and in turn derives from their advancement an increased energy. The passions develope themselves along with genius; ambition takes strength, political conditions lend to it always vaster views, victories have results more durable, and empires are formed whose laws, manners, and government, acting diversely upon genius, become a sort of general education for nations, and put between one people and another the same difference that education puts between one man and another.

United, divided, one raised on the ruins of others, empires rapidly succeed each other. Their revolutions bring about all possible states, they combine and separate all the elements of political bodies. There occurs an ebb and a flow of power, from one nation to another, and in the same nation from princes to the multitude, and from the multitude to princes. From these settlements and unsettlements everything approaches by degrees to an equilibrium, and takes at last a more permanent and tranquil condition. Ambition, by forming great states out of the fragments of many smaller ones, places limits to its own ravages; war does not desolate except around the frontiers of empires; towns and country places begin to breathe in the bosom of peace; the ties of society unite a greater number of men; the communication of ideas becomes more prompt and further spread; the arts, sciences, and manners make progress at a more rapid rate. Thus, like the tempest which has agitated the waves of the sea, the evils inseparable from revolutions disappear, the good remains, and Humanity perfects itself. . . .

Genius, whose steps are at first slow, unknown, buried in the general oblivion into which time precipitates human affairs, emerges with them from obscurity by the invention of writing. Inestimable invention, that seemed to give to those peoples who first possessed it wings that enabled them to distance other nations—inestimable invention, that snatches from the power of death the memory of great men and the examples of virtue, unites places and times, fixes fugitive thought and assures for it a durable existence, by which the productions, the opinions, the experiences, the discoveries of all ages accumulated, serve as a basis and a step to posterity that it may raise itself still higher.

But what a spectacle is presented by the succession of the opinions of men! I seek there the progress of the human mind, and I see almost nothing but the history of its errors. Why is its march, which is so sure from the very first steps in the study of mathematics, so unsteady on all other roads, and so subject to wander astray? Let us try to discover the reasons. In mathematics the mind works out a chain of propositions, the one deduced from the other, the truth of which is demonstrated by their mutual dependence. It is different with the other sciences, in which it is not through the comparison of ideas between themselves that the truth of knowledge is reached, but through their conformity with a sequence of real facts. In order to discover truth and to establish it, the point in question is no longer the mere laying down of a small number of simple principles from which the mind has only to let itself be carried on along the line of consequences; it is necessary to start from Nature, just as she is, and from that infinite diversity of effects towards which have concurred so many causes counterbalanced one by another. Notions are no longer assemblages of ideas that the mind forms at its will, and the extent of which it knows exactly. Ideas rise and collect themselves in our mind almost unconsciously; the images of objects come assailing it in the cradle; by degrees we learn to distinguish them, less in respect to what they are in themselves than by their relation to our habits and to our needs. The signs of language impress themselves on the mind while yet feeble, connect themselves by means of habit and imitation at first to particular objects, then succeed in calling up more general notions. This chaos of ideas and of expressions is incessantly increased and confused, and man when he begins to seek for truth finds himself in the midst of a labyrinth which he enters blindfold. Can we wonder at his errors?

Spectator of the universe, his senses, while experiencing effects, leave him ignorant of causes; to seek by the examination of effects for their unknown cause is to divine an enigma, to imagine one or several words to solve it, to try each successively until one is met with which fulfils all the conditions. The natural philosopher forms hypotheses, follows them to their consequences, applies them to the enigma of Nature, tries them, so to speak, upon the facts, as one verifies a seal by applying it to its impression. Suppositions imagined according to a small number of deficiently known effects yield to other suppositions less absurd but still incorrect. Time, research, chance, accumulate observations, and unveil the hidden connections that unite the several phenomena.

The curiosity of man, ever unsatisfied, incapable of finding repose elsewhere than in the truth, ever excited by the image of that truth which it believes itself to have touched, but which flies before it, still multiplies questions and disputes, and compels him to analyse ideas and facts in a manner always more exact and more profound. Mathematical truths becoming from day to day increased in number, and hence more fruitful, lend themselves to develope more extended and more precise hypotheses, and indicate new experiences which, in their turn, present new problems for mathematics to resolve. Thus the need perfects the instrument, thus mathematical science rests in and illumines physics, thus everything is connected, thus, in spite of the inequality in their steps, all sciences acquire, each from all the others, a mutual support, and thus by dint of grouping, by multiplying of systems, one after another, and by exhausting these of errors, man arrives at last to the certain knowledge of a vast number of truths. . . .

Ill-fated are those nations which, by a blind zeal for the sciences themselves, wish to confine them within the limits of existing knowledge. It is from this cause that the regions which were the first to be enlightened are not those which have made the most real progress. The respect which the grandeur of novelty in an expanding philosophy impresses upon men tends to perpetuate their first conceptions, and then the spirit of sect is introduced. This spirit was natural to the first philosophers because pride nourishes itself upon ignorance; because the less we know the less we doubt, the less we have discovered, the less we see what remains to be discovered. In Egypt, and for long before in India, superstition which treated the dogmas of ancient philosophers as the patrimony of sacerdotal families by consecrating them, incorporated them with the dogmas of a false religion. In Upper Asia political despotism, the effect of the establishment of great empires during the barbarous ages, and the civil despotism born of slavery and of the plurality of wives, which is a consequence of it, the effeminacy of princes, the degradation of their subjects; in China the very care that the emperors took to regulate studies and to mingle sciences with the political constitution of the state, all tended to retain for ever the sciences in mediocrity. . . .

Time flows on and new peoples are formed through the inequality in the progress of nations. Peoples civilised surrounded by barbarians, sometimes conquerors, sometimes conquered, mix themselves with them, and either as conquered receive arts and laws along with servitude, or as conquerors yield to the natural empire of reason and of policy over force, and thus barbarism is always mitigated. The Phœnicians, inhabitants of an arid coast, made themselves the ministers of the exchanges between peoples. Their vessels, spread over the Mediterranean, began to reveal nations to nations. Astronomy, navigation, geography developed themselves, the one by the other. The coasts of Greece and Asia Minor were covered with Phœnician colonies. But colonies are like fruits, which hold to the tree only until their maturity; the colonies, having become sufficient to themselves, will do as Carthage did, and as, some day, America will do.

[The lecturer next takes a survey of the rise of the power of Greece and of its character as a nation, of the Greek language, philosophy, and government.]

Happy age! when all the fine arts throw forth their light

on every side, when the fire of a noble emulation communicates itself with rapidity from city to city; when painting, sculpture, architecture, poetry, history, culminate everywhere simultaneously.

Athens, governed by the decrees of a multitude whose tumultuous waves were at the will of orators, calmed down or again raised into fury; Athens, in which Pericles taught its magistrates to buy up the State at the State's own expense, to dissipate its treasures in order to save themselves from rendering an account of them; in which the art of governing the people was the art to amuse them, the art to delight their ears, their eyes, their curiosity, always greedy of novelties, with fêtes, pleasures, and renewed spectacles; Athens, to whose very vices of government, which led her to succumb to Lacedæmon, were due the eloquence, the taste, the magnificence, the splendour in all the arts that have made her the admiration of nations. . . .

Commerce and the arts rendered Alexandria the rival of Athens. Astronomy and the mathematical sciences were there carried to a height they had reached nowhere else. Above all there shone there that erudition only slightly possessed by the Greeks, that kind of study which employs itself less upon things than upon books, which consists less in producing and discovering than in generalising and comparing, in judging of what has been produced and been discovered; not bent on marching forward, but turning its gaze backwards to observe the road it has come. The studies which demand the most genius are not always those which infer the most progress for the mass of mankind. There are minds to whom Nature has given a faculty for comparing ideas, of giving them that arrangement which puts them in their full light, but to whom, at the same time, she has refused the ardour of that genius which invents and which opens for itself new paths. This learned culture, with its purpose of bringing together under the same point of view the discoveries of the past in order to show them in clear distinctness, and even to further perfect them, if it be not the torch that shines by its own light, is the diamond that reflects with splendour a borrowed light, but which only a total darkness would confound with stones of a lower order. . . .

Meanwhile, for several ages past, Rome, as a world apart, was marching in a continued succession of triumphs to the conquest of the universe. Victorious over Carthage, she appeared suddenly in the midst of nations. Peoples trembled and were subjected. The Romans, conquerors of Greece, became cognisant of a new empire—that of Mind and Knowledge—and their rudeness grew less austere. Athens in her victors found disciples, and in the course of time almost rivals. Cicero displayed in his declamations at the Capitol and in the tribune an eloquence drawn from the lessons of the Greeks, of which his degenerate masters knew only the rules. The Latin tongue, softened and enriched, educated Africa, Spain, and Gaul. The limits of the civilised universe became those of the Roman power, and two rival languages, the Greek and the Latin, divided it between them.

From the age of Augustus to the fall of the Roman Empire I see but a general decadence into which everything precipitates itself. Is man elevated, therefore, only to fall? A thousand causes unite to deprave taste more and more: tyranny, which degenerates the public mind from everything that is great; senseless luxury, born of vanity, judging of works of art less as objects of cultivated taste than as signs of opulence, which is as much opposed to their perfection as an enlightened love of true magnificence is favourable to it; the ardour for new things by those who, without the genius to invent them, have too often just wit enough to spoil the old; the imitation of the faults of great authors and even the misplaced imitation of their beauties. Writers multiply in the Roman provinces and corrupt the language. Some remnants, imperfectly known, of ancient Greek philosophy, mixed with a mass of vain allegories, or with the illusions of magic, take possession of men's minds, smothering all the sound philosophy of Nature which had been born of the works of Seneca and of Pliny the Elder. Soon the Empire, abandoned to the caprices of an insolent military faction, becomes the prey of a long line of tyrants, who, in snatching it from each other, carry ravage and desolation into the provinces. Military discipline is annihilated. The barbarians of the North penetrate on all sides. Peoples dash themselves on peoples; towns become deserted, the country uncultivated, and the Empire of the West weakened by the transport of all its strength to Constantinople, ruined in detail by so many repeated ravages, on a sudden collapses, and leaves the Burgundians, the Goths, and the Franks to dispute over its vast ruins and to found kingdoms in the different countries of Europe.

It should not be for me, in this sanctuary, to pass in silence that new light which, while the Empire marched to its ruin, was shed on the universe—light more precious a thousand times than even that of letters and philosophy. Holy Religion! can we forget that it was through you that manners were improved, that the darkness of idolatry at last was dissipated, and that mankind were enlightened on the true character of God? During the almost total ruin of literature, you alone formed the writers who inspired the desire to instruct the faithful and to repel the attacks of the enemies of the faith. When Europe was the prey of the barbarians, you alone reclaimed their ferocity; you alone have perpetuated the knowledge of the Latin tongue become dead; you alone have transmitted to us, across the abyss of so many ages, the mind, if I may say so, of so many grand men, which was stored up in that language. The conservation of a vast treasure of human knowledge, when at the point of being dissipated, we owe to you.

But the malady of the human race was too deep; it required ages to cure it. . . . In what are called the middle ages we see kings without authority, the nobles lawless, the people slaves, the countries covered with fortresses, ravages incessant, war aflame between town and town, village and village, penetrating almost the whole mass of kingdoms; no commerce, all communication interrupted, cities inhabited by artisans, poor and without emulation; the only riches, the only leisure which some men yet enjoy, lost in the idleness of a nobility scattered here and there in their castles, who could only give themselves up to combats useless for their country. The most gross ignorance spread over all nations, over all the professions. Deplorable picture, but too true of Europe during several centuries. And yet, in the midst of this barbarism shall one day spring forth the perfected sciences and arts. In the midst of this ignorance an insensible progress prepares the way for the striking success of later centuries. Under this unpromising soil are being nourished and developed the feeble roots of a distant harvest. Among civilised people the towns are by their nature the centre of commerce and the focus of society. They already existed; if the spirit of the feudal government, born of the ancient customs of Germany, combined with some accidental circumstances, depressed them, it was in the constitution of such states an anomaly which was certain to be effaced in the long run. We soon see the towns raising themselves under the protection of princes, who sought, by holding out their hand to the oppressed citizens to gain their aid, to increase their own power by reducing the power of their vassals. [In the larger towns rose the universities.] Already Latin and theology, along with the dialectics of Aristotle, were studied in the universities. Long before that the Mussulman Arabs had been instructed in the philosophy of the Greeks, and this light spread itself over the West. Through them mathematics was extended and expounded, a science less dependent than the other sciences on the perfection of taste, and perhaps even on justness of mind. One can study it without being conducted to any great truth. The verities of mathematics, always certain, always pure, were surrounded by the errors of judicial astrology. The chimerical hopes to discover the great secret, by animating the Arab philosophers to separate and to combine all the elements of bodies, had brought forth under their hands the immense science of chemistry, and had spread it wherever men could be deceived by their greedy desires.

At last on all sides, and in all circumstances, the mechanical arts perfect themselves, because even in the decline of the sciences and of taste the needs of life conserve them, and because in the crowd of artisans who cultivate them successively it is impossible not to meet, now and again, one of those men of genius who are mixed with the rest of mankind as the gold is with the lower metal of the mine. Hence a number of inventions unknown to the ancients appeared in an age almost of barbarism: our art of recording music, our bills of exchange, our paper, window-glass, plate-glass, windmills, clocks, spectacles, gunpowder, and the magnetic needle leading to the perfection of navigation and commerce. Arts are but the practice of Nature translated, and the prosecution of arts is a sequence of physical experiments, more and more unveiling Nature. Facts accumulate in the shade of the times of ignorance, and the sciences, whose progress although for a time concealed is not the less real, emerge some day increased by new riches.

Different causes of events take their rise in the different countries of the world, and all, by however many separate roads, concur at last to the same end—to advance the human mind. . . . Germany, Denmark, Sweden, Poland, by the influence of Charlemagne and the Othos, and Russia by her commerce with the empire of the Greeks, cease to be uncultivated forests. . . . The nations, by the quarrels between nobles and princes, begin to form for themselves the principles of a more stable government, and to acquire, by the variety of circumstances into which they are brought, the particular character which distinguishes them. The wars against the Mussulmans in Palestine, in giving to all the Christian States a common interest, taught them to know each other and be united, and set the seeds of that modern policy by which so many nations seem to constitute but one great republic. Already is seen royal authority rising in France; the power of the people establishing itself in England; the cities of Italy forming themselves into republics, and presenting the image of ancient Greece; the little monarchies of Spain driving the Moors before them and gradually forming themselves into one. Soon the sea, which until now caused the separation of nations, becomes by the invention of the mariner's compass a band of connection. The Portuguese in the East, and the Spaniards in the West, discover new worlds. The universe is at last known. Already the mixture of barbarous tongues with the Latin has produced, in the course of ages, new languages, while the Italian, less distant from the common source, less mixed with the foreign elements, is the first to be refined into elegance of style and fitted for the beauties of poetry. The Ottomans, pouring over Asia and into Europe with the rapidity of a tempest, finish by overthrowing the empire of Constantinople, and disperse into the west of Europe the feeble sparks of the sciences which Greece had yet preserved.

An art suddenly rises by which are spread, in all directions, the thoughts and the glory of the great men of the past. Until now how slow, in every sense, progress has been! For two thousand years back medals have presented to all eyes characters impressed on bronze, and, after so many ages, it occurs for the first time to some obscure man that characters might be impressed on paper! As soon as the treasures of antiquity, drawn from the dust, pass into all hands, penetrate into all places, enlightenment is brought to the minds that were losing themselves in ignorance, and then genius is called forth from the depth of its retreat. The time has come.

Emerge, Europe, from the darkness that covered you! Immortal names of the Medicis, of Leo X., of Francis I., may you be consecrated for ever, may the patrons of the arts share the glory of those who cultivated them! I salute you, Italy, happy land, for the second time the country of letters and of taste, the source whence their waters are shed to fertilise our regions. Our France, as yet, views your progress, but from a distance. Her language is still infected with some remnant of barbarism. . . .

And now that multiplicity of facts, of experiences, of instruments, of ingenious operations, which the practice of the arts had accumulated during so many ages, has been drawn from obscurity by the work of the printing press, the productions of the two worlds, brought together by an immense commerce, have become the foundation of a natural history and philosophy hitherto unknown, and freed at last from grotesque speculations. On all sides attentive eyes are fixed on Nature. Slight chances turned to profit bring forth discoveries. The son of an artisan in Zealand, while amusing himself, brings together two convex glasses in a tube, and the limits of our senses are removed. In Italy the eyes of Galileo have discovered a new celestial world. Now Kepler, while seeking in the stars the numbers of Pythagoras, has found the two famous laws of the course of the planets which will become one day, in the hands of Newton, the key to the universe. Bacon had already traced for posterity the road she had to follow. . . . Great Descartes! if to find truth has not been always given to you, you have at least destroyed tyranny and error [that obscured it]. . . . At last all the clouds are dissipated. What a glorious light is cast on all sides! What a crowd of great men on all paths of knowledge! What perfection of human reason! One man, Newton, has submitted the infinite to the calculus; has unveiled the nature and properties of light, which, while revealing to us everything else, had concealed itself; he has placed in his balance the stars, the earth, and all the forces of Nature.

. . . . . . . .

Amidst these vicissitudes of sciences, of arts, of all that is human, rejoice, gentlemen, in the satisfaction of seeing that the Religion to which you have consecrated your hearts and your talents, always herself, always pure, always entire, stands perpetuated in the Church, preserving all the characters of the seal which the Divinity has stamped upon it. You will be her ministers and you will be worthy of her. The Faculty expects from you her glory, the Church of France her enlightenment, Religion her defenders; genius, learning, piety, unite to give foundation for their hopes.[1]

[1] *Œuvres de Turgot*, i. 527–691.

# NOTES ON UNIVERSAL HISTORY (1750)

## Introduction

### *Man's Place in Creation*

PLACED by his Creator in the midst of eternity and of immensity, and occupying in them but a point, man has necessary relations with a multitude of things and of beings. At the same time his ideas are concentrated in the individuality of his mind, and in the supremacy of the present moment. He knows himself only by sensations which are all connected with exterior objects, and the present moment is a centre at which a crowd of ideas, linked one with another, all issue. It is from this connection between his ideas, and from the order of the laws which all these ideas follow in their continual variations, that man acquires the consciousness of reality. By his connection with all the different sensations he learns the existence of exterior objects. A similar connection in the succession of his ideas shows him the past. The connections between different phenomena are not chance connections. All must act, the one on the other, according to the different laws, and according to their distances. We are ignorant of the limits of our world, and the comparatively little of it that we know depends more or less upon the perfection of our senses. We know a few links in the chain, but the extremities in the infinitely great and in the infinitely little equally escape us. The laws that govern bodies form physics; they are always constant, we simply describe them, we do not narrate them. The history of animals, and, above all, that of Man, offers a spectacle quite different. Like the animals, man succeeds to other men to whom he owes existence, and he sees as they do his fellows spread over the surface of the globe he inhabits. But, endowed with more comprehensive reason and a more active liberty, his connections with his fellows are much more numerous and more varied. Possessor of a treasure of signs which he has the faculty of multiplying almost to infinity, he can insure himself the possession of all his acquired ideas, communicate them to other men, and transmit them to his successors as a heritage continually augmented. A constant combination of these progressions, with the passions and the events they have produced, forms the history of the human race.

*Object of History.*—Thus universal history embraces the consideration of the successive progressions of the human race and of the detail of the causes that have contributed to them—the beginnings of man, the formation, the mingling of nations; the origin, the revolutions of governments; the progress of languages, of physics, of morals, manners, of sciences and arts; the revolutions by which empires succeeded to empires, nations to nations, religions to religions; humanity being ever the same amidst all these confusions, and ever marching onwards to its perfection. To unveil the influence of general and necessary causes, along with that of particular causes, and that of the free action of great men, to discover the springs and mechanism of moral causes by their effects—this is History in the eyes of a philosopher. It rests upon geography and chronology, which measure the distance of times and places. In laying down, on the following plan, a view of the human race, and in following as nearly as possible the historical order of its progress, and in dwelling on its principal epochs, I wish merely to indicate, I do not attempt to elucidate causes. I give but a sketch of a great study and open up the view of a vast field unexplored, just as we see through our narrow window all the immensity around and above us.

## Plan of the First Discourse, being on the Formation of Governments and the Commingling of Nations.[1]

*A Creator implied.*—The whole universe announces to us a Supreme Being. We see everywhere the print of the hand of God. But if we wish to know anything definitely, we are surrounded by clouds.

*Age of the World.*—We see every day arts invented; we see in some parts of the world peoples civilised and enlightened, in other parts peoples wandering in the heart of forests. In an eternity of duration this inequality of progress would have disappeared. The world, then, is not eternal, but we must at the same time conclude that it is of a vast age. To what extent we know not. Historic times cannot be traced further back than the invention of writing, and even when writing was invented we at first received from it but the narration of vague traditions or some leading facts, fixed by no date, and so mixed up with myths as to render discernment impossible. The pride of nations has induced them to throw back their origin far into the abyss of antiquity. But in respect to duration, men, before the invention of numbers, could scarcely have stretched their ideas beyond the few generations that they could know, that is, three or four. It is only to a century, or to a century and a half, that traditions, unaided by history, could indicate the epoch of a known fact. . . .

*Man's primitive Life; the Chase.*—Without provisions, in the midst of forests, he could be occupied only with his subsistence. The fruits of the earth produced without culture would not be much to him, it would be necessary for him to resort to the hunting of animals, and these being of limited number and, within a certain district, insufficient to furnish nourishment to many men, the dispersion of

[1] This discourse is given here necessarily in a greatly abridged form.

peoples and their rapid diffusion were thus accelerated. Families, or little nations, a long distance from each other, because it was necessary for each to have a vast space in order to sustain them—this was the necessary state of hunters. They had no fixed dwelling; they transported themselves with extreme facility from place to place. The difficulty of getting a living, a quarrel, the fear of an enemy, would suffice to separate families of hunters from the rest of their nation. Then they would follow wherever the chase might conduct them. . . . Thus peoples speaking the same language would find themselves at distances of more than 600 leagues, and surrounded by peoples who could not understand them. This is common among the savages of America, where we find, owing to the same cause, nations even of from fifteen to twenty men. . . .

*Pastoral Life.*—There are animals which suffer themselves to be subjected to man, as the ox, the sheep, the horse; and men find it more advantageous to gather these into herds than to run after wandering animals. The pastoral life has not failed to be introduced wherever these animals are met with; oxen and sheep in Europe, camels and goats in the East, horses in Tartary, reindeer in the North. . . . Pastoral peoples, by having their subsistence more abundant and better assured, have been the most numerous. They became richer, and were soon influenced by the idea of property. Ambition, or rather greed, which is the ambition of barbarians, inspired them with the inclination to plunder, and at the same time with the determination and the courage to hold their own. Flocks, to be properly tended, brought troubles from which hunters were free, but they sustained more men than were necessary to guard them.

Hence was brought about a disproportion in the promptness of movement of fighting men and that of nations. A nation would not shun the fight against a body of determined men, whether hunters, or members of other pastoral nations, who would remain masters of the flocks if they were conquerors, or who, on the other hand, might be repelled by the cavalry of pastors, if the herds of these consisted of horses or camels. And as the conquered could not escape without the risk of death by starving, they shared the fate of the cattle and became the slaves of the conquerors, who employed them in tending their flocks. The masters, on their side, relieved from all cares, went on subjecting others in the same manner. Thus little nations were formed which in their turn formed larger nations, thus peoples spread themselves over a whole continent until they were stopped by barriers felt to be impenetrable.

*Migrations.*—The incursions of pastoral peoples left more traces than those of hunters. Susceptible, by the idleness they enjoyed, of many desires, they sought for booty and seized upon it. They remained wherever they found pasturage, and mixed with the inhabitants of the country. The examples of the first encouraged others. These streams widened in their course, peoples and languages ever mixing. The conquering invaders, however, soon dispersed. When there was nothing more to pillage, their different hordes had no longer interest in remaining together, and, besides, the multiplication of flocks compelled them to separate. Each horde had its chief; and some principal chief, or the one most warlike, would hold a certain superiority over the others throughout the nation, exacting from them some presents, as signs of homage. . . .

*Aggressions.*—At last false ideas of glory would come in; what had been undertaken at first in view of pillage was now done in order to dominate, to lift their own nation above others, and, when commerce had taught them the qualities of different countries, in order to exchange a poor country for one rich and promising. Every prince, a little ambitious, made raids on the lands of his neighbours and extended his power until he met with some one capable of resisting him; then they fought; the conqueror increased his power by that of the conquered, and made use of that for new conquests. Hence all the inundations of barbarians which have ravaged the earth and those fluxes and refluxes which make up their whole history. . . . All conquests were not equally extensive: what would not have arrested a hundred thousand men would arrest ten thousand. . . . Rivers, and still more, chains of mountains and the sea, formed impassable barriers for these small would-be Attilas. . . . Beyond these first natural barriers conquests have been vaster, and the mingling of peoples and languages less frequent. Particular customs and dialects form different nations. Every obstacle that lessens communication, and consequently distance, which is one of these obstacles, strengthens the distinctions that separate nations; but in general the peoples of a continent are mixed together, at least indirectly, as the Gauls with the Germans, these with the Sarmatians, and so on, up to the extremities if the course be open. Hence those customs and those words common to peoples very distant and very different. Like a set of coloured bands, stretching across all the nations of a continent, we may see their languages, their manners, their faces even, forming a series of sensible degrees of distinction, each nation being the shade between the nations its neighbours. Sometimes all the nations mingle, sometimes one carries to another what it has itself received. But nearly all these revolutions are historically unknown, they have left no more traces than tempests on the sea. It is only when they have in their course embraced civilised peoples that their history has been preserved.

*Rise of Agriculture.*—Pastoral peoples who found themselves in fertile countries were undoubtedly the first to pass into the condition of labourers. . . . Labourers are not naturally a conquering class; the work of the soil occupies them too fully. But, richer than other peoples, they were obliged to defend themselves against violence. Besides, the earth was able to sustain many more men than were required to till it. Hence (in a greater degree than in the case of pastoral peoples) men free for other work, hence towns, commerce, all the arts of utility and of a simple refinement, hence progressions more rapid and of every kind, for everything follows the general march of the mind; hence a greater ability in war than that of barbarians, the division of employments, the inequality of men, slavery rendered domestic. . . . At the same time arise preciser ideas of government.

*Introduction of Government.*—The inhabitants of towns, more energetic than those of the country, subjected these. Or, more likely, a village, which by its situation as a centre to which the neighbouring population gathered for the convenience of commerce, growing stronger in inhabitants, and richer, became dominant, and leaving in the surrounding country only those who were necessary to the cultivation of the land, drew to itself, either by means of slavery, or by the attraction of government and of commerce, a still further increase of inhabitants. The union of different functions of the government became more intimate and more stable. In the leisure of towns passions are developed as well as genius. Ambition gathers strength, policy lends to it designs, the progress of the mind extends them; hence a thousand forms of government. The first were necessarily the work of war, and assumed consequently the government of one leading man. It is not necessary to believe that men ever voluntarily gave themselves a *master*, but they have often agreed in recognising a *chief*; and the ambitious themselves, in forming great nations, have unconsciously contributed to the will of Providence, to the progress of enlightenment, and consequently to the increase of happiness of the human race. . . . Hence the passions of individuals have multiplied ideas, extended knowledge, advanced men's minds, in default of that Reason, whose day has not yet come, and which would have been less powerful had it reigned earlier.

*In the early Times War a Civiliser.*—Reason, which is Justice herself, would not have sanctioned the taking away from anyone of what belonged to him, would have banished for ever war and usurpations, and would have left men divided into a multitude of nations, separated the one from the other, all speaking different languages. Limited thus in their ideas, incapable of that progress in every quality of mind, in science, arts, and government, which takes its rise from the collective genius of different provinces, the human race would have remained for ever in a state of mediocrity. Reason and justice, better listened to, would have fixed everything, as has almost been the case in China. But what is never perfect ought never to be entirely fixed. Tumultuous and dangerous passions become a principle of action, and consequently of progress; everything that draws men from their actual state, that brings under their eyes varied scenes, that extends their ideas, that enlightens them, that animates them, in the long run conducts them to the good and the true, to which they are attracted by their natural bent. . . . There are the soft passions which are always necessary, and which are developed in the degree to which humanity is perfected; there are the other passions, violent and terrible, such as hatred and vengeance, which are more developed in the times of barbarism; they are natural also, consequently also necessary. Their explosions call back the soft passions to mitigate them. . . . Men instructed by experience become more and more humane. But before laws had formed manners, these odious passions were necessary for the defence of individuals and of peoples. They were, if I may so, the leading-strings, with which Nature and its Author have conducted the infancy of the human race. It is by subversions and ravages that nations have been extended, that society and government have been perfected in the end; like in those forests of America, as ancient as the world, where from age to age oaks have succeeded to oaks, where from age to age, falling into the dust, they have enriched the soil with all those fruitful juices which the air and the rains have helped to furnish, where the *débris* of some, becoming a new principle of fecundity for the earth that had produced them, have served to the production of new offspring, still stronger and more lasting. In the same manner, over all the surface of the world, governments have succeeded to governments, empires have been raised on the ruin of empires, their *débris*, dispersed, have been gathered together again; the progress of reason, freed from the constraint of imperfect laws imposed by absolute power in the early governments, played a greater part in the constitution of governments succeeding. Repeated conquests extended states; the weakness of a barbarous legislation and of a limited executive encouraged divisions to take place. Here, a people fatigued with anarchy threw themselves into the arms of despotism; elsewhere tyranny carried to excess produced liberty. No mutation has been made which has not brought about some benefit, for none has been made without evolving experience, and without extending or improving, or at least preparing for man's education.

*Monarchy.*—In the first quarrels of nations a man superior in strength, in valour, or in prudence, induced, then compelled to obey him those whom he defended. That superiority alone sufficed, as we have said, to give a chief to men gathered together. It is not exactly true that ambition was the only motive to authority. Peoples are disposed to choose a chief, but they have always wished him to be one reasonable and just, not senseless nor arbitrary. With nations of a small size it is impossible for despotic authority to continue established. . . . All the state is under the eye of each individual. . . . There is no populace; a sort of equality reigns. . . . The means and the art of enforcing by the smallest number of men the obedience of the largest number cannot exist. Five hundred thousand men can keep in subjection fifty millions; two hundred men cannot subject twenty thousand, although the proportion is the same. . . . In states limited to a single town it is also impossible for royalty to be long maintained. Its least aggressions are and appear there the most tyrannical; tyranny there has less power, finds there more energetic resistance. . . . Royalty there more easily degenerates. The passions of the man are there confounded with those of the prince. . . . Hence republics arise, at first aristocratic and more tyrannical than monarchy, because nothing is so perilous as obedience paid to a party, which can always erect its passions into virtues. . . . The powerful and the feeble unite against a single tyrant; but an aristocratic senate, especially if it be hereditary, has only the populace to combat. In spite of that, republics limited to the extent of a city tend naturally to democracy, which also has its serious drawbacks. . . .

*Despotism.*—Despotism is easy. To do whatever one wills, this is a code that a king learns very fast; it requires art in order to persuade, none is needed in order to command. . . .[1] The larger a state is, the easier despotism is, and the greater difficulty exists in establishing a moderate government. For that there is necessary a connected order in all the parts of the state; the demarcations must be fixed for each province, and for each town, with its municipal government left for itself to manage in full liberty. What a multitude of springs to combine to balance, and what a difficulty presented to him who does not believe in the necessity for it! . . . The prince forgets the people. The best government was that which gave him the most money, and which could the more easily gain the habitual ministers and flatterers of the palace. The governors had their subalterns acting in the same spirit. Despotic authority rendered the governors dangerous; the Court treated them with the utmost rigour, their existence hung on the most trifling caprice. Pretexts were sought to strip them of the treasures they had pillaged, but the people got no relief by this, for greed is the natural quality of barbarian kings. . . . Despotic princes, not having found laws, scarcely dreamt of making any. They were their own judges. When the power that makes the laws and the power that applies them are identical, laws are useless. . . .

[1] 'Anyone can govern in a state of siege.' (Cavour.)

But a despotic government which comes subsequent to the establishment of laws and manners does not involve all the same evils as in the early conquests made by barbarians. The Neros and the Caligulas, I dare say, had more wickedness in them than the evil they were able to commit. By the principles established for the state under the first Cæsars the people were not oppressed, the provinces enjoyed a sort of tranquillity, justice was, generally, equitably exercised. The governors dared not gratify their greed; they would have been punished by the emperors. . . .

The despotism of the Roman emperors led to less evil than that of the Turks. With them despotism enters into the very constitution of their government; it acts upon every spring. Each pasha exercises over the people submitted to him the same authority the grand seignior holds over himself. He is alone charged with, and is responsible for, all the tributes of his province. He has no revenue except what he can exact from the people beyond what he is obliged to furnish to the sultan, and he is compelled to increase his exactions in order to provide for the countless presents necessary to secure himself in his post. There is no law in the empire regulating the levy of taxes, no system in the administration of justice. Everything is transacted in military fashion. The people find no protectors at the Porte against the abuses of power by the great, for the Porte itself partakes their fruits. . . .

*European Freedom.*—Military discipline necessarily supposes despotism and rigour. But we must not confound nations administered by military government with the nations wholly composed of warriors, like the barbarians, ancient Germans, and others. Far from that, their government gave rise to liberty, war was not an exclusive profession which required to be specially studied, and which gave to those who exercised it a superiority over the rest of society. Such a nation could guard its right. A prince could subject his people by soldiers because the people were the feebler party. But how could a people of soldiers be subjected? . . . The kingdoms of Europe conquered by the barbarians of the North were then preserved from despotism because these barbarians were free before the conquest, and it was made in the name of the people, and not in that of the king. The Roman customs which had been established, and the religion which the barbarians embraced, contributed to maintain the freedom existing.

*Asian Despotism.*—It was not the same in Asia, where the conquered peoples found themselves already accustomed to despotism, because the first conquests, at a time before manners could be formed, had been vast and rapid. Despotism gave birth to revolutions, but these were only a change of tyrant, because in the great despotic states the strength of the monarch is only established by means of his troops, his own safety by his guards. The people are neither strong enough nor united enough to arrest that military power which substitutes one monarch for another, and makes itself the same instrument of the tyranny of the new monarch as it was of the old. In these vast despotic states there was introduced also a despotism which extended itself over social manners, and, worst of all, enfeebled men's minds; which deprived society of the greatest part of its resources, of its gentle graces, of the co-operation of woman in the administration of the family; which, by interdicting the free communion of the two sexes, brings everything into monotony and throws the members of the state into a lethargic repose which is opposed to all change, consequently to all progress. By conducting everything by mere force (as is necessary to be done in a society where a crowd of slaves and of women is, in each wealthy house as in the state itself, immolated to one master) the flame of the intellect is extinguished. . . . Despotism perpetuates ignorance, and ignorance perpetuates despotism. What is more, this despotic authority becomes usage, and usage confirms the abuses.

*Slavery.*—In early times men were cruel in their wars, it was long before they learned moderation. Peoples living by the chase massacred the prisoners, or when they did not kill them they incorporated them with their own nation. A mother who had lost a son chose a prisoner who served her as a son; she loved him because he was useful to her. It was common for their old people to adopt children. There were few or no slaves, therefore, among the primitive or hunting tribes. Pastoral people began to know slavery. Those who captured flocks were obliged, as has been said, to keep those who guarded them before applying themselves to new expeditions. An agricultural people studied slavery still further. They had for the employment of slaves more varied services and more fatiguing works, and in the degree to which the manners of the masters grew more refined, slavery became harsher and more degraded, because the inequality was the greater. The rich ceased to work, slaves became a luxury and a merchandise, parents even sold their children. But the greatest number of slaves was always those captured in war or who were born of slave parents.

*Polygamy.*—Female slaves belonged to the pleasures of the master. We see that in the manners of the patriarchs (and it is still a point in ancient jurisprudence) the crime of adultery was not one reciprocal as with us. The husband only believed himself to be outraged. This was a sentiment of the inequality of the sexes belonging to barbarism. Women had no rights in the marriage relation in ancient times. It was only poverty that prevented polygamy from being everywhere established. . . . In the first empires the plurality of wives became a custom as general as the limits of private fortune permitted. Jealousy is a necessary consequence of love, it wisely inspires in man and wife a spirit of mutual property which insures the fate of the children. This passion, and still more the prejudice of dishonour, attached to the husband by the infidelity of any of his wives, increased along with polygamy. The impossibility to subject woman to this one-sided law of fidelity, when neither her heart nor her senses could be satisfied, dictated the practice of immuring them. Princes, and afterwards all those who were rich enough, made for themselves seraglios. . . . Princes shut themselves up with their wives and their slaves; their subjects, whom they never saw, were scarcely regarded as men. Their political government was always that of barbarians. It was simply because they were ignorant and idle and cruel; because less time was needed to cut down a tree than to gather its fruits, and because the art to render men happy is of all the arts the most difficult, the one in which the most elements have to be combined. This same effeminacy spread itself over all the state, hence the sudden declension of the monarchies of the East. That of the Chaldeans, the Assyrians, the Medes and Persians, scarcely survived the first conquerors who had founded them. . . . If sometimes those monarchies, by the multitude of their soldiers, have crushed weaker nations, they were overthrown by any courageous resistance, and as soon as Greece was united she demolished almost without effort this immense colossus. There is but one resource against this general debasement of such nations, a body of troops kept up in warlike discipline, like the Turkish janissaries, or the mamelukes of Egypt, but such a body becomes often terrible to its masters. One thing I ought to remark is, that the evils of despotism and of the plurality of wives have never been carried so far as under Mahometanism. This religion, which does not permit other laws than those of the religion itself, opposes the wall of superstition to the natural march of improvement. . . . We do not find in the history of ancient monarchies, nor in the manners of China or Japan, the excesses of abasement seen among Mahometan peoples.

*Longevity of Despotism.*—Despotism, uniformity and consequently imperfection of manners, of laws and government, are preserved in Asia, and wherever the great empires were formed at an early stage in the world's history, and I doubt not that the existence of the vast plains of Mesopotamia has contributed to this effect. When despotism was afterwards extended elsewhere, along with Mahometanism, it was in some degree only the transport of manners from one country to another.

*Peoples preserved from Despotism* are those who remained pastoral or followed the chase, those who formed small societies and republics. It is among such peoples that revolutions have been useful, and the nations participating in them have been advanced; among them tyranny has not been able to consolidate itself enough in order to enthral the mind. The fall of an old, and the rise of a new sovereign authority which again and again subjected laws to criticism, have, in the long run, perfected legislation and government. Thus equality has been preserved, public spirit has taken more activity, and the human mind has made rapid progress. Thus manners and laws have at length learned to direct themselves towards the greatest happiness of the peoples.[1]

---

## Plan of the Second Discourse, being on the Advance of the Human Mind.[2]

*Men by Nature intellectually unequal.*—A fortunate arrangement of the fibres of the brain, a greater or less strength or refinement in the organs of sense and the memory, a certain degree of quickness in the blood, these are probably the only differences that Nature herself puts between one man and another; all the rest is the result of education. Their minds, or the power and character of their minds, have a real inequality, the causes of which will be always unknown by us.

*Genius dependent on Circumstances.*—Genius permeates the human race in some manner as gold exists in a mine.

[1] *Œuvres de Turgot*, ii. 626–42.

[2] Of this we select only a few salient paragraphs.

The more you take of the mineral the more you gather of the precious metal. The more men you draw forth (educate) you will have the more great men, or men fit to become great. The chances of education and of events develope them, or leave them buried in obscurity, or sacrifice them before their age, like fruit struck down by the wind. We are obliged to admit that if Corneille, brought up in a village, had followed the plough all his life, that if Racine had been born in Canada among the Hurons or in Europe in the eleventh century, they would never have unfolded their genius. If Columbus and Newton had died at fifteen, America would possibly not have been discovered until two centuries later, and perhaps we should have been still ignorant of the true system of the world. And if Virgil had perished in infancy we should have had no Virgil, for we have had only one.

*Climate and Civilisation.*—A cause of the difference between nations has been sought in the difference of their climates, but the inductions made are at least precipitate and in many respects are contradicted by experience, since, under the same climates, peoples are different, and under climates unlike we often find the same character of people and the same turn of mind. . . . The metaphorical language of Eastern nations, which some have considered due to the proximity of the sun, was that of the ancient Gauls and Germans (according to the accounts of Tacitus and Diodorus Siculus), and is still that of the Iroquois in the icy regions of Canada. It is in fact the style of all peoples whose language is very limited, and who, wanting appropriate words, have to multiply comparisons, metaphors, allusions, in order to make themselves understood, and who succeed in that sometimes forcibly enough, but always with little exactitude and clearness.

*Music, the Dance, and Poetry* have their source in the nature of man. Designed to live in society, his joy makes exterior signs, he leaps or he cries. . . . By degrees he accustomed himself to leap in a similar manner to represent a similar feeling; the steps were marked by sounds, these were separated by regular intervals. The ear, by a short experience and by following Nature alone, learned to appreciate the leading connections of sounds. When one wished to communicate the motives of his joy by words, he regulated them on the measure of sounds; thus the origin of the dance, of music, and of poetry, which is at first made in order to be sung.

*Ancient Poetry.*—Among uncultivated peoples, national vanity and the facility to retain verses induced them to record their most memorable actions in songs. Such are the songs of the savages of our own day, those of the ancient bards, the runic rhymes of the Scandinavians, some old songs inserted in the old historical books of the Hebrews, the chou-king of the Chinese, and the romances of modern peoples of Europe; these were the only histories before the invention of writing, histories without chronology, and, as we might expect, often full of invented circumstances.

*Mythology.*—The myths of all peoples resemble each other, because the effects to be explained and the patterns of the causes which they imagined in order to explain them, were similar. . . . The mythological beings supposed as existing were attached to the history of facts, and hence became varied. The sex of divinities, which often depended on the gender of a word in a language, would also vary the myths with the different peoples. A thousand circumstances might belong to these myths without destroying their general connection. The commingling of nations and their commerce created, by ambiguities, new myths, and words ill understood augmented the number of the old ones. Regarding imaginary beings as real, sometimes the gods were held to be the same if their attributes were somewhat similar. Hence the confusion in the history of the gods.

Hence the multitude of their actions, especially when two or more peoples having a similar mythology happen to commingle, as in the case of India. A knowledge of physical causes occurred, but the myths had still their influence by the double love of antiquity and of the marvellous, and because recital transmitted them from century to century.

*Origin of the Fine Arts.*—The arts of design, sculpture and painting have many connections with poetry by the emotions felt by the artist, and by those he strives to communicate. They had a natural origin in the desire to preserve historical or mythological monuments; and genius was there exalted by the patriotic or religious zeal which demanded to express with feeling, with depth, and with force the ideas and the memories which these monuments were intended to recall.

*Rise of Science.*—Before arriving at the knowledge of the relations between physical effects, there was nothing more natural for man than to suppose that they were introduced by some intelligent beings, invisible, and similar to himself—for the gods were only men more powerful and more or less perfect according as they were the creation of an age more or less enlightened. When philosophers had recognised the absurdity of these myths, but were still without new light on natural history, they imagined they could explain the causes of phenomena by abstract expressions, such as *essences* or *powers* (which, however, explained nothing), on which they reasoned as if these terms were beings, new divinities substituted for the old ones. Analogies were followed out and *powers* multiplied in order to account for each effect. It was only after a long lapse of time, by observing the physical action of bodies in themselves and upon each other, that philosophers arrived at such hypotheses as mathematics could develope and experience verify. Physics did not rise from its degradation as a form of bad metaphysics until a long progress in the arts and in chemistry had multiplied the combinations of bodies, and until, the communication between nations having become more intimate, and geographical knowledge more extended, the facts themselves became better ascertained. Printing, literary and scientific journals, and transactions of academies have increased certitude to such a point that now only the details are doubtful.[1]

[1] *Œuvres de Turgot*, ii. 642–71.

## ON SOME SOCIAL QUESTIONS, INCLUDING THE EDUCATION OF THE YOUNG

*Addressed to Madame de Graffigny* [1] (1751)

. . . I HAVE again read the *Lettres péruviennes.* Zilia is a quite worthy sister of Cénie. I am like Henri Quatre, for the last one I have heard. I would indeed prefer the constantly discovering new beauties (which I am always astonished not to have already admired) to amusing myself by making poor criticisms. But you do not wish praise, and I must renounce gratifying myself.

In obedience to the request you have honoured me by making, I begin by suggesting the additions which I imagine might be made to the work. You seem to me to approve of the principal of these, which would be to show Zilia as Frenchwoman, after having shown her as Peruvian; to show Zilia judging no longer according to her prejudices, but comparing her prejudices with our own, making her regard objects from a new point of view, making her remark how far she has been wrong in being astonished at so many

[1] See *supra*, p. 15. Graffigny (Françoise). Born 1695. Belonged to a noble family fallen in fortune. Made when very young an unhappy marriage; after many years of suffering obtained a judicial separation. Spent with Voltaire and Madame du Châtelet at Cirey six months, 1738–39, of which she has left a narrative. Admitted to the closest literary intimacy, Voltaire's poem 'La Pucelle' was read to her; suspected of having spoken to others of this work, desired to be kept secret, she was unceremoniously expelled from Cirey by Madame du Châtelet in Voltaire's absence. He, more lenient, gave her the best introduction to Paris society. She published between 1745 and 1758, the year of her death, several romances and plays. The *Lettres d'une Péruvienne*, of 1747, was her greatest success, and went through many editions. It has been translated into English (1805).

things, and making her search out the causes of those arrangements, derived from the ancient constitution of government, bearing upon the distribution of social conditions as well as on the progress of knowledge.

The distribution of conditions is a very important feature in the social state, and one very easy to justify by showing its necessity and its utility. Its necessity, because men are not born equal, because their strength, their mind, their passions, would constantly disturb the equilibrium which laws might attempt to set, because all men are born in a state of feebleness, which renders them dependent on their parents, and which forms between them indissoluble ties. Families unequal in capacity and in strength redoubled the causes of inequality; the wars of savages required a chief. What would society have been without this inequality of conditions? Each would have been reduced to a life concerning itself merely with necessities, and there would be many to whom even these would not be assured. One cannot labour at the soil without having utensils and the means of sustenance until the harvest. Those who have not had the intelligence or the opportunity to acquire these means have not the right to deprive of them him who has earned and won them by his work. If the idle and the ignorant robbed the laborious and the skilful, all work would be discouraged, misery would become general. It is more just and more useful for all that those who are deficient in mind or in good fortune should lend their strength to others who can employ them, who can, in advance, give them wages, and thus guarantee them a share of the future products. Their subsistence then is assured, but so is their dependence. It is not unjust that he who has invented a productive work, and who has supplied to his co-operators the sustenance and the instruments necessary to execute it, who has made with them, in that, only a free contract, should reserve for himself the better part, and, for the price of his advances, should have less hard work and more leisure. This leisure enables him to reflect more, and still further to increase his mental resources. What he can save from the portion, equitably greater, which he will have of the products, increases his capital and his power to undertake new enterprises. Thus inequality will arise, and will increase, even among the most capable and most moral peoples. . . . It is not an evil, it is a blessing for mankind: where would society be if every man laboured only at his own little field? It would be necessary for him also to build his own house, to make his own clothes. The work of each would be limited to himself and to the productions of the little piece of ground surrounding him. How would the inhabitant of the land which did not produce wheat manage to live? Who would transport the products of one country to another? The humblest peasant now enjoys many commodities gathered often from distant countries. A thousand hands, perhaps a hundred thousand hands, have worked for him. The distribution of employments necessarily leads to the inequality of conditions. Without it who would perfect the useful arts? Who would succour the infirm? Who would spread the light of the mind? Who would give to men and to nations that education, particular as well as general, which forms their manners? Who would decide peacefully men's quarrels? Who would check the ferocity of some men, or support the feebleness of others? Liberty! I say it in a sigh, men are perhaps not worthy of thee! Equality! they desire thee, but they cannot attain to thee!

Let your Zilia weigh again the relative advantages of the savage and of the civilised man. To prefer the condition of the savage is a ridiculous declamation. Let her refute it, let her show that the vices which we regard as produced by civilisation are the appanage of the human heart; that he who has no gold may be as avaricious as he who has it, because, in all circumstances, men have the hunger for property, the right to preserve it, the avidity which actuates them to accumulate its products. But let not Zilia be unjust; let her, at the same time, unfold the compensations, unequal indeed but still real, belonging to the condition of uncivilised people. Let her show that our arbitrary institutions too often lead us away from Nature; that we have been the dupes of our own progress, that the savage, without knowing how to consult Nature, knows often how to follow her.

Let Zilia criticise, above all, the method of our education; let her criticise our pedantry, for it is in that to-day that our education consists. Our teaching is applied quite against the grain of Nature. See the 'Rudiments.' We begin by wishing to cram into the heads of children a perfect crowd of the most abstract ideas. We deluge them with words which can offer to them no meaning, because the meaning of words can only be presented along with ideas, and these ideas can come only by degrees, by proceeding from sensible objects. Then we suppress their imagination, we keep from their view the objects by which Nature gives to the savage the first notion of all things, of all the sciences, even of astronomy, of geometry, of natural history. A man, after a very long education, is still ignorant of the cause of the seasons, cannot fix the cardinal points, does not know the most common animals and the most common plants. We have not an eye for Nature. It is the same with us in morals; general ideas again spoil everything. We take enough care to say to a child that he must be just, temperate, virtuous, but has he the least idea of virtue? Do not say to your son, *Be virtuous*, but make him find pleasure in being so. Develope in his heart the germ of the sentiments which Nature has put there. We often need more barriers against our education than against Nature. Place the child in the opportunities to be true, liberal, compassionate, rely upon the heart of man, let the precious seeds of virtue expand in the air that surrounds them. Do not smother them under a load of straw-mattings and wooden frames.

Another point in our education which seems to me to be bad and ridiculous is our severity in respect to these poor children. They have done some mere foolishness, and we reprehend them as if it were a most important fault. There are many of these childish follies which age itself will correct, but we do not think of that. We wish our son to be 'well brought up,' and we overwhelm him with petty rules of civility, often frivolous, which cannot but annoy him, for he does not see the reasons for them. It would be quite sufficient to prevent him from being troublesome to those he meets. The rest will follow by degrees. Inspire in him the desire to please, he will soon know more in that respect than all that masters could teach him. We wish our child to be serious, we make it a virtue in him not to run about; we fear every instant that he is going to fall. What happens? We weary and vex him, and we enfeeble him. We have forgotten that above all it is a part of education to form the body.[1] We can trace the cause of this to our ancient manners and our old government. Our ignorant nobility indeed knew nothing but the body; it was men of the people who studied, and that only in order to become priests or monks. Latin was then the whole education, because it was not men who were to be formed, but priests, capable of passing an examination required of them. And again, to-day we study philosophy, not to be a philosopher, but to pass Master of Arts. What has followed from this? When the nobility have desired to study they have studied according to the forms of colleges established for ecclesiastical objects, and this has often had the effect of disgusting them with study altogether.

I know that you wish to take the conceit out of men by placing woman's constancy above man's. This reminds me of the lion in the fable, who, seeing a picture in which a man had overcome a lion, observed, 'If lions could paint, they would show another story.' You, who can paint, wish to abase them too. But, candidly, I advise you

[1] 'This was the education of the time. Let us bless Rousseau, who delivered youth from it; but let us also admire Turgot, who wrote this several years before the publication of *Émile*.' (Dupont.) It is not improbable that Turgot in these observations affords us a glimpse of his own early home life. See *supra*, p. 4.

not to blemish your romance for the glory of women—you have no need to do so.

I have long thought that our nation has need to have marriage preached to her—good marriage. We make our marriages with sordidness, from views of ambition or self-interest, and for this reason many of them are unhappy. We see becoming stronger day by day a fashion of thinking which is hurtful to the State, to manners, to the duration of families, to happiness and the domestic virtues. We dread the ties of marriage, we dread the care and the expense of children.[1] There are many causes of this mode of thinking, but this is not the place to detail them. It will be useful to the State and to manners that we set ourselves in this to reform our opinions less by reasoning than by sentiment. Assuredly there is no lack of matter to be urged; it is Nature that brings about marriage, it is she who adds to the attraction of pleasure the still more delightful attraction of love, because, man having a longer need of help than other young beings, it is necessary for the father and the mother to be united by a durable tie in order to guide the education of their children. It is this same Nature which, by the wise providence of the Supreme Being, endows animals with a maternal tenderness, which endures precisely to the time when the little ones cease to need it. It is Nature that renders the caresses of the little ones so agreeable to their parents. You might introduce this topic by making Zilia dilate upon the happiness she promises herself with Aza. She might see Céline playing with her young children, might envy the sweetness of those pleasures so little tasted by people of the world; she could—and this is still a point in the comparison between man civilised and man uncivilised—she could reprehend this blot on our manners. We blush at our children, we regard them as an embarrass-

[1] 'Looseness of opinion as to the family and the conditions of its well-being and stability was a flaw that ran through the whole period of revolutionary thought. . . . It is a proof of the solidity of Turgot's understanding that he should from the first have detected the mischievousness of this side of the great social attack.' (John Morley, *Crit. Misc.* ii. 71.

ment, we keep them away from us, we send them to some college or convent, in order to be troubled with them as little as possible. It is a true reflection that the ties of the natural society of the family have lost their strength proportionally as society in general has expanded. General society has jostled out Nature; we have taken away society from the family to give it to the public. It is true that this general society is advantageous in many respects, and will some day destroy the prejudices it has established; for although the first effect of society is to render individuals slaves to public opinion, the second, but more distant effect is to embolden everyone to judge for himself. . . . The most courageous venture to say aloud what others think only in secret, and, in the long run, the voice of the public becomes the voice of Nature and of truth, because in the long run it becomes the judgment of the greatest number.

Returning to the question of marriage, I would that Zilia should dwell a little on the abuse of which I have already spoken—the manner in which we make marriages without the two parties we join together for life being known to each other, merely by the authority of the parents who determine their own choice only by the fortune of rank or of money, or of rank which it is hoped will one day be translated into money, and who give point to their ideas by the saying we hear every day, 'He has done a foolish thing—*married for love*. . . .' I believe it will take a long time to correct society on this matter. I know that even marriages of inclination are not always happy; but because in choosing we are sometimes deceived, it is concluded that we must never choose. The consequence drawn is amusing.

And this leads me to another matter very important for our happiness, of which I would like your Zilia to speak. I would examine closely into the causes of the inconstancies, and even occasional dislikes, that occur between those who at heart love each other. I believe that as we live longer in the world we see that the bothers, the teasings, and the bad temper, brought about by trifles, place more trouble and divisions between people than serious things do. It is deplorable to see so many quarrels, and so many people made unhappy actually on account of mere nothings. How much acrimony rises on the foundation of a word, or on some presumed forgetfulness of respect! If we only put ourselves in the place of others, if we were only to think of the many times we ourselves have had movements of temper, how often we ourselves have forgotten things! A word spoken in depreciation of our judgment is enough to render us irreconcilable, and yet how many times *we* have found ourselves wrong in forming opinions!—how many men of mind we have sometimes taken for fools!—and why should not others have the same right to err as we? But *their* self-love, it is said, makes them find pleasure in preferring themselves to us. Honestly, without our own self-love being concerned, should *we* be thus shocked? Pride is the greatest enemy of pride: they are two inflated balloons which mutually repel each other. Let us pardon the pride of others and let us fear our own. Nature, by forming men so subject to error, has given them but so many claims to tolerance. Why should we refuse it because it is ourselves who are concerned? It is here the evil is; because it is so rare for us to judge fairly, because almost no one weighs truly himself with others. . . . How much tact is needed in those living together to be compliant without lowering one's self, to blame another without harshness, to correct without dominating, to complain without ill-temper! Women, above all, whom we train up to believe that every deference is due to them, are not able to bear contradiction. This is of all the dispositions the most liable to render them unhappy and all those surrounding them. Nothing is more miserable for us than to be ever dwelling on the respect we think due to us; it is the sure way to our becoming insufferable, it is to make for others a burden of that respect we desire. Respect is tendered with pleasure only where it is not exacted. The best advice that can be given to persons living together is to be quite frank with each other in dealing with any serious difference as soon as it appears; this arrests at their source many of the annoyances often proceeding from mere prejudiced dislikes. But this must be done with full sincerity; we must habituate ourselves to criticise, to examine, and to judge others with a perfect impartiality. I do not speak of tempering our criticisms by giving to them some agreeable turns, and of seasoning them with some mixture of praise and tenderness. How difficult this art is! . . . It is true that, even with the best tact used by us to soften reproaches, there are persons who do not know how to receive them; advice they mistake for scolding, they imagine always to see in him who gives it them an assumption of superiority and authority which repels them. It must be admitted that this is a defect belonging to many givers of advice. I have often met with persons who say in self-defence: 'I am so made, and I cannot help it.' These are persons whose self-love embraces even their defects. This bad disposition proceeds, perhaps, from the manner in which we have had advice given us in childhood, always under the form of reproach, of correction, with the tone of authority, often of threatening. Hence a youth when once free from the hands of his masters or his parents places all his happiness in having no longer to give account of his conduct to anyone, and the most friendly advice appears to him an act of domination, a yoke, a continuance of childhood. Ah! why not accustom children to listen to advice with sweetness by our giving it to them without bitterness? Why exercise authority? I would that children really felt that it is from our affection for them that we reprehend them; but how can we make them feel this if we do not express it in our own softness with them? I have no sympathy with Montaigne when he censures the caresses given by mothers to their children. Who can know better than mothers themselves? It is the instinct that Providence has given them. It is the seasoning which reason teaches should be added to instruction in order to give it genial growth. We forget that it is the caresses of a courageous mother that inspire courage, that they are the most powerful medium of opening the young soul to the inlet of all fine and pure feelings.

I complain above all that our system of educating the young is, for the most part, a mass of most frivolous rules for the teaching of most frivolous things. Why should not children be taught, instead, the art to know themselves, to acquire that fairness of mind which would in time banish from society, if not ill temper, at least the quarrels which ill-temper occasions? How many men would have been happier had they but learnt earlier that tact in giving advice, that docility to receive it and to follow it, of which I have spoken! It is supposed that such quiet impartiality as this is only a gift of Nature, the result of a fortunate temperament, and that education is powerless to effect this constant attention to oneself. We little know the power of education. I will mention one of the reasons of its failure; it is that we content ourselves with giving *rules* where it is necessary to create *habits*. . . . I believe that Nature has sown in all hearts the seeds of all the virtues, that they require only to be developed; that education (but indeed only a skilful education) can render virtuous the most of men. I know that human progress cannot be rapid; man slowly trails himself along step by step. We must commence by teaching parents to feel the necessity of this true education and to know how to impart it. Each generation will learn a little from the preceding one, and books will thus become the preceptors of nations. And you, Madame, who are so zealous for the good of humanity, who can work better than yourself to spread these principles? They are not quite unrecognised. We have already begun in our time to have a glimpse of them, to render justice to them, even to favour them. But we do not yet know how to instil them. What slovenliness there is in home education, and how easy it would be to penetrate the hearts of children with the sentiments of compassion and of good-will! I have seen parents who taught their children that 'nothing is so beautiful as to make people happy.' And I have seen the same rebuff their children when they wish to invite some young friends. These, perhaps, might not be quite suitable, but the parents should be careful not to intimidate the rising sensibility of their children, they should rather encourage it, and should make evident the pain they feel in refusing their children's request and the necessity there is for refusing it. But only the present moment is thought of. Again, we reproach children for having been foolish in making some generous gift, as if they would not be corrected of that soon enough! . . . . Thus we contract the heart and mind of a child. I wish, too, that we could avoid exciting in them a shyness when doing a good action, and that we did not believe in inducing them to do it by praises. These repel a timid child; they cause him to feel that we are watching him, and they throw him back upon himself. It is the perfection of tact to bestow praise appropriately. We should teach our children to seek out and to seize occasions of being helpful to others, for this is an art which can and ought to be taught. I do not speak of the delicacy to be used with the unfortunate while we relieve them, for which natural benevolence, without some knowledge of the world, is not sufficient. But above all the great point in home education is to preach by example. Morality in the general is well enough known by men, but the particular refinements of virtue are unknown by most persons; thus the majority of parents, without knowing it and without intending it, give very bad examples to their children. . . .

You might also have alluded in your work to the abuse in the capital absorbing the provinces, &c.[1]

[1] *Œuvres de Turgot*, ii. 785–94.

## ON PAPER-MONEY[1]

### *Letter to the Abbé de Cicé*

Paris, April 7, 1749.

. . . I HAVE not forgotten my engagements with you [to discuss certain subjects]. That I may broach at once some matter worth our study, I may tell you that I have read the three letters which the Abbé Terrasson published in favour of Law's system a few days before the famous edict of May 21, 1720,[2] which, as you can believe, covered it with ridicule. . . .

The main portion of the work treats of credit and of its nature, and as this is the foundation of the 'system,' or rather is the whole system, I will give you a note of the reflections that occurred to me on reading it. I believe that the principles which he sets forth are those of Law himself, for the Abbé wrote undoubtedly in concert with him. From this evidence before us I cannot help thinking that Law had really no fixed or comprehensive views in respect to the work he had undertaken.

'First,' says the Abbé, 'it is an axiom received in commerce that the credit of a well-regulated merchant amounts to tenfold his capital.' But this 'credit' is not a credit in the shape of *notes*, as in the case of Law's bank. A merchant who would buy goods to tenfold his capital and who would pay for them by notes, payable to the bearer, would soon be ruined. . . . A merchant borrows a sum of money in order to cultivate it, and he derives from this sum not only what is necessary to pay the stipulated interest and to reimburse

[1] See *supra*, pp. 11, 12.

[2] Which virtually announced the collapse of Law's bank.

the sum itself at the end of a certain time, but also a considerable profit for himself. This credit is not founded on any ascertained capital of the merchant, but on his probity and on his industry, and it necessarily supposes an exchange at the term foreseen and fixed in advance; for if the bills were payable at sight, the merchant would not be free to turn to use the money he had borrowed. Thus it is a contradiction in terms for a bill at sight to bear interest, and such a credit cannot exceed the capital of the borrower. Thus the gain which the merchant makes by his credit, and which it is pretended may be tenfold what he makes by his capital alone, is due entirely to his industry; it is a profit which he draws from the money which passes through his hands, due to the confidence placed in his ability and in his exactitude to restore it, and it is ridiculous to conclude, as I think I have read in 'Dutot,' that he can make bills for ten times the amount of money or of goods in his possession. . . . Observe that the State draws no interest from the sum that it borrows; it has need of it either to pay off former debts or for some extraordinary expenditure; the State consequently cannot restore the amount borrowed except from its natural revenue, hence it ruins itself if it borrows more than it possesses in reserve. . . . In a word, every credit is a borrowing, and has an essential relation to its repayment. . . . The State, the King, the Clergy, and the states of the provinces are necessarily ruined if their revenue is not sufficient to pay every year, besides current expenses, the interest and a part of the capital they have borrowed in the time of extraordinary necessity. The Abbé Terrasson thinks very differently. According to him, 'the king can exceed considerably the proportion of tenfold to which merchants or private individuals are fixed.' The bill of a merchant, he says, being liable to be refused in commerce, does not circulate like money, and consequently returns to its source; its author, in being obliged to pay, finds himself deprived of the benefit of credit. It is not the same with the king; everyone being obliged to take *his* bill, and this bill circulating like money, 'he pays validly with his very promise.' This doctrine is manifestly an illusion.

If the note be the same as money, why promise to *pay*? If it takes the place of money absolutely, it is no longer a credit. Law had seen that, and declared that his circulating paper was truly a money, and as good as gold and silver. 'These two metals,' says Abbé Terrasson, 'are only the signs that represent real wealth, that is to say, commodities. A *crown* is a note conceived in these terms: "Any seller shall give to the bearer the article or merchandise of which he may have need to the amount of three livres, for as much of another merchandise which has been delivered to me," and the effigy of the prince stands for the signature. Now what does it signify, whether the sign be of silver or of paper? Is it not better to choose a material that costs nothing and which we are not obliged to withdraw from commerce where it is employed as merchandise—one, in fine, that is fabricated in the kingdom and does not subject us to a necessary dependence on foreigners and owners of mines, who greedily profit by the seduction into which, by the glamour of gold and of silver, other nations have fallen—a material which we can increase according to our needs, without fear of its ever being deficient? Paper has all these advantages, which render it preferable to hard money.'

Here would be a benefit as grand as the philosopher's stone if all these reasonings were just. We should have need of neither gold nor silver to buy all kinds of commodities. But, has it been left to Law to remain ignorant that gold falls in value like everything else by becoming more plentiful? If he had read and studied Locke, who wrote twenty years before him, he would have known that all the commodities of a country are balanced between themselves, and with gold and silver, according to the proportion of their quantity and the demand for them; he would have learned that gold has not a value which corresponds always to a certain quantity of merchandise, but that when there is more gold it is cheaper, and one gives more of it for a determinate quantity of merchandise; that thus gold, when it circulates freely, suffices always to the need of the State, and that it becomes a matter indifferent to have one hundred millions of marks or one million, if we are to buy all commodities dearer in the same proportion. It is ridiculous to say that metallic money is only a *sign* of value, the credit of which is founded on the stamp of the king. This stamp is only to certify the weight and the title. Even in its relation to commodities the metal uncoined is of the same price as that coined, the marked value is simply a denomination. This is what Law seems to have been ignorant of in establishing his bank.

It is then as merchandise that coined money is (not the sign) but the common measure of other merchandise, and that not by an arbitrary convention, founded on the glamour of that metal, but because, being fit to be employed in different shapes as merchandise, and having on account of this property a saleable value, a little increased by the use made of it as money, and being besides suitable of reduction to a given standard and of being equally divided, we always know the value of it. Gold obtains its price from its rarity, and so far from its being an evil that it is employed at the same time as merchandise and as money, these two employments maintain its price.

Supposing that the king could establish paper-money, which, with all his authority, would not be easy, let us examine what he would gain by it. First, if he increased the quantity he would lower its value by the same act; and as he reserves the power to increase it, it is impossible for people to consent to give their commodities, at the same nominal price, for a bill when by a stroke of the pen that could be made to lose its real value. 'But,' says Abbé Terrasson, 'the king, to preserve his credit, is interested in restricting the paper within just limits, and this interest of the king is sufficient to establish public confidence.' What should the just limits be? and how are they to be determined? Let us follow out the system into the different suppositions that may be made, and let us see in each case what would be its solidity in respect to the utility it proposes.

I observe, first of all, that it is absolutely impossible for the king to substitute the use of paper for that of gold and silver. Gold and silver themselves, regarding them only as signs, are, by the fact of their very circulation, actually distributed among the public according to the proportion of the commodities, of the industry, lands, and real wealth of every kind existing. Now this proportion can never be primarily known, because it is hidden, and because it varies continually by a new circulation. The king will not proceed to distribute his paper-money to each person in the proportion that he holds gold and silver money, forbidding him at the same time to employ the metal in commerce; it would be necessary for the king to take to himself the gold and silver of his subjects, giving them his paper in their place. . . . But it is a point, equally of theory and of experience, that the people would never receive the paper except as representing real money, and consequently convertible into it.

One of the ways in which the king could draw to himself metallic money in exchange, and perhaps the only way, would be for him to take back his notes, conjointly with the coin, but to give out only his notes, while keeping the coin. Then he would choose between these two expedients: either to melt the coin in order to use it as merchandise, reducing his subjects to the use of paper, or to leave the coin and to circulate conjointly with it the paper as representatives of each other. I commence by examining this last supposition.

I assume, then, that the king puts into circulation a quantity of paper-money equal to that of coin (Law would have put ten times more). Now as the total quantity of signs (instruments of exchange) always balances itself with the total of commodities, it is plain that the sign will be worth the half less, or, what is the same thing, commodities will be worth as much again more. But independently of their function as signs of value, gold and silver possess their real value as articles of merchandise, a value which also balances itself against the commodities proportionately to the quantities of these metals, and which they do not lose by their function as money—but on the contrary; that is to say, their value will be balanced with more merchandise as metal than the paper can be with which it was balanced as money, and, as I shall afterwards show, the king being always obliged to increase the number of his notes if he would not have them rendered useless, this disproportion will go on increasing to the point when specie and paper will be no longer reciprocally convertible, and the paper must become discredited from day to day, while the value of metallic money will be always sustained. . . .[1]

[1] *Œuvres de Turgot*, i. 94–102. 'If, more than forty years afterwards, the majority of the Constituent Assembly had had as much enlightenment on this question as Turgot already showed while almost a youth, France would have been saved from the *assignats*.' (Dupont.)

# RELIGIOUS LIBERTY

## '*Le Conciliateur*.'[1] (1754)

[Of Turgot's writings this was the first that was published. It is noteworthy for having exercised a real influence on the settlement of the question in dispute. Its length is about equal to an octavo pamphlet of forty pages. The extracts we give are sufficient to show the nature of his argument and the spirited manner in which it was developed. The form is that of 'Letters of an Ecclesiastic to a Magistrate.' 'In 1754,' says Dupont, 'after prolonged quarrels between the parliaments and the bishops on the subject of tickets of confession and the refusal of sacraments, it was proposed to the king as a means of contenting both parties to grant to the parliaments the right to compel the bishops to administer the Communion to the Jansenists, and to console the clergy by restoring to them the power of persecuting the Protestants; thus withdrawing from the latter the actual half-tolerance which the Government, now become milder than the law, had been allowing them to enjoy.' A second edition of the work was published in 1788, a third in 1791.]

### Letter I

**. . . May 1, 1754.**

Can it be true what I heard, as I was leaving Paris, that the king intends to renew the old laws against the Protestants, and at the same time to support the Parliament in its cause against the clergy? It seems to me impossible that, by so astounding an inconsistency, the Council should propose to adopt, at the same time, two such opposite extremes, and to take towards both matters in dispute the course which is the least just and the least reasonable. What next? While the bishops are to be permitted to exclude

[1] See *supra*, p. 18

Protestants from the rank of citizens, they themselves are to be ordered to dispense divine grace to those whom they consider unworthy of it . . .!

The king has four parties to content—the Protestants, the Jansenists, the Bishops, and the Parliament. Each party has its prejudices; but it is not prejudices which we have to consider. Favour ought to form no part in the act of our deliberations; justice alone ought to decide. The king should act exactly as he has a right to do. Each party may complain at first that it has not gained more for its own side, but in time each party will bless a settlement which has done equal justice to all.

Now this is what the king would be in the right to do; he ought to say to the Protestants: 'I grieve, and shall always grieve, to see you separated from Unity. With the belief in which I rest, that the truth can be found only in the bosom of the Catholic Church, and with the affection I have for you, I cannot see your condition without feeling pain. But, in error though you be, I shall not the less treat you as my children. Submit yourselves to the laws; continue to be useful to the State of which you are members, and you will receive from me the same protection as my other subjects enjoy. My mission is to render justice and happiness to all.'

He ought to say to the Jansenists: 'I would that the Church should be without divisions, but it does not belong to me to end them. I would that no one should pronounce anathema against you, but it belongs to me neither to pronounce it nor to suspend it. I am faithful, but I judge not. All that concerns me is to see you tranquilly enjoying your life as citizens. It is only in this connection that I am interested in you. Fear then neither exile, penalty, nor prison. Pray to Heaven that peace be restored to the Church. But evil be to me if these divisions are dragged into the State.'

He ought to say to the bishops: 'No one respects your judgments more than I do. I submit myself to your decision; I have no other faith than yours; but I shall never meddle with the affairs of religion, I have no right to exact that all my subjects should believe as I do. Use your example, your exhortations, to convert them, but do not count on my authority. Had I been unfortunate enough not to have been a Christian, should I have had the right to compel you to cease to be so? You have your own laws in dealing with divisions; I leave to you the control of them. But I shall not lend the temporal arm to the spiritual authority. Needlessly will you press me to molest the Protestants and the Jansenists, to exile the one body, to imprison the other, or to deprive them of their charges. I shall reply to you in the same spirit which you admire in Gamaliel: "If their doctrine be undoubtedly the work of men, it will, in God's time, be overthrown." Count upon my personal submission as a faithful son of the Church, but, as king, count only on receiving from me the same justice which I owe to all my subjects.'

He ought to say to the Parliament: 'My authority and yours should harmonise. I have endowed you with my power, and I have no thought of withdrawing it. But you cannot use it beyond its province. I have myself no power in the spiritual order, my kingdom is not established to save souls. Your own jurisdiction, then, cannot have greater extent. Leave to the bishops the care of terminating the divisions in the Church; make it your care only that my subjects be not troubled in their honour, in their estate, in their life; preserve for them all that belongs to them as citizens. Leave to the Church all that belongs to itself.'

## Letter II

. . . May 8, 1754.

All that I have said in my first letter was founded on the principle of civil tolerance. Although all men seem disposed to admit it, we are so accustomed to hear civil tolerance proscribed, that one almost fears, in defending it, to be thought guilty of religious indifference. We have our heart tolerant, but custom has rendered our mind fanatical. This fashion of thinking, too common in France, is perhaps the effect of the approbation lavished on the revocation of the Edict of Nantes. We have dishonoured religion in order to flatter Louis XIV. It is necessary for me to show, then, that ecclesiastical tolerance is the only one which [the Catholic] religion excludes, and that religion itself proscribes civil intolerance. To prove this I shall not draw upon any reasons, purely human, which, while enlightening the faith of a Christian, are not accepted for guiding it; I shall give as authorities for my statement Jesus Christ and the Fathers of the Church.

I have already alluded to Jesus Christ reprehending his apostles, who desired that the fire of heaven should fall upon the Samaritans. Every incident in his recorded life is marked by the same spirit. He does not instruct his disciples to implore the assistance of kings to constrain unbelievers, to employ human authority in order to make converts. He tells them to let grow the tares along with the good grain until the time of harvest, when the master himself will discern them. He performs miracles in order to influence minds, not to subjugate bodies. When his apostles propose to Him to repulse the soldiers coming to seize Him, he replies to them that a legion of angels would be at his command to exterminate his persecutors, but that his 'kingdom is not of this world.' He performs a miracle that He may teach them not to confound the rights of God with those of Cæsar, the things of heaven with the things of earth. . . . It was less exterior homage that He demanded than the sacrifice of the heart and the adhesion of the mind. A consent due to fear and self-interest does not make a Christian; it is not by such means that Jesus Christ desired his religion to be spread. . . .

But, it is said, it is not the prince who interferes to decide—he only follows and executes the decisions of the Church. The Council of Trent proscribes the Protestants, the Constitution proscribes the Jansenists; the prince has made these decisions into laws of the State, persons who contravene them infringe the laws of the kingdom and they can be punished, without its being held that the prince has meddled in the affairs of religion. But has the king a right to make a law of the State of the decision of the Council of Trent, or of the Constitution? The first Fathers of the Church did not require of the pagan princes to make the gospel a law of the empire. They demanded only the liberty to profess their religion, and they were grateful to the emperors when they had the happiness to obtain that liberty. It is to those early times that we must go back in order to fix the limits of the two powers. When the princes became Christians, the bishops, in order to concern themselves in matters of State, demanded that their decisions should be made laws of the kingdom. The princes, either through zeal or through self-interest, complied with this, imagining to have thereby a greater authority over their subjects. The step was prejudicial to both parties. . . .

But let us go back to the origin of things. We shall see Religion, as she should be, separated from the Government; the Church occupied with the salvation of souls; the empire occupied with the welfare of the people; the one and the other having its laws distinct, as the things of heaven ought to be from the things of earth.

To make an edict of a decision of the Church . . . is to compel the people to adopt an opinion because it appears truth to us. Is not this overruling consciences? . . . If the King of France can make of the Council of Trent and of the Constitution laws of his State, has not the King of England the right to establish for himself the supremacy, the Turk the right to establish the Koran, each prince his own religion? This idea revolts us, because in foreign countries *we* should be the persecuted. Ought it not to revolt us all the same when we would be the persecutors?

'But,' it is said, 'the prince would thus be obliged to tolerate in his states all sorts of religion, even those contrary to social good, as human sacrifices, &c.' God forbid that I should advance such a principle! *Actions* are the only things that interest the State in respect to religion.

As for doctrine, or even morals, in the objects of pure speculation, the State ought to be indifferent to them. Actions are either contrary to social welfare or they are not. If they are not contrary, why forbid them to be made acts of religion? If they are contrary they are already proscribed and cannot be authorised. It is indifferent to the State that each day I purify my body by different ablutions; the practice may be superfluous, but it is not dangerous. Kings have no right to hinder it from being made a religious ceremony. But it is another thing to shed human blood. If I preach a religion which permits it, the prince has a right to proscribe me; it is less the religious action than the criminal action that is forbidden. It would be a crime to immolate, because it is already a crime to kill. . . .

Then it is said, 'if the king is to permit all religions whose doctrine is not contrary to the good of the State, what a monstrous assemblage of sentiments you would introduce! Do you believe that peace could exist between minds filled with principles so opposed? Is not unity in religion necessary in a government? The fields of our country reek yet with the blood shed in the wars of religion.' I know of how many wars heresies have been the source, but is not this because we have persisted in persecuting them? The man who believes earnestly believes with still more firmness if we would force him to change his belief without convincing him; he then becomes obstinate, his obstinacy kindles his zeal, his zeal inflames him; we wish to convert him, we have made of him a fanatic, a madman. Men, for their opinions, demand only liberty; if you deprive them of it, you place arms in their hand. Give them liberty, they remain quiet, as the Lutherans were at Strasburg. It is then the very unity in religion we would enforce, and not the different opinions we tolerate, that produces trouble and civil wars. . . .

[After a further vindication of the principle of tolerance in all its applications, Turgot sums up the anticipated results from the policy of neutrality he recommends.]

I can easily imagine that each party will at first be ill-pleased at being denied the rights it would usurp, but as it is still gratifying not to lose those rights it possesses, and ought to possess, each party will in time be grateful to the Government for having preserved these. . . . The bishops will thank the king for having left them masters in the affairs of religion; the Parliament for having confided to it his authority; the Jansenists for having no longer to fear punishment, exile, imprisonment; and, finally, the general public will bless a government so wise, whose authority will be exercised only in allowing each party to enjoy tranquilly its own rights, this being the end for which government is established.

I should finish, but as there have occurred to me some reflections that tend to make these principles more sensibly felt, I feel I ought not to omit them.

*First Reflection.*—In France we have always proscribed the Inquisition, that odious power which has carried sword and fire into the world of the God of peace and charity. Now, odious as this tribunal is, he who establishes intolerance would not be less odious. If the prisons of the Inquisition were terrible, France itself has had only too many which have echoed the cries of the oppressed conscience. If the former were unjust, why should the latter be authorised? We who condemn with horror the minister of the Church who, by torture, compelled the mind, should we give to our king the right still to subjugate it? We regard with indignation the inflictions which, in Italy and in Spain, obstruct the rights of conscience; the least reflection should prevent our feeling less for the conscience of our own citizens.

*Second Reflection.*—To justify what I have advanced, let us suppose that these actual disputes had occurred in a country where the prince was neither Jansenist nor *constitutionnaire*; at Berlin, for example, the King of Prussia, although Protestant, has permitted the Catholics to build a church in his capital. If among them were found some Jansenists to whom the sacraments were refused, should we not be astonished to see that prince entering into their disputes and pretending to dictate their laws to them? We should feel shocked to see the Protestant prince meddling with Catholic affairs. Does the faith of the prince, then, make all the difference? . . . What we consider the King of Prussia ought to do, is that not the principle for our own kings to follow?

*Third Reflection.*—It has been usual to compare the salvation of the soul to the health of the body. The bishops themselves style themselves spiritual physicians. Errors are the maladies that affect the mind; those who rule the consciences are established in order to apply the remedies. Let us judge then of the liberty that ought to reign in the sphere of salvation by that liberty which every one must have in order to govern his own health. However excellent a remedy may be, should we not find it rather hard if a prince compelled his subjects to make use of this particular one in preference to all others? Should we not say to him that confidence cannot be prescribed, that each is master of his health, that we cannot cure a man in spite of himself? If the king did more and if the confidence he had in his remedy induced him to order that all physicians in his kingdom should use that remedy on all occasions, would they not have the right to represent to him that no one could better know the utility of a remedy than they could, that its application varies according to different temperaments and conditions, of which they are the best judges, that they cannot all be kept within the same fixed lines, that they would rather suffer a thousand penalties than administer a remedy that they knew might be dangerous? . . . If, in spite of these just representations, the king persisted in compelling all his subjects to take this remedy, and all the physicians to administer it, even when they believed it dangerous, what should we think of such conduct? I leave to you to make the application of this comparison; I avoid for myself the mixing overmuch things profane with things sacred.

I believe, Sir, that I have thus justified Toleration. There was a time when these principles would have shocked many persons, but we become every day more enlightened, and we learn to distinguish in religion what is essential to it and what men have added. We detest more than ever the Inquisition, we admire the edict of tolerance of the empress-queen. The King of Prussia appears to us wise in having, although a Protestant, accorded to Catholics the free exercise of their religion. The revocation of the Edict of Nantes revolts us; our soldiers murmur when they are employed against the Protestants. The cause of Civil Toleration has been sustained even in some theses of the Faculty of Theology, it is being advocated in many writings; everywhere discussion is tending to establish it. Let us, the one and the other, be happy if we can help towards this end.[1]

[1] *Œuvres de Turgot*, ii. 688–703.

# ENDOWMENTS

## *Article 'Fondation' in the 'Encyclopédie'*[1]

[Written in 1756. Much has been done since Turgot's time, and much in the direction he has indicated. But we give the article as written, nearly *verbatim*. It is still not without some application to present-day discussions.]

To *found*, in the sense in which we are now using the word, is to assign a fund or a sum of money in order to its being employed in perpetuity for fulfilling the purpose the founder had in view, whether that purpose regards divine worship, or public utility, or the vanity of the founder—often the only real one, even while the two others serve to veil it. . . .

Our intention in this article is limited to examining the utility of *foundations* in general, in respect to the public good, and chiefly to demonstrating their impropriety. May the following considerations concur with the philosophic spirit of the age, in discouraging new foundations and in destroying all remains of superstitious respect for the old ones!

1. A founder is a man who desires the effect of his

[1] See *supra*, p. 19. The publication of the *Encyclopédie*, the most famous literary achievement of the eighteenth century, was begun in July 1751, unde the editorship of Diderot and D'Alembert. During the long course of its issue (twenty-nine years) it was several times suppressed by the Government, in deference to the Church, but influential sympathisers from time to time succeeded in gaining its reappearance. The original edition consists of thirty-five volumes folio. There were about one hundred and sixty contributors, including Voltaire, Rousseau, Euler, Marmontel, Montesquieu, D'Anville, Quesnay, Turgot, Daubenton. Diderot was general editor to the last, but D'Alembert retired in 1758.

own will to endure for ever. Now, even if we suppose him to be actuated by the purest motives, how many reasons are there to question his enlightenment! How easy it is to do harm in wishing to do good! To foresee with certainty that an establishment will produce only the effect desired from it, and no effect at variance with its object; to discern, beyond the illusion of a near and apparent good, the real evils which a long series of unseen causes may bring about; to know what are the real sores of society, to arrive at their causes, to distinguish remedies from palliatives; to defend oneself against the prestige of a seductive project, to take a severe and tranquil view of it amidst that dazzling atmosphere in which the praises of a blind public, and our own enthusiasm, show it us surrounded; this would need the effort of the most profound genius, and perhaps the political sciences of our time are not yet sufficiently advanced to enable the best genius here to succeed.

By these institutions support is often given to a few individuals against an evil the cause of which is general, and sometimes the very remedy opposed to the effect increases the influence of the cause. We have a striking example of this kind of abuse in the establishment of houses designed as asylums for repentant women. In order to obtain entrance, proof of a debauched life must be made. . . . I know well that this precaution has been made in order to prevent the *foundation* being diverted to other objects; but that only proves that it is not by such establishments, powerless against the true causes of libertinage, that it can be combated. What I have said of libertinage is true of poverty. The poor have incontestable claims on the abundance of the rich; humanity and religion alike make it a duty on us to relieve our fellow-creatures when under misfortune. It is in order to accomplish these indispensable duties that so many charitable establishments have been raised in the Christian world to relieve necessities of every kind, that so many poor are gathered together in hospitals and are fed at the gates of convents by daily distributions. What is the result? It is that precisely in those countries where gratuitous resources are most abundant, as in Spain and some parts of Italy, there misery is more common and more widely spread than elsewhere. The reason is very simple, and a thousand travellers have observed it. To enable a large number of men to live gratuitously is to subsidise idleness and all the disorders which are its consequences; it is to render the condition of the ne'er-do-well preferable to that of the honest working-man. Consequently it diminishes for the State the sum of labour and of the productions of the earth, a large part of which is thus left necessarily uncultivated. Hence frequent scarcities, the increase of misery, and depopulation. The race of industrious citizens is displaced by a vile populace, composed of vagrant beggars given up to all sorts of crime. . . . From this loss of the labour and wealth of the State there results a great increase of public burdens, thrown on the shoulders of the industrious man, and an increase of all the disorders we see in the present constitution of society. It is thus that the purest virtues can deceive those who surrender themselves without precaution to all suggestions that they inspire. But if these pious and respectable designs contradict in practice the hopes that were conceived for them, what must we think of those endowments (undoubtedly numerous) whose only motive and object is the satisfaction of a frivolous vanity? I do not fear to say that were we to weigh the advantages and the disadvantages of all the foundations in Europe, perhaps there would not be found one which would stand the test of an enlightened scrutiny.

2. But of whatever utility a *foundation* might be at its conception, it bears within itself an irremediable defect which belongs to its very nature—the impossibility of maintaining its fulfilment. Founders deceive themselves vastly if they imagine that their zeal can be communicated from age to age to persons employed to perpetuate its effects.

There is no body that has not in the long run lost the spirit of its first origin. There is no sentiment that does not become weakened, by mere habit and by familiarity with the objects which excite it. What confused emotions of horror, of sadness, of deep feeling for humanity, of pity for the unfortunates who are suffering, does that man experience who for the first time enters the ward of a hospital! Well, let him open his eyes and look around. In this very place, in the midst of these assembled human miseries, the ministers provided to relieve them walk about with an air careless and expressionless; they mechanically and without interest distribute from invalid to invalid the food and the remedies prescribed, and sometimes do so even with a brutal callousness; they give way to heedless conversation, and sometimes to ideas of the silliest and the grossest; vanity, envy, hatred, all the passions reigning there, as elsewhere, do their work, and the groans from the sick-bed, the cries of acute pain, do not disturb the *habitués* any more than the murmur of a rivulet interrupts an animated conversation. Such are the effects of habit in relation to objects the most capable of moving the human heart. Thus it is that no enthusiasm can be constantly sustained. And how without enthusiasm can ministers of a foundation fulfil its purpose always and with precision? What interest, in their case, can counteract idleness, that weight attached to human nature which tends constantly to retain us in inaction? The very precautions which the founder has taken in order to insure for them a constant revenue dispenses them from meriting it by exertion. Are there superintendents, inspectors, appointed to see the work of the foundation carried out? It will be the same with these inspectors. If the obstacle to the right working comes from idleness, the same idleness on their part will prevent them from exposing it; if the abuse proceeds from pecuniary interest, they will too readily share in it. Supervisors themselves would need to be supervised. . . . Thus almost all old foundations have degenerated from their primitive institution. Then the same spirit which had devised the first has created new ones on the same plan, or a different plan, which, after having degenerated in their turn, are displaced in the same manner. Measures are ordinarily so well taken by the founders to protect their establishments from exterior innovations, that generally it is found to be easier to found new establishments than to reform the old; but, through these double and triple renovations, the number of useless mouths in society and the sum of wealth kept from general circulation are continually increased. [After having alluded to the case of foundations being affected, and often prevented, by changes in the value of money, he proceeds :—]

3. I will suppose that a foundation has had at its origin an incontestable utility, that sufficient precautions have been taken against its degeneration through idleness and negligence, that the nature of its funds has sheltered it from the revolutions of monetary changes, then I say that the very immutability which the founders have succeeded in giving it is still a great public impropriety, because time brings about new revolutions which will sweep away the utility, the foundation once fulfilled, and will render its continued operation even injurious. Society has not always the same needs; the nature and dispositions of properties, the divisions between different orders of the people, opinions, manners, the general occupations of the nation or of its different sections, the climate even, the maladies and the other accidents of human life—all experience a continual variation. New needs arise, others cease to be felt. The proportion of those remaining declines from day to day, and along with them the utility of the foundations designed to relieve them diminishes or disappears. The wars of Palestine gave rise to innumerable foundations whose utility ceased with the wars. Without speaking of the military religious orders, Europe is still covered with leper hospitals (*maladreries*), although for long leprosy has been almost unknown. The greater number of foundations long survive their utility: first, because there are always men who profit by them, and who

are interested in maintaining them; secondly, because even when we become convinced of their inutility, we make long delays before deciding either upon the measures or the formalities necessary to overthrow establishments consolidated for many centuries, or deciding upon the use or the distribution we should make of their property.

4. I have said nothing of the splendour of the buildings and of the pomp connected with some of the grand foundations. It would be perhaps to value very favourably the utility of these objects if we estimated them at one hundredth part of the whole cost.

5. Woe to me if my object be, in presenting these considerations, to concentrate man's motives in his mere self-interest, and to render him insensible to the sufferings or the happiness of his fellow-creatures, to extinguish in him the spirit of a citizen, and to substitute an indolent and base prudence for the noble passion of being useful to mankind. In place of the vanity of founders, I desire that humanity, that the passion of the public good, should procure for men the same benefits, but more surely, more completely, and at less cost, and without the drawbacks of which I have complained.

Among the different needs of society intended to be fulfilled by means of durable establishments or foundations, let us distinguish two kinds. One belongs to society as a whole, and is just the result of the interest of each of its members, such as the general needs of humanity, sustenance for everyone, the good manners and education of children, for all families. . . . It does not require much reflection to be convinced that the first kind of social needs is not of a nature that can be fulfilled by foundations, or by any other gratuitous means, and that, in this respect, the general good ought to be the result of the efforts of each individual for his own interests. Every able-bodied man ought to procure his subsistence by his work, because if he were fed without working, it would be so at the cost of those who work. What the State owes to all its members is the destruction of the obstacles which impede them in their industry, or which trouble them in the enjoyment of the product which is its recompense. While these obstacles subsist, particular benefits will not diminish the general poverty, for the cause will remain untouched. For the same reason every family owes education to the children who are born to it, and it is only from the efforts of each in particular that the general perfection of education can arise. If you amuse yourself to endow masters and bursaries in colleges, the utility of which will be felt only by a small number of scholars, favoured by chance, who have not perhaps the necessary talents to profit by them, that will be, for the whole nation, but a drop of water spread on a vast sea, and you will have procured, at very great expense, very small results. And then you have accustomed people to be ever applying for these endowments, and (not always) receiving them, and to owe nothing to themselves. This sort of mendicity spread over all conditions of men degrades a people and substitutes for the high impulses a character of lowness and intrigue. Are men powerfully interested in that good which you would procure for them? Leave them free to attain it; this is the great, the only principle. Do they appear to you to be actuated by less ardour towards it than you would desire to see? Increase their interest in it. You wish to perfect education—propose prizes for the emulation of parents and children, but let these prizes be offered to whosoever can *merit* them, offered at least to every order of citizens; let employments and places become the recompense of merit, and the sure prospect of work, and you will see emulation struck up at once in the heart of all families. Your nation will soon be raised above its old level, you will have enlightened its spirit, you will have given it character, you will have done great things, and you will have done all at less expense than founding one college.

The other class of public needs intended to be provided for by foundations comprise those regarded as accidental, which, limited to particular places and particular times, enter less into the system of general administration, and may demand particular relief. It is desired to remedy the hardships of a scarcity, or of an epidemic, to provide for the support of some old men, or of some orphans, for the rescue of infants exposed, for the working or maintaining works to improve the amenity or the salubrity of a town, for the improving of agriculture or some arts in a backward condition in a locality, for rewarding the services rendered by a citizen to the town of which he is a member, to attract to it men celebrated for their talents. Now, it is before all necessary that the means taken by public establishments or foundations should be the best in order to procure for their subjects all these benefits as fully as possible. The free employment of a part of the revenues of a community, some contribution of all its members in the case of the need being pressing and general, with a free association of, and voluntary subscriptions of some generous citizens, in the case of the need being less urgent and less generally felt—here is the true means of fulfilling all kinds of schemes really useful, and this method will have the inestimable advantage over foundations, that it is subject to no great abuse. As the contribution of each is entirely voluntary, it is impossible for the funds to be diverted from their destination. If they were, their source would be soon dried up. There would be no money sunk in useless expenses, in luxury, or in building. It is a partnership of the same kind as those made for business, with the difference that its object is only the public good; and as the funds are employed only under the eyes of the shareholders, these are able to see them employed in the most advantageous manner. Resources would not be permanent for needs that are temporary; succour would be given only to the portion of society that suffered, to the branch of commerce that languished. If the need ceased, the liberality would cease, and its course would be directed to other needs. There would never be useless repetitions of schemes, because the generosity of the public benefactors would be determined only by the actual utility recognised. In fine, this method would withdraw no funds from general circulation, the lands would not be irrevocably possessed by idle hands, and their productions under the hands of an active proprietor would have no limit except that of their fecundity. Is it said that these ideas are chimerical? England, Scotland, Ireland are full of such voluntary associations, and they have experienced from them, for many years, the happiest effects. What has taken place in England can take place in France, and the English have not the exclusive right to be citizens. We have already in some provinces examples of such associations, which prove their possibility. I would cite in particular the city of Bayeux, whose inhabitants are associated in order to banish begging entirely from their town, and have succeeded in providing work for all able-bodied mendicants, and alms for all those unfit for work. This fine example deserves to be proposed for the emulation of all our towns. Nothing would be so easy, if we really willed it, as to direct to objects of certain and general utility the emulation and the tastes of a nation so sensible to honour as ours is, and so easy to lend itself to all the impressions which the Government might know how to give.

6. These reflections ought to strengthen our approval of the wise restrictions which the king, by his edict of 1749, has made to the liberty of creating new foundations. Let us add that they ought to leave no doubt on the incontestable right possessed by the Government—in the first place, in the civil order, next, by the Government and the Church, in the order of religion—to dispose of old foundations, to extend their funds to new objects, or, better still, to suppress them altogether. Public utility is the supreme law, and it ought not to be nullified by any superstitious respect for what we call the *intention of the founder*—as if ignorant and short-sighted individuals had the right to chain to their capricious wills the generations that had still to be born. Neither should we be deterred by the fear to infringe upon the

pretended rights of certain bodies—as if private bodies had any rights opposed to those of the State. Citizens have rights, and rights to be held sacred, even by society—they exist independently of society, they enter into it with all their rights, only that they may place themselves under the protection of these same laws which assure their property and their liberty. But private *bodies* do not exist of themselves, nor for themselves; they have been formed by society, and they ought not to exist a moment after they have ceased to be useful.

We conclude. No work of man is made for immortality; and since *foundations*, always multiplied by vanity, would in the long run, if uninterfered with, absorb all funds and all private properties, it would be absolutely necessary at last to destroy them. If all the men who have lived had had a tombstone erected for them, it would have been necessary, in order to find ground to cultivate, to overthrow the sterile monuments and to stir up the ashes of the dead to nourish the living.[1]

[1] *Œuvres de Turgot*, i. 299-309.

# PORTRAIT OF A MINISTER OF COMMERCE

## *Éloge de Gournay* (1759)[1]

[This *Éloge* was not published in Turgot's lifetime. It was written within a few weeks of the death of his friend (June 27, 1759) to supply materials for Marmontel, whose duty it was as Academician to deliver the *Éloge*. We have not included in these translations his principal economical work, the '*Réflexions sur la Formation et la Distribution des Richesses*,' for two reasons: first, because its construction as a chain of ratiocination demands that, if given at all, it must be given entire, and being of considerable length, its reproduction would be unsuitable in a volume intended for general readers; secondly, for those specially interested in Economical Science, the work has been already translated in full in Lord Overstone's 'Collection of Economical Tracts,' London, 1859. In these circumstances, that we may as fairly as possible enable our readers to form an estimate of Turgot's economical doctrine, we give this *Éloge de Gournay*, which, in fact, in its course embodies in less scientific form the general principles of Turgot and his school. The *Éloge* is besides in great part worth reading for its own sake, as giving a view of the extraordinary degree to which Government interference with industry and manufactures was carried in France in the middle of the eighteenth century.]

Jean Claude Marie Vincent, Seigneur de Gournay, honorary Councillor of the Grand Council, honorary Intendant of Commerce, died at Paris June 27, 1759, aged forty-seven years.

He was born at St. Malo in May 1712. His father was Claude Vincent, one of the most considerable merchants of that town. His parents destined him to a commercial life,

[1] See *supra*, pp. 20, 21.

and sent him to Cadiz in 1729, when under seventeen. Left at this early age to his own direction, he was yet able to avoid the rocks and the dissipations that too commonly wreck youth, and during all the time he spent at Cadiz his life was divided between study, the work of his business, and the many connections which his business and his personal merit soon procured for him. His assiduous application won the time for him to enrich his mind with a mass of useful knowledge, without neglecting the higher literature, but it was, above all, to commercial science that he felt himself drawn, and to this study he directed all the vigour of his mind.

To compare the productions of nature and art belonging to different countries; to arrive at the value of these different productions, or, in other terms, their relation to the needs and wealth of our own country and to those of the foreigner, the cost of transport, according to the nature of the commodities and the diversity of routes, the several duties to which they are subject, &c., in a word, to comprehend all its relations, and to follow in its continual revolutions, the current history of natural productions, of industry, of population, of wealth, of finance, the needs, and even the caprices of fashion in all nations that commerce unites, in order to found, upon the thorough study of all these details, trustworthy speculations—this is, as a merchant, to cultivate the science of business, and it is still but a part of the science of commerce.

But to discover the causes and effects of that diversity of revolutions; to search out the simple forces whose action always combined with, and sometimes disguised by, local circumstances, directs all the operations of commerce; to recognise those special and radical laws, founded in Nature itself, by which all the values existing in commerce are balanced against each other, and settle at last into a fixed value, as bodies left to themselves take their place according to their specific gravity; to discern those complicated relations by which commerce connects itself with all the branches of political economy; to perceive the reciprocal dependence of commerce and agriculture, the influence of the one and the other on national wealth, on the population and the strength of states, their intimate connection with the laws and customs, and with all the operations of Government, especially with the distribution of its finances ; to weigh the advantages which commerce receives from the existence of a military navy and those it can render in return, the changes it produces in the respective interests of states, and the weight it places in the political balance of nations ; in fine, to distinguish in the particular character of events, and the principles of administration, affecting the different nations of Europe, the true causes of their progress or of their decadence in commerce—this is to approach the subject as a philosopher and a statesman.

If the position in life of M. Vincent obliged him to concern himself with the science of commerce under the first of these two points of view, the bent and depth of his mind did not permit of his confining himself to that. To the enlightenment which he drew from his own experience and his reflections, he added the reading of the best works on this subject produced by the different nations of Europe, and particularly those of the English nation—the richest of all in such works, of which, for that reason, English has become almost the special language. The works which he read with most pleasure, and of which he most imbibed the doctrine, were the Treatises of the famous Josias Child (which he afterwards translated into French) and the Memoirs of the Grand Pensionary John de Witt. We know that these two great men are considered (the one in England, the other in Holland) as the legislators of commerce, that their principles have become national principles, that the observance of these principles is regarded as one of the sources of the immense superiority which these two nations have acquired in commerce over all the other powers. M. Vincent constantly found in the practice of an extensive business the verification of these simple and luminous principles ; he made them his own, and without foreseeing that he was destined one day to spread the light through France and to merit from his country the same tribute of gratitude which England and Holland have rendered to these two benefactors of their nation and of humanity.

. . . During his stay at Cadiz he made several visits to the Court of Spain, as well as voyages through the different provinces of the kingdom. In 1744 some commercial enterprises which had to be concerted with the Government led him to France and brought him into relation with the Count de Maurepas, then Minister of Marine, who soon discovered M. Vincent's value.

He quitted Spain, having formed a resolution of spending some years in travelling through the different parts of Europe in order to increase his knowledge, as well as to extend his business connections. He visited Hamburg, travelled through Holland and England. Everywhere, as he went, he made observations and wrote out memorandums on the state of commerce and matters of marine, and on the principles of administration adopted by the different nations in respect to these great objects. He kept up, during his travels, a regular correspondence with M. de Maurepas. . . . The Court of Vienna, as well as that of Berlin, wished to attach him, and made to him very seducing proposals, but he declined them. He had no other view than to continue in business and to return to Spain, after having again seen Germany and Italy, when an unforeseen event interrupted his projects and restored him to his own country.

M. de Villebarre, his partner and his friend, died in 1746, and being without children, he made M. Vincent his sole legatee. He was in England when he received this news; he returned to France. The amount of his fortune was sufficient for his moderate desires. He decided it would be best to remain in his country, and he quitted commercial life in 1748. He then took his name from his property of Gournay, which was included in the legacy of M. de Villebarre.

. . . M. de Maurepas adhered to his desire to render the talents of M. de Gournay useful to the Government; he advised him to turn his views towards the position of intendant of commerce, and to enter, in the meantime, into one of the higher courts. Consequently M. de Gournay bought in 1749 a place of councillor of the *Grand Conseil*. An intendancy of commerce having become vacant in 1751, M. de Machault [Prime Minister], to whom also his merit was well known, conferred the office upon him. From this point the life of M. de Gournay became that of a public man; his entry into the Ministry of Commerce marked itself as a revolution. . . . His principles appeared new to some of the magistrates who composed the Board of Commerce. M. de Gournay imagined that every man who works deserves the gratitude of the public [instead of discouragement]. He was astonished to see that a citizen could neither make nor sell anything without having bought the right to do so at great expense in a corporation, and that, after having bought it, it was still sometimes necessary for him to sustain an action at law to determine whether by entering into such or such corporation he had really acquired the right to make or to sell precisely this or that article. He imagined that a workman who had manufactured a piece of stuff had made a real addition to the mass of wealth of the State; that if this stuff happened to be inferior to others, there might yet be found among consumers some one to whom this inferiority might be more suitable than a more costly perfection. He was far from imagining that this piece of stuff, for not being conformable to certain regulations, must be cut up into fragments of three ells length, and that the unfortunate man who had made it must be condemned to pay a penalty, enough to bring him and his family to beggary. He could not see the necessity that a workman in making a piece of stuff should be exposed to risks and expenses from which an idle man was exempt. He could not see it to be useful to society that a manufactured piece of stuff should involve legal procedures and tedious discussions in order to ascertain whether it was conformable to a complicated system of regulations, often difficult to understand, nor that such discussions ought to be held between a poor manufacturer, who perhaps could not read, and an inspector who could not manufacture, nor that this inspector should be the final judge of the unlucky man, &c. . . . M. de Gournay could not see the propriety of the Government regulating by express laws the length and breadth of each piece of stuff, the number of threads it was to contain, and to stamp with the seal of the executive power four volumes in quarto filled with these important details, nor could he see the need of innumerable statutes dictated by the spirit of monopoly, the whole effect of which is to discourage industry, to concentrate trade within a limited number of persons by the multiplication of formalities and expenses, by the subjecting of industry to apprenticeships and journeymanships (*compagnonnages*) of ten years for some trades which might be learned almost in ten days, by the exclusion of those not being the sons of 'masters,' or of those born beyond certain bounds, and by the prohibition of employing women in manufacture, &c.

He had not imagined that in a kingdom under the same monarch all the towns should reciprocally regard themselves as enemies, should arrogate the right to prohibit work within their precincts to Frenchmen (described under the name of *étrangers*), to set themselves in opposition to the sale or the free transit of commodities of a neighbouring province—thus, for a slender interest of their own town, to contend against the general interest of the State.

He was not less astonished to see the Government concern itself in regulating the course of each commodity, in proscribing one kind of industry in order to encourage another, in subjecting to special restraints the sale of provisions the most necessary to life, in forbidding stores to be made of a product, the crop of which varies from year to year and the consumption of which is nearly always equal, in forbidding the export of an article subject to deteriorate, in expecting to insure the abundance of corn by rendering the condition of the labourer more uncertain and more unhappy than that of other men, &c.

[In condemning these anomalies, M. de Gournay did not believe himself to deserve being called] an 'innovator' and a 'man of systems,' for he felt himself to be only developing those principles which experience in business had taught him, and which he saw were unanimously recognised by the enlightened merchants with whom he had associated. Those principles appeared to him as only the maxims of simple common sense. All this despised 'system' was founded on the ordinary maxim that in general a man knows his own interest better than another man can know it for him. Hence he concluded that as the interest of individuals is, on the whole, precisely the same as the general interest, we should leave every man free to manufacture whatever he considers desirable, because, with industry and commerce left free, it would be impossible for the aggregate individual interests not to concur with the general interest.[1]

Commerce can be related to the general interest, or, which is the same thing, the State can interest itself in commerce only under two points of view. As protector of the individuals who compose it, it is its interest that no one should in the course of business suffer any wrong from another against which he cannot secure himself. Next as being a political body, having to defend itself against exterior invasions, it is the interest of the State that the mass of the wealth of the community and the yearly productions of the land and of industry should be the greatest that is possible. Under each point of view it has a special interest in insuring the value of necessaries of life against those sudden shocks which, by plunging the people into the horrors of famine, endanger public tranquillity and the safety of citizens and magistrates. Now, it is clear that the interest of all the individuals, kept free from restraints of all kinds, necessarily fulfils all these conditions of general utility.

[1] 'Adam Smith has unreservedly adopted this part of the physiocratic doctrine. Liberty, in the economic order, does not suppose, as some apparently believe, the abandonment of the moral rights, and of the right of the Government to defend that liberty against the selfish aggressions of individuals. (Eugène Daire, *Œuvres de Turgot*, i. 270.)

As for the first object, that in trade none should be injured by others, it is evidently sufficient that the Government should always protect the natural liberty of the buyer to buy and of the seller to sell. For the buyer being always the master to buy or not to buy, it is certain that he will select among the sellers the man who will give him at the best bargain the merchandise that suits him best. It is not less certain that every seller, it being his chief interest to merit the preference over his competitors, will sell in general the best merchandise and at the lowest price profitable, in order to attract customers. It is not true therefore that a merchant has an interest to deceive—unless at least he has some exclusive privilege. But if the Government limits the number of sellers by exclusive privileges or otherwise, it is certain that the consumer will be wronged and that the seller, made sure of selling, will compel him to buy dearly bad articles. If, on the other hand, it is the number of buyers which is diminished by the exclusion of foreigners or of certain persons, then the seller is wronged, and if the injury be carried to the point when the price cannot cover his expenses and risks, he will cease to produce the commodity, its regular supply will thus be endangered, and a famine may be the consequence. The general liberty of buying and selling is therefore the only means to insure on the one side to the seller a price sufficient to encourage production; on the other side to the consumer the best merchandise at the lowest price. If we descend to particular cases, we may indeed find a merchant who is a cheat and a consumer a dupe, but the cheated consumer will instruct himself and will cease to frequent the cheating merchant, who will become discredited and punished for his knavery; but that will never happen very frequently, because in general men will be enlightened upon their evident self-interest.[1]

[1] This principle of the non-interference of Government with commercial transactions is, as M. Daire observes, liable to only one exception—in the case where it is *beyond the ability* of the consumer to protect himself from the fraudulent greed of the merchant.

To desire that Government should be obliged to prevent fraud from ever occurring would be to desire it to provide head-pads (*bourrelets*) for all children who might fall. To assume, by regulations, successfully to prevent all the possible malversations of this nature, is to sacrifice to a chimerical perfection the whole progress of industry; it is to restrict the imagination of artificers to the narrow limits of what is already done; it is to interdict all new experiments; to renounce even the hope of our competing with foreigners in the making of the new stuffs which they invent every day—because, as victims to regulations, our workmen cannot imitate these articles without having first obtained the permission of the Government, and obtained, if at all, after the foreign fabric, having profited by the first run of consumers for the novelty, has been already displaced by another.

. . . We forget, too, that these regulations, these inspectors, these stamp offices and examinations, always involve expenses, and that these expenses are always a tax on the merchandise, and that while overcharging the home consumer they keep back the foreign consumer. Thus a palpable injustice is done to commerce and consequently to the nation, and this heavy burden is maintained in order to save a few idle people from the trouble of instructing themselves in respect to what they buy! To suppose all consumers to be dupes, and all merchants and manufacturers to be cheats, has the effect of authorising them to be so, and of degrading all the working members of the nation.

As for the second object of Government in this connection, that there should be the greatest possible production of wealth by the nation, is it not evident that the only real wealth of the State being the yearly productions of its land and the industry of its inhabitants, its wealth will be at its greatest when the produce of each acre of land and the industry of each individual shall be carried to the highest possible point? and is it not evident that each proprietor has more interest than any other person to draw from his land the greatest possible return, that each labourer and artisan has the same interest to gain by his work all the wages he can get?

. . . To imagine that there are commodities which the State ought to favour, in order that the land may produce more of them than of others, that it ought to favour certain manufactures more than others, and consequently to prohibit certain productions and encourage others, to interdict certain kinds of industry from fear of injuring other kinds, to attempt to sustain manufactures at the expense of agriculture by forcing the price of provisions to be under what it would naturally be, to establish certain manufactures at the cost of the Treasury, to accumulate on them privileges, favours, exclusions of all other manufactures of the same kind, for the object of procuring for the privileged manufacturers a profit which it is assumed their productions could not obtain naturally—all this is to misapprehend greatly the real advantages of commerce, it is to forget that no operation of commerce can be otherwise than reciprocal, for to desire to sell everything to foreigners and to buy nothing from them is absurd.

. . . The market value of each commodity, all expenses on it paid, is the only rule by which to judge of the advantage which the State derives from a certain class of productions; consequently every manufacture whose natural market value does not compensate the manufacturer with profit after the expenses of production is of no advantage to the State; the sum spent on sustaining it against the natural course of commerce is a charge made on the nation, to its absolute loss.

M. de Gournay concluded that the only end the administration should propose to itself was:—1. To render to all branches of commerce that precious liberty which the prejudice of ignorant ages, the facility of the Government to lend itself to particular interests, and the desire for an ill-understood perfection in workmanship had caused them to lose. 2. To free the road for work to all members of the State, for the purpose of exciting the greatest competition in the market, from which would necessarily result the greatest perfection in manufacture and a price most advantageous to the *buyer*. 3. To give at the same time to the buyer the greatest possible number of competitors by opening for the *seller* all the outlets for his commodity—the true means of assuring to labour its recompense and of developing production.

He held, besides, that the Government ought to remove those obstacles which retard the progress of industry by diminishing the measure or the extent of its profits. He considered the chief of these obstacles to be the high interest of money, which, offering to all possessors of capital the means of living without working, encourages luxury and idleness, withdraws from commerce and renders unproductive for the State the riches and industry of a multitude of citizens; which excludes the nation from all branches of commerce not yielding one or two per cent. above the actual rate of interest; which consequently gives to foreigners the exclusive privilege of all these branches of commerce, and enables them to gain the preference over us in almost all other countries by selling at a price which would be unremunerative to us; which gives to the inhabitants of our colonies a powerful interest to carry on contraband trade with the foreigner, and through that to weaken the natural affection they ought to have for the mother-country; which secures for the Dutch and for the Hanse Towns the coasting trade of Europe, including France itself; which renders us yearly tributaries to the foreigners by the high rate on their loans to us; which, finally, condemns to be left uncultivated all the land of the kingdom that cannot yield more than five per cent., since with the same capital one could, without working, procure the same return. But he believed also that the commerce of capital itself, whose price is the interest of money, can only be led to attain this price equitably and with all necessary economy, as in the case of every other commerce, by competition and by reciprocal liberty, and that the Government could assist towards this end only, on the one hand, by abstaining from making laws for its rate while agreements can accomplish this much better, and, on the other hand, by the Government avoiding to swell the number of debtors and consumers of capital in contracting loans, or in not paying its obligations with exactitude.

Another kind of obstacles to the progress of industry which he considered could not be too soon cleared away was that multiplicity of taxes, which, owing to the necessities of the State, had been imposed upon labour of every kind, entailing vexatious modes of collection which were often more onerous than the taxes themselves: the arbitrary *taille*, the multiplicity of dues on every sort of merchandise, the complexity of tariffs, the inequality of the dues in the different provinces, the innumerable custom-houses on the frontier of the provinces, the frequency and importunity of official searches and examinations to provide against fraud, the necessity to have recourse, for proof of the frauds, to the solitary testimony of mercenary men of low moral character; the interminable contentions, so fatal to commerce that there is hardly a merchant who does not prefer in this respect a disadvantageous compromise to the most evidently just appeal to law; for if the merchant, instead of yielding to injustice, decides to give up meanwhile the charge of his business that he may carry on a prolonged action at law, he runs the danger of losing it, and even when he triumphs he remains always at the mercy of a powerful body, which has, by the rigour of the laws suggested by it to the Government, easy means of crushing him. Finally, he condemned the impenetrable obscurity and mystery resulting from the complexity of local dues and regulations published at different dates, an obscurity which is always interpreted in favour of officialism and against commerce.

Fiscal finance is necessary, for the State has need of revenues, but agriculture and commerce are, or rather agriculture animated by commerce is, the ultimate source of these revenues.[1] If State finance is injurious to commerce,

[1] There can be little doubt that Turgot here uses the term 'agriculture' in the philosophical meaning of the 'physiocratic' school, as including the whole productions of the earth. See *supra*, p. 64.

it is injurious to itself. These two interests are essentially united, and if they have appeared opposed to each other it is perhaps because we have confounded the interests of finance in relation to the State, which always exists, with the interest of the *financiers*, who being charged with the collection of revenues only for a certain time, think more of increasing these for the moment than of conserving the source which produces them.

He considered that the Board of Commerce was less useful for the management of commerce (which ought to go its own way) than for defending it against the enterprises of State finance. He would have desired that the financial arrangements of the State could permit it to free commerce from duties of all kinds. He believed that a nation fortunate enough to have arrived at this point would necessarily draw to itself the greatest part of the commerce of Europe. He believed that all taxes, of whatever kind they may be, are in the last analysis paid by the proprietor of the land, who sells by so much the less the produce of his land, and that if all the taxes were assessed on landed property the proprietors and the kingdom would thereby gain all that was absorbed in the cost of administration, the unproductive employment of men wasted in collecting the various taxes, or engaged in contraband trade, or in preventing it, and without reckoning the natural gain from the immense increase of capital and of income that would result from the increase of commerce.

He did not absolutely limit the duties of Government towards commerce to removing the obstacles that oppose the mere march of industry. He was quite convinced of the utility of the encouragements that could be given to industry either by recompensing the authors of useful inventions, or by exciting by prizes or gratuities the emulation of artists aiming at perfection.

. . . He had soon to battle with a crowd of opponents to his principles. He gave himself with pleasure to discussions which could only elucidate principles and bring about, in one way or another, a better knowledge of the truth.

Free from every selfish interest, from all pride, without the slavery to his opinions which self-love might have induced, he lived only for, and aspired only towards, the public good. His opinions were expressed with as much modesty as courage. Equally incapable of taking a dominant tone and of speaking against his thought, he delivered his sentiments in a simple manner; they were emphatic only by virtue of the reasons for them, which he had the art of placing within the reach of all minds with a kind of luminous precision. When he was contradicted he listened with patience; however sharp the attack might be, he never lost his sense of politeness or his usual suavity, or the presence of mind necessary to distinguish with nicety the bearings of the reasoning opposed to him. His zeal was mild because it was purged of all selfishness; but it was not the less earnest, for the love of the public good was in him a passion. He acted on his convictions, but his mind, always without prejudice, was always ready to receive new light.

He had the good fortune to find in M. Trudaine, who was then at the head of the administration of commerce, the same love of truth and of the public welfare which animated himself. It was by M. Trudaine's advice that he translated, in 1752, the treatises on commerce and on the interest of money of Josias Child and Thomas Culpeper. . . . His reputation became widespread, and his zeal communicated itself to others. It is to the ardour with which he sought to direct towards the study of commerce and political economy all the men of talent he could meet with, and to the alacrity with which he communicated all the knowledge he acquired, that we owe that propitious fermentation which sprang up two or three years after he had been Intendant of Commerce, and which since has already procured for us several works full of laborious researches and of profound views, works that have wiped away from our nation the reproach of frivolity it had too deservedly incurred by its indifference to studies the most truly useful. His zeal induced him to form a scheme of visiting the whole kingdom, in order to see for himself the state of commerce and manufactures and to discover the causes of the progress or the decadence of each branch of commerce, to expose abuses and to recognise needs and resources. Between July and December 1753, he travelled through Burgundy, Lyons, Dauphiny, Provence, and Languedoc. A severe attack of illness interrupted his plans for 1754. In 1755 he visited Rochelle, Bordeaux, Montauban, Guienne, and Bayonne. In 1756 he followed the course of the Loire from Orleans to Nantes, journeyed through Maine, Anjou, the coasts of Brittany from Nantes to St. Malo, and he returned to Rennes at the time of the sitting of the States in 1756. The weakness of his health prevented him from undertaking further voyages. He found at each step new reasons to confirm him in his principles, and new arguments against the restrictions of commerce. He took up the complaints of the friendless, poor artificer, who, unable to write and to represent his claims, having no representative at the Court, has always been the victim of a misguided Government. The fruits of his voyages were the reform of an infinite number of abuses of this kind; a knowledge of the real state of the provinces giving more certainty to the operations of the Ministry, a more exact appreciation of complaints and of applications, and a facility afforded to the people and to the simple artisans themselves to make known their complaints. . . . He sought to inspire the magistrates and notable persons in each place with an ambition to promote the prosperity of their town or their canton; he interviewed men of letters, proposed to them subjects for discussion, encouraged them to direct their studies to questions of commerce, agriculture, and political economy.

Full of respect for all persons charged with the administration of the provinces he visited, he gave them no room to think that his mission conveyed the least reflection on their authority; always forgetting himself in the good of the object, it was as far as possible by them and with them that he acted; he seemed only to second their zeal, and he enabled them often to obtain great credit with the ministry for views which were really inspired by himself. . . .

Meanwhile, in the course of giving himself so entirely to public work, his fortune became deranged as well as his health. He had sustained losses in the funds he had left in Spain, and the state of his affairs determined him in 1758 to resign his place of Intendant of Commerce. Those around him, who felt how useful he was, offered to make application for the bounty of the Court to make good to him what he had lost. But he replied that he did not estimate himself so high as to believe that the State should thus buy his services; he had always regarded these favours as having dangerous consequences, especially in the present circumstances of the State, and he did not wish that anyone should ever reproach him for having in his own interest abandoned his principles. He added that in his retirement he still hoped to interest himself in the cause of commerce, and with that view he asked for a chair in the Board of Commerce, to be merely honorary, which was granted to him.

His retirement detracted in no way from the consideration paid to him. His zeal was not abated; (a higher position was kept in view for him), when he was attacked by the malady of which he died.

---

The opposition which his principles encountered has given rise to M. de Gournay being represented as an enthusiast, and as a 'man of systems.' This phrase, 'a man of systems,' has become a favourite epithet directed against all who propose reform by prejudiced men or by those interested in maintaining abuses. The philosophers of recent times have indeed, with as much strength as reason, striven against the spirit of *system*. They intend by the word those arbitrary suppositions by which it is sometimes attempted to explain phenomena, but which really explain nothing,—that blind presumption which, dazzled by an idea, sees it everywhere.

But when men of the world condemn systems it is not in the philosophic sense. These men, accustomed to receive successively all opinions, as a glass reflects images without retaining any of them, accustomed to find everything probable without ever being convinced, to ignore the intimate connection of effects with their cause, to contradict themselves continually without being aware of it or placing any importance on it—these men are only astonished when they meet with a man inwardly convinced of a truth, and deducing from it consequences with the rigour of an exact logic. They let themselves listen; they listen next day to propositions quite contrary; they are surprised not to see in a thoughtful man the same flexibility. Then they do not hesitate to call him a fanatic and a *man of systems*. . . .

Every man who really thinks has in fact a system; a man without a system of reasoned links between his ideas could only be an imbecile or a madman. Nevertheless the two senses of the word are confounded, and he who has a system in the sense of the men of the world, that is a settled opinion holding to a chain of observations, incurs the reproach made by the philosophers to the spirit of system [theory] taken in a quite different sense—that of an opinion which is not founded on sufficient observation. If the arbitrariness or the folly of making everything bend to his ideas instead of bending his ideas to things, is the characteristic of the spirit of system, assuredly M. de Gournay was no man of systems.

The general principles in respect to commerce are accepted by nearly everyone. We know M. Le Gendre's words to Colbert: 'Let us alone' (*Laissez-nous faire*). . . . M. de Gournay differed often from men, otherwise good economists, in rejecting, with the strictness of a just mind and honest heart, those *exceptions* which they claimed in favour of their own interest. The world is full of men who condemn exclusive privileges, but who believe that there are certain commodities for which these privileges are necessary, and this exception is ordinarily founded on their personal interest, or on the interest of some individuals connected with them. The great majority is naturally attracted to the beneficent principle of liberty of commerce, but almost all, either by interest, or routine, or suasion, place upon it some little modifications or exceptions. M. de Gournay, in rejecting each exception while obtaining on the general question a majority of votes, raised against him each claimant for a particular exception. The result was a jumbled unanimity against the severity of his principles and an imputation to him of being *doctrinaire.* Contradiction only excited his courage. He knew that by pronouncing less openly the universality of his principles he would have saved himself from suffering much prejudice. But he believed it best that principles should be developed to their full extent, he desired that the nation should be instructed, and knew that it could be instructed only by the clearest exposition of the truth. Any 'management' in the art of setting it forth would be advisable only for his own sake, and he counted himself as nothing.

It was not that he believed, as several people have accused him of believing, that it is not necessary to keep any bounds in the reform of abuses; he knew how well prepared for all ameliorations need to be, how dangerous sudden shocks are; but he held that the necessary moderation should be shown not in a confined *exposition of principles,* but in the application of them to circumstances. He did not wish to pull down all the old edifice before laying any foundation for the new, but he held that before putting our hand to the work, we should have a plan, made in full detail, in order that we should not act blindly, in destroying, or in conserving, or in reconstructing.

Finally, M. de Gournay's special personal glory was his virtue, recognised so widely that, in spite of the many oppositions he met with, even the shade of suspicion never for an instant tarnished the brightness of his reputation. This virtue was sustained during his whole life. Founded on a deep sense of justice and beneficence, it made of him a man gentle, modest, indulgent in society, irreproachable and even austere in his conduct and his manners; but austere to himself only, well-balanced, free from bad temper in his home life, occupied in making happy everyone who surrounded him, always ready to sacrifice to compliancy whatever could not be regarded as a duty. In his public life we have seen him, although free from all self-interest, from all ambition, and even all love of fame, to have been not less active, nor less indefatigable, nor less adroit in advancing his schemes, whose only object was the public welfare; a citizen concerned above all with the prosperity and the glory of his country and the happiness of humanity. This respect for humanity was one of the sentiments that attached him the most closely to what was called his 'system,' and what he reproached most sharply in the principles he attacked was their tendency to favour the rich and idle classes of society to the prejudice of the poor and labouring classes.

It is a kind of misfortune that the men commendable for possessing those virtues, which are the most deserving of respect and the most useful to the world, share least of all in the distribution of renown. Posterity rarely judges but of public and striking actions, and is perhaps more sensible of the *éclat* than of their utility. But, supposing even its judgment to be always equitable in this respect, the motives, the spirit that evoked these actions, and which only can impress on them the character of virtues, are unseen and unknown; such delicate features of conduct are lost in the recital of history, as the complexion and the refinement in physiognomy vanish under the colours of the painter. There remain only lineaments without life, and actions of which we mistake the character, and the judgment of posterity on the character of some men is left fluctuating between a verdict ascribing to it the purest virtue, and one ascribing to it the mere knavery clever enough to wear virtue's mask.

We are, however, not so readily misled in our moral estimate of men while they live with us, and there is still an interval of time when malignity can in vain attempt to tarnish recognised virtue, and when flattery that would award unmerited honours can be repelled. This moment passes with the life of the man. Thus, the only means we have of securing public esteem for that small number of men of true excellence, and of fixing the perfume of virtue exhaled by them, is to challenge the testimony of their own generation by presenting to it a statement of facts still recent.

In rendering to the character of M. de Gournay the public homage which it merits, we feel sure no voice will be lifted against us.[1]

[1] *Œuvres de Turgot*, i. 257–91.

# PROTECTION TO NATIVE MANUFACTURES

## *Letter to the Abbé Terray 'sur la Marque des Fers'* [1]

Limoges, December 24, 1773.

I HAVE the honour to report to you on the state of the ironworks and manufactures in the Generality of Limoges. . . .

As to the observations you seem to desire on the means of giving more activity to this branch of industry (or of restoring to it what it is said to have lost), I have few to offer. I know of no means of stimulating any trade or industry whatever but that of giving to it the greatest liberty, and of freeing it from all those burdens which the ill-understood interest of the revenue has multiplied to excess upon all kinds of merchandise, and particularly upon the manufactures in iron.

I must not conceal from you that one of the chief causes of the delay in my responding to your inquiries has been the rumour spread that they had for their object the establishment of new burdens or the extension of old ones. The opinion, founded on too much experience, that the investigations of Government have for their sole object the finding of means to extract more money from the people, has given rise to a general mistrust, and the most of those to whom inquiries have been addressed either have not replied, or have sought to mislead the Government by replies sometimes incomplete, sometimes false. I cannot believe that your intention is to impose new charges upon a commerce which, on the contrary, you announce your desire

[1] See *supra*, p. 73.

to favour. If I thought so, I confess I should congratulate myself on the involuntary delay in my furnishing you with the information you have requested, and I should regret my not being able to prolong the delay still further.

If, after complete liberty has been obtained by the relief from all taxes on the fabrication, the transport, the sale, and the consumption of commodities, there remains to the Government any means of favouring a branch of trade, that can only be by the means of instruction; that is to say, by encouraging those researches of scientific men and artists which tend to perfect art, and, above all, by extending the knowledge of practical processes which it is the interest of cupidity to keep as so many secrets. It would be advisable for the Government to incur some expense by sending young men to foreign countries in order to instruct themselves in processes of manufacture unknown in France, and for the Government to publish the result of these researches. These means are good; but liberty of movement and freedom from taxes are much more efficacious and much more necessary.

You appear, in the letters with which you have honoured me on this subject, to believe that certain obstacles which might be placed to the import of foreign irons would act as an encouragement to our national trade. You intimate even that you have received from different provinces several representations to the effect that the demand which these foreign irons obtain acts to the prejudice of commerce in manufacture of the native iron. I believe, indeed, that iron-masters, who think only of their own iron, imagine that they would gain more if they had fewer competitors. It is not the merchant only who wishes to be the sole seller of his commodity. There is no department in commerce in which those who exercise it do not seek to escape from competition, and who do not find sophisms to make the State believe that it is interested, at least, to exclude the rivalry of foreigners, whom they easily represent to be the enemies of national commerce. If we listen to them, and we have listened to them too often, all branches of commerce would be infected by this spirit of monopoly. These foolish men do not see that this same monopoly is not, as they would have it believed, to the advantage of the State, against foreigners, but is directed against their own fellow-subjects, consumers of the commodity, and is retaliated upon themselves by these fellow-subjects—sellers in their turn—in all the other branches of trade. They do not see that all associations of men engaged in a particular trade need only to arm themselves with the same pretexts in order to obtain from the misled Government the same exclusion of foreigners; they do not see that in this balancing of vexation and injustice between all kinds of industry, in which the artisans and the merchants of each kind oppress as sellers, and are oppressed as buyers, there is no advantage to any party; but that there is a real loss on the total of the national commerce, or rather a loss to the State, which, buying less from the foreigner, must consequently sell him less. This forced increase of price for all buyers necessarily diminishes the sum of enjoyments, the sum of disposable revenues, the wealth of the proprietors and of the sovereign, and the sum of the wages to be distributed among the people.[1]

Again, this loss is doubled, because in this war of reciprocal oppression, in which the Government lends its strength to all against all, the only one left outside excepted is the small cultivator of the soil, whom all oppress in concert by their monopolies, and who, far from being able to oppress anyone, cannot even enjoy the natural right to sell his commodity, either to foreigners or to those of his fellow-subjects who would buy it; so that he remains the only one

[1] 'Here Turgot puts his finger on the evil. Let A be the body of the privileged; B the rest of the nation; 100,000,000 the yearly gain to the monopolisers. This sum must evidently come out of the pocket of B, to enter the pocket of A. But B, again, evidently represents the non-privileged capitalists, the proprietors, and the mass of simple workmen. Now, if the tithe levied by A strikes these three classes without distinction, it is clear that it takes from the two first but a portion of their superfluities, while it attacks the third in its circumscribed means of subsistence, represented in the *sum of wages* of which Turgot speaks.' (E. Daire, *Œuvres de Turgot*, i. 381, *note*.)

who suffers from monopoly as buyer, and at the same time as seller. There is only he who cannot buy freely from foreigners the things of which he has need; there is only he who cannot sell to foreigners the commodity he produces, while the cloth-merchant or any other buys as much wheat as he wants from the foreigner and sells to him as much as he can of his cloth.

Whatever sophisms the self-interests of some commercial classes may heap up, the truth is that *all* branches of commerce ought to be free, equally free, *entirely* free; that the system of some modern politicians who imagine they favour national commerce by prohibiting the import of foreign merchandise is a pure illusion; that this system results only in rendering all branches of commerce enemies one to another, in nourishing among nations a germ of hatred and of wars, even the most feeble effects of which are a thousand times more costly to the people, more destructive of its wealth, of population and of happiness, than all those paltry mercantile profits imaginable *to individuals* can be advantageous to their nations. The truth is, that in wishing to hurt others we hurt only ourselves, not only because the reprisal for these prohibitions is so easy that other nations do not fail in their turn to make it, but still more because we deprive our own nation of the incalculable advantages of a free commerce—advantages such, that if a great state like France would but make experience of them, the rapid advancement of her commerce would soon compel other nations to imitate her in order not to be impoverished by the loss of their own.

But supposing these principles not to be perfectly demonstrated, supposing even that we admit the expediency of prohibition in some branches of commerce, then I contend that the article of iron ought to be excepted, for a particular and decisive reason. This reason is, that iron is not merely a commodity of itself useful for the different purposes of life; the iron employed in household utensils, in ornaments and in armour, is not the most considerable portion of the metal worked and sold. It is principally as an article necessary in the practice of all the arts, without exception, that this metal is so precious and is so important in commerce. It is the chief material employed in all the different manufactures —in agriculture even, to which it furnishes the greater part of its instruments. For this reason it is a commodity of the first necessity. For this reason, even were we to adopt the idea of favouring manufactures by prohibitions, iron ought never to be subject to them, because these prohibitions, in the opinion even of their partisans, ought to be placed only on an article manufactured for consumption, and not on the necessary materials used in manufactures. According to this very policy, the buyer of instruments of iron, of service to his manufacture or to his land culture, ought to enjoy the advantages which the policy gives to the seller over the consumer. To prohibit the import of foreign iron is therefore to favour the ironmasters, not only, as in the ordinary cases of prohibition, at the cost of the home consumers of the simple article; it is to favour them at the cost of all manufactures, of all branches of industry, at the cost of agriculture, and of the production of all food stuffs.

I feel convinced that this reflection, which doubtless has occurred also to yourself, will restrain you from yielding to the indiscreet solicitations of the ironmasters and all those who look upon this branch of commerce as one by itself, and isolated from all the other branches with which it has connections of the first necessity. . . . A great number of arts have need not only of iron, but of iron of different qualities, and adapted to the nature of each work. For some is needed an iron more or less soft, for others an iron more brittle; the most important manufactures employ steel, and steel varies still more in quality; that of Germany is suited for certain purposes, that of England, which is more valuable, for other purposes. Then there are certain kinds of iron which our kingdom does not yield, and which we are obliged to procure from the foreigner. With regard to steel, it is notorious that we make very little of it in France, that we are still at our first experiments of making it, and that, however fortunate they may eventually turn out, perhaps a half-century may pass before we can make enough steel in France to supply, even in a moderate degree, the needs of our manufactures. We are now obliged to procure for our manufacturers' use instruments ready made from the foreigner, because we cannot in France make them of the necessary perfection, and because our manufacture would lose too much of its value and its price if it were made with imperfect instruments. Thus, to prohibit the import of foreign irons would be to cripple our own manufacture; it would be almost to ruin those in which steel is employed, and all those which have need of particular qualities of iron. To admit these irons, but only under excessive duties, would still bring our manufactures, in time, into an inevitable decay; it would be to sacrifice a large part of our national commerce to the self-interest, ill understood, of the ironmasters.

From narrow views of policy, to be obstinate in desiring everything we need to be of our own make, is just what the proprietors of Brie did, who believed themselves to be wisely economical in drinking the bad wine of their own growth, which really cost them much more, by their sacrifice of land suited for pasture, than the best Burgundy, which they could have bought from the sale of their cheese; they thus sacrificed a very large profit in order to maintain a very small one.

Our true policy consists in following the course of Nature and the course of commerce (not less necessary, not less irresistible than the course of Nature), and without pretending to direct the course. Because, in order to direct it without deranging it, and without injuring ourselves, it would be necessary for us to be able to follow all the changes in the needs, the interests, and the industry of mankind. It would be necessary to know these in such detail as it would be physically impossible to arrive at; in such a study the Government the most able, the most active, the most painstaking, would risk always to be wrong in half the cases. . . . Even if we had in all these particulars that mass of knowledge impossible to be gathered, the result would only be to let things go precisely as they would have gone of themselves, by the simple action of men's interests, influenced by the balance of a free competition.

But, if we ought not to drive away the foreign irons of which we have need, it does not follow that we should burden our own irons by taxes on their fabrication or on their transport. Quite the contrary, the fabrication and transport of French irons should be left perfectly free, in order that the contractors may work our mines and our forests to the best advantage, and may by their competition supply to our agriculture and to our arts, as cheaply as possible, the instruments they require.

I have felt it as a satisfaction to my own sense of duty to communicate to you all the reflections which have been suggested to me by a fear that you might yield to proposals which would injure the trade you desire to favour. . . .[1]

[1] *Œuvres de Turgot,* i. 376–88. In almost the same words the greatest French writer of our own century has given expression to the same truth: 'In the matter of commerce, encouragement does not mean *protection.* A nation's true policy is to relieve itself of paying tribute to other nations, but to do so without the humiliating assistance of custom-houses and prohibitory laws. Manufacturing industry depends solely on itself; competition is its life. Protect it, and it goes to sleep; it dies from monopoly as well as from the tariff. The nation that succeeds in making other nations its vassals will be the one which first proclaims commercial liberty. . . . France can attain this result much better than England.' (Balzac, *Médecin de Campagne* [published in 1835], Eng. tr. 1887, p. 63.)

# RELIGIOUS EQUALITY

## *Memorial to the King 'on Toleration'* (*June* 1775) [1]

[To appreciate the style of thought and of composition adopted in the following Memorial, the reader must be reminded of two things: first, that it was written for the purpose of instructing the young king in the very elements of religious liberty; and, second, that at that time the doctrine of toleration was, by the religious classes, still deemed a *heresy*.]

SIRE,—When I proposed to your Majesty to alter the form of the oaths to be pronounced at your consecration, I could only indicate to you, summarily, the reasons which I considered warranted my proposals. I undertook to develope to you, in more detail, the principles pertaining to the most essential object of the alterations proposed, that is to say, to the use of the prince's power in matters of religion. Your Majesty, while rendering justice to my views, dreaded the explosion which might result, in certain quarters, from the step I recommended. You know how deeply I have regretted your submission to formulas of obligation drawn up in times so deficient in enlightenment. But all is not lost, for your Majesty cannot hold yourself bound to take any action that would be unjust.

Your oaths, Sire, have been pronounced in presence of God and your subjects. Your subjects have an interest in, have a right to your justice; God has given you a law. To commit an injustice in order to execute the formulas which you have been induced to pronounce would be to violate the duty you

[1] See *supra*, p. 103.

owe to God, to your people, to yourself. You must, therefore, Sire, examine if the engagements included in the formulas of consecration with respect to heretics are just in themselves; and if they are unjust, it cannot be your duty to fulfil them. . . .

I have never concealed from your Majesty my own way of thinking. You saw it in a letter with which I accompanied the new forms of oath which I proposed to you. I venture to repeat to-day that your Majesty is bound, as a Christian, as a just man, to leave to all your subjects the liberty of following and of professing the religion which in their conscience they believe to be true. I add, Sire, that your own political interests on this point are entirely conformable with what Christianity and justice prescribe. These three points of view form the natural division of this Memorial. I shall examine first the rights of conscience according to the principles of religion; I shall next establish these rights according to the principles of natural law; in the third place, I shall discuss the question of this liberty of conscience in its connection with the political liberty of the State.

1. What, Sire, is religion? It is the binding together of the several duties of man towards God; duties of worship to be rendered to the Supreme Being, duties of justice and of benevolence to men; those duties known by the simple light of reason which constitute what we call Natural Religion, and those which the Divinity Himself has taught to men by a supernatural revelation which constitute Revealed Religion.

All men do not agree in acknowledging divine Revelation, and those who do acknowledge it do not agree in interpreting alike particular revelations. It is notorious that there are on the surface of the earth a multitude of religions, the votaries of which believe that the one they profess is the only one that is the work of the Divinity, and which is agreeable to Him.

The principal religions, such as Mahommedanism and even Christianity, are divided into a multitude of sects, each of which believes itself to hold exclusively the true religion.

All, or almost all religions, in exacting from man certain beliefs and the accomplishment of certain duties, add to this obligation the sanction of rewards and punishments in the life to come. A great number of religions teach that these punishments and these rewards are eternal. This is the doctrine of nearly all the Christian communities, and in particular of the Roman Catholic Church, whose doctrine your Majesty professes. So that on the belief and on the practice of a true or a false religion depends for man an eternity of happiness or of misery.

I can conceive that the men who believe all religions to be equally false, and who regard them as inventions of policy in order to govern more easily the people, can make no scruple about compelling them to follow the religion which it is thought most expedient to prescribe for them. . . . But if there is a true religion, if God is to demand account from each man of what he has believed and practised, if an eternity of punishment must be the portion of him who shall reject the true religion, how can we imagine that any power on earth can have the right to order a man to follow another religion than the one which he believes true in his soul and conscience?

If there is a true religion a man must follow it, and profess it in spite of all the powers of the earth, in spite of the edicts of emperors and kings, in spite of the judgment of proconsuls and of the executioner's sword. It is for having had this courage, for having fulfilled this sacred duty, that we have had held up to our veneration the martyrs of the primitive Church. If the martyrs were right in resisting the civil power, and following the voice of their conscience, their conscience, by that fact, did not recognise the civil power as judge.

All sovereigns have not the same religion, and each religious man feels himself, in his conscience, by his duty and for his salvation, obliged to follow that religion which he believes to be the truth. Sovereigns have not the right to order their subjects to disobey their conscience. God, in judging men, will demand of them whether they have believed and practised true religion; not whether they have believed and practised the religion of their sovereign. How could He demand that of them if all the sovereigns have not the true religion? Cast your eyes, Sire, on the map of the world; and see how few countries there are of which the sovereigns are Catholics. How can it be that with the greatest number of sovereigns of the world existing in error, they have received from God the right to judge of the true religion? If they have not the right, if they have neither infallibility nor the divine mission which alone could give it them, how dare they take upon themselves to decide the fate of their subjects, of their happiness or their misery during eternity? Every man, by the principles of religion, has his soul to save; he has all the light of reason and of revelation in order to find the way of salvation; he has his conscience in order to apply these lights—but this conscience is for himself alone. To follow his own conscience is the right and duty of every man, and no man has the right to make his conscience a rule for another. Each one is in this responsible for himself to God, none is responsible for another.

This principle is so clearly evident, that it would seem a waste of time to prove it, if the illusions opposed to it had not blinded the greater part of the human race, if they had not inundated the earth with blood, if even to-day they did not make millions unhappy.

Will the defenders of intolerance say that the prince has only the right to command when his religion is true and that then he ought to be obeyed? No, even then we cannot and ought not to obey him, for if we ought to follow the religion he prescribes, it is not because he commands it but because it is true, and it is not and it cannot be because the prince commands it that it is true. There is no man so irrational as to believe a religion true for such a reason. The man who submits himself to it in good faith does not obey the prince, he obeys only his conscience, and the order of the prince does not add, and cannot add, any weight to the obligation which conscience alone imposes. Let the prince believe or not believe a certain religion, let him command or not command his subjects to follow it, it is neither more nor less than it is—either true or false. The opinion of the prince is thus absolutely foreign to the truth of a religion, and consequently to the obligation to follow it; the prince then has, as prince, no right to judge, no right to command in this respect; his incompetence is absolute on things of this order, which are beyond his jurisdiction, and in which the conscience of each individual has only, and can have only, God Himself for Judge.

Some theologians say: 'We admit that the prince has not the right to judge of religion, but the Church has this right, and the prince, in submission to the Church, ordains in conformity with its judgments. . . . He himself does not judge, but orders his subjects to submit themselves to a legitimate judgment.' As this reasoning has been used and is still used seriously, it has to be answered seriously.

The Church has the right to judge of the things of religion—yes, without doubt; it has the right to exclude from its body, to anathematise, those who refuse to submit to its decisions, its decisions are obligatory [upon those who belong to it, and who believe that] what the Church binds and looses shall be bound and loosed in heaven. But the Church is not a temporal power, it has neither the right nor the power to punish in this world; its anathemas affect only the penalties which God reserves in the future life for the obstinately refractory. The prince, if he is a Catholic, is the child of the Church; he is subject to her, but only as a man concerned with his personal salvation; as a prince he is independent of the ecclesiastical power. The Church, then, can order him in nothing so far as he is prince, but only so far as he is a man; and as it is only in quality of prince that he could compel his subjects to submit to the judgment of the Church, it follows that the Church cannot make it a duty for him to use his authority to compel his subjects against their conscience. The Church cannot give him the right to do so, because she has it not herself, and besides, because the prince, as prince, not only does not acknowledge the superiority of the Church, but is not competent to judge for others what are the rights of the Church, or whether such a society is the true Church.

Is there an infallible Church? Is the society of Christians united with the Pope that Church? This is precisely the question that divides all Europe into two parties nearly equal—the question of judgment between the Protestants and the Catholics. There is even another question to be judged on before that. The Protestants and the Catholics both recognise the truth of Christianity and the divinity of the Scriptures, on which all Christian Communions profess to found their beliefs. But the Jews do not accept all the Scriptures; a great part of Asia follows the religion of Mahommed and rejects that of Jesus Christ. The Mussulman countries are as extensive as those where Christianity is established; the rest of the earth, still vaster, recognises neither Mahommed nor Jesus Christ, and follows different religions.

[This doctrine of making the prince the creature of the Church is] the same doctrine, the same spirit, which produced the infernal St. Bartholomew and the detestable League, placing alternately the sword in the king's hand to massacre the people, and in the people's hands to assassinate their kings. This, Sire, is a subject of meditation which should ever be kept in princes' minds. But, without ascending to those high principles, would the simplest common sense allow it to be imagined that princes could have any right over the conscience and the salvation of their subjects? If the fate of men during eternity could depend upon other men, should there not be a reasonable certitude that these other men should be endowed with natural or acquired enlightenment, superior to those of common men? Without such light—or even with it, without an express mission from the Deity, what man could dare to take upon him the eternal happiness or misery of other men?

The mission of kings is to make the happiness of their people on earth. This mission is noble enough, beautiful enough, and the work it involves is weighty enough for the strength of anyone, whoever he may be. He who has fulfilled with success this sublime and laborious career can die content with himself, and need not fear to render an account of his life. With attention, straightforwardness, and diligence, a prince has every enlightenment and assistance to discover what is really just and truly useful; he has no need to know anything else. He may make mistakes; this is an evil no doubt, but it is an inevitable result of the nature of things.

Sire, I speak to a king, but to a king just and true; let him ask himself what he thinks on this matter, and let him answer himself. There are in the different universities and among the ministers of the different Protestant sects, men who, endowed with great mind, have grown white-haired in the study of religion, have all their life read the Holy Scriptures, have researched thoroughly into all ecclesiastical antiquity; and although in all religions there are men who concern themselves less to discover truth than to find means to prop up the doctrine they are interested to maintain, yet one cannot doubt that a great number of these learned men are quite sincerely convinced that the doctrine of which they make profession is the only true one. Who among Catholic princes would feel himself fit to convince these men, fit even to defend himself against their objections? Doubtless the Protestant princes would not be less embarrassed if their turn came to dispute against the learned Catholic doctors. Princes, to whatever religion they may belong, are not made to fathom theology. I recollect only one king who had this fancy, and he was a Protestant—James I. of England. It did not succeed with him, and Europe felt that he would better have employed his time to become a great king than to be a middling theologian. Too many are given up only to pleasure and dissipation. Those who reflect apply themselves to the affairs of their state and to do good. I venture to ask you, Sire, if among the princes of different times and of different countries of whom you have read in history, there is a single one whom you would have taken as authority in the choice of a religion. And yet all those princes were believed to have the right to ordain the religion of their subjects, to render religion's laws, to pronounce its penalties, and to subject to torture men whose only crime was having religious opinions different from those of the prince, and desiring to follow the dictates of their own conscience. What increases our astonishment is that the most of these princes, at the very time of issuing these orders, were violating in a thousand ways the precepts of their own religion, and were allying the scandal of debauch with the barbarity of persecution. Louis XIV., deservedly thought a great prince because he had probity, honour, character (although somewhat spoiled perhaps, being inflated by an excessive love of glory), but above all because he possessed that firm will without which kings can neither do good nor prevent evil, even Louis XIV. knew very little. He candidly confessed that his education had been neglected. He made that confession, and he dared to judge what the religion of his subjects should be; he believed he had the right to deprive the Protestants of the liberty of conscience solemnly insured to them by Henry IV., whose succession to the crown had been cemented with their blood. Louis XIV. reduced the Protestants to despair by a continued vexatious persecution, the details of which make us shudder while we read of them in the memoirs of the time, and the errors into which this despair drove them he punished with the most relentless cruelty. He believed himself to be doing a praiseworthy and pious action. This was a deplorable blindness in a prince otherwise well-intentioned, who knew not how to distinguish his duties as man from his rights as prince. . . . But the interest of the priests about the Court has always been to confound these two things, and, in order to support their credit and serve their ambition, to misuse the prince's ignorance on these matters. That was not the only fault of the kind they caused Louis XIV. to commit. The miserable disputes of Jansenism and Molinism, which have been the ruin of so many and which served as pretexts for commotions dangerous to the royal authority, existed only as a consequence of the passion of the clergy to force the Government to interfere in questions with which it has neither interest nor right to meddle.

How can religion command sovereigns to use their power to constrain their subjects in matters of religion? Can religion then command, can it permit, crimes? To order a crime is to commit one; he who orders to assassinate is regarded by all the world as an assassin. Now the prince who orders some of his subjects to profess a religion they do not believe, or to renounce one they do believe, commands a crime; the subjects who obey act a lie, they betray their conscience, they do an act which they believe God forbids. The Protestant who through self-interest or fear makes himself a Catholic, and the Catholic who by the same motives makes himself a Protestant, are both guilty of the same sin. For it is not the truth or the falsity of an assertion that constitutes a perjury; the man who affirms on oath a true thing, but which he does not believe, is as much a liar, as much a perjurer, as if the matter were really false. The lie or the perjury consists in the contradiction between the assertion and the real belief of him who affirms or makes the oath.[1] . . .

[The remainder of the Memorial has unfortunately been lost.]

[1] *Œuvres de Turgot*, ii. 492–501.

# LOCAL GOVERNMENT AND NATIONAL EDUCATION

*Introduction to the Memorial to the King 'sur les Municipalités'* (1775)[1]

SIRE,—In order to judge whether it be expedient to establish municipalities in France in the cantons where they do not exist, and whether we should improve or should modify those that already exist, and how we should constitute those which we may believe to be necessary, there is no need for us to go back to the origin of municipal administrations, to make an historical relation of the vicissitudes which they have undergone, nor even to enter with much detail on the different forms they assume to-day. We have been too much in the habit, when dealing with seriously urgent questions, of deciding what is to be done by the examination into, and by the example of, what our ancestors have done in times which we ourselves confess to have been times of ignorance and barbarism. This method is only fit to lead justice astray through the multiplicity of facts presented to us as authorities. It tends to disgust rulers with their most important functions when they are told that in order to acquit themselves with effect and with honour it is necessary to be prodigiously learned. All that is necessary is to thoroughly understand and to correctly weigh the rights and the interests of men. These rights and these interests are not very numerous, so that the science which embraces them, being founded on the principles of justice which every one of us carries in his heart, has a great

[1] See *supra*, pp. 113–115.

degree of certitude without having any great complexity. It does not exact a very deep study, and is not beyond the powers of any straightforward man.

The rights of men gathered in society are not founded on their history as men, but in their nature. There can be no reason to perpetuate establishments which were made without reason. The kings, your Majesty's predecessors, pronounced, in the circumstances in which they found themselves, laws which they judged to be expedient. They were sometimes wrong. They were often led by the ignorance of their age, and still oftener their views were obstructed by the very powerful self-interests of parties whom they were not strong enough to conquer, and with whom they judged it wiser to compromise. There is nothing in that to subject you to retain the ordinances your ancestors made or the institutions they supported, when you come to recognise that a change is now just, useful, and possible. None of your courts, the most accustomed to make complaints, would venture to contest your Majesty's right, in order to reform abuses, to a legislative power as extensive as that of the princes who created or permitted the abuses we now deplore. The greatest of all powers is a pure and enlightened conscience in those to whom Providence has entrusted authority, shown in their governing for the good of all. So long as your Majesty does not stray beyond the lines of justice, you may regard yourself as an absolute legislator, and may depend on your well-affected subjects for the execution of your decrees.

Your nation is large, it is necessary to have some confidence in the means of well governing it, and for this end it is necessary to know its situation, its needs, its possibilities, and these even in some detail. This will be much more useful than the history of past positions. But it is a knowledge to which your Majesty cannot hope to arrive in the present state of things, a knowledge which your ministers cannot furnish, or the intendants themselves, and which the sub-delegates appointed by the intendants can gather only very imperfectly, owing to the limited duties confided to their care. Hence arise in the assessment and division of the taxes, in the means of levying them and in the administration connected with them, an infinity of errors which excite as many murmurs, and which, bearing most upon the lower classes of people, contribute so effectively to keep their condition unhappy. . . .

The cause of the evil, Sire, lies in the fact that your nation has no constitution. It is a society composed of different orders ill-united, and of a people the members of which have between them very few social ties, where consequently each is concerned almost exclusively with his own private interest, since there is no opportunity for anyone to fulfil his social duties, or even to know what his relations are to his fellow-citizens; so that in this continual war of individual pretensions and violations, reason and enlightenment bearing upon the circumstances have no regulating effect. Your Majesty is obliged to decide everything by yourself or by your mandatories. The issue of your special orders is waited for before the public good can be served, before the rights of others can be respected, sometimes even before one's own rights can be exercised. You are compelled to decree upon everything (and very often through private importunities), while you would govern as God does, by general laws, if the integrant parts of your empire had a regular organisation and had recognised connections.

Your kingdom is composed of provinces; these provinces of cantons or of *arrondissements*, which are named, according to the provinces, *bailliages*, *élections*, *sénéchaussées*, or some such other name. These arrondissements are formed of a certain number of villages and towns. These towns and villages are inhabited by families. These families are composed of individuals who have many duties to fulfil towards each other and towards society, duties founded on the benefits which they have received in the past from these others, and which they every day continue to receive. But the individuals are very ill-instructed upon the duties in the family, and they are not instructed at all upon the duties that bind them to the State. The families themselves scarcely know that they belong to the State of which they form part; they are ignorant by what title. They regard the exercise of authority in requiring contributions to serve to maintain public order as merely the law of the stronger party, to which there is no other reason to yield than the powerlessness to resist it, and which one ought to elude whenever the means can be found. Hence everyone seeks to deceive you and to escape his social obligations. His income is concealed, and can be discovered very imperfectly by a sort of inquisition, in which, we might say, your Majesty is at war with your own people, and in this kind of war no one has any interest in taking part with the Government; the man doing so would be regarded with an evil eye. There is no public spirit, because there is no point of common interest visible and recognised. The villages and the towns, the members of which are thus disunited, have no connection between themselves in the arrondissements to which they are attributed. They cannot come to an arrangement for any of the public works which are necessary. The different districts are in the same case, and the provinces themselves find themselves in the same towards the kingdom.

In order to dissipate this spirit of disunion (by which the work of your adminstrators and of your Majesty is ten times multiplied, and which necessarily and increasingly diminishes your power), in order to substitute for it a spirit of order and of union, by which the strength and the resources of your nation may concur towards the common good, we must devise a plan which shall link, one to the other, all the parts of the kingdom by an education which we must see to be nowhere neglected, by a common interest made clearly evident. The individuals must be attached to their families; the families to the village or town to which they belong; the towns and the villages to the arrondissement in which they are comprised; the arrondissements to the provinces of which they form part; finally, the provinces to the State.

The first and the most important of all the institutions which I believe to be necessary, the one most fit to immortalise your Majesty's reign, to have the most influence over the whole extent of the kingdom, is, Sire, the formation of a Council of National Education, under whose direction will be placed the academies, the universities, the colleges, and all the smaller schools. The backbone of a nation is its morality; the first basis of morality is the instruction imbibed from the time of childhood on all the duties of man in society. It is astonishing that this science is so little advanced. There are schemes and establishments for forming geometers, physicians, painters. There is not one devised for forming citizens.[1]

It would be the duty of one of the Councils to get composed a series of classic books, according to a regular plan, so that one would lead on to another, and that the study of the duties of the citizen, member of a family and of the State, might be the foundation of all other studies, which would be graduated in the order of utility they have for the State.

The Council of National Education should supervise the whole machinery of education. It should endeavour to render all literary bodies really useful. The efforts of these at present tend only to form savants, men of intellect and of taste; those who cannot arrive at this eminence remain abandoned and come to nothing. A new system of education which can only be established by the authority of your Majesty, seconded by a well-chosen council, would conduce to form in *all* the classes of society men virtuous and useful, just souls, pure hearts, zealous citizens. Those among them

[1] Turgot's ideas on social and civic education deserve more attention, even among ourselves, than they have yet obtained. Our educational codes, school-manuals (or most of them), are defective in this respect, in spite of the life-long efforts of the great and good William Ellis, of London (founder of the Birkbeck Schools), to improve them. Like Turgot, he held the strange opinion that schools, besides the three R's, &c., &c., should teach the young *good conduct and good manners*, along with some knowledge of the laws of social economy.

who in time could and would give themselves specially to science and literature, being drawn away from frivolous things by the importance of the principles instilled into them during their early education, would display in their subsequent work a character more manly and more coherent. Taste itself would gain by this, and so would the national moral tone; it would become less frivolous and more elevated, and would above all be more concerned with things praiseworthy.

There is at present only one kind of instruction possessing any uniformity—that is religious instruction. But religious instruction is particularly limited to things of heaven. Your kingdom, Sire, is of this world, and it is with the conduct due from your subjects towards each other and towards the State that your Majesty is bound to concern yourself. Without placing any obstacle in the way of instructions whose object is higher, and which already have their regulation and their ministers, I can propose nothing to you more advantageous for your people, more fit to maintain peace and good order, to give activity to all useful works, to make your authority to be cherished, to attach to you each day more and more the affections of your subjects, than to give to all of them an instruction which opens their mind to the obligations they have to society and to your power that protects them, the duty which these obligations impose, the self-interest that all have to fulfil these duties, for the public good and for their own. This moral and social instruction requires books made for the purpose, by competition, selected with great care. It requires a schoolmaster in each parish who will teach these books to the children, with the arts of reading, writing, counting, weighing, and with the principles of mechanics. A higher instruction, embracing progressively the knowledge necessary to citizens from whom the State requires more scientific training, would be given in the colleges.

If your Majesty approves of this scheme, I will place before you the details of it in a special memorial. I venture to promise that in ten years your people will not be ungrateful for it, and that by their enlightenment, their higher moral life, their sincere zeal for your service and for that of the nation, your people will stand above all other peoples. The children who are now of ten years will then find themselves men of twenty, prepared for the State, attached to our country, submitting, not by fear but by reason, to authority; assisting their fellow-citizens, accustomed to recognise and to respect justice, which is the permanent foundation of societies. Such men would fulfil all the duties towards their families which Nature lays upon them, and would form in time families which would well conduct themselves in the village to which they would belong.

But in order to interest existing families in the public good and your Majesty's service, it is not necessary to wait for the fruits appearing of this good education. There is nothing to prevent our employing families, such as they are, towards the constitution of regular villages, which would be something quite different from the present mere assemblage of houses, and cottages, and of inhabitants not less passive.

[Turgot then proceeds to develope in great detail his scheme of the representative bodies for the villages, the towns, the arrondissements, and the provinces, and he concludes with another appeal to the king's heart, picturing in enthusiasm the future fruits of the beneficent policy suggested.]

The civic education which the Council of Education would promote through the whole extent of the kingdom, the appropriate books it would introduce and direct to be taught, would contribute still more to form an instructed and virtuous people. There would be sown in the heart of the young the principles of humanity, of justice, of benevolence, of love for the State; these principles, finding their application as the young advanced in age, would grow more and more. In time your Majesty would have a people renovated, and the first of peoples. Instead of corruption, meanness, intrigue, and greed, which are found everywhere, we should find virtue, disinterestedness, honour, and zeal. It would be common to be a man of probity. Your kingdom, connected in all its parts, each part acting as a support to the rest, would appear to be (and indeed would be) increased in its strength beyond measure. Your kingdom would flourish each day as a fertile garden. Europe would regard you with admiration and respect, and your loving people with a felt devotion.[1] . . .

[1] *Œuvres de Turgot*, ii. 502–50.

# CORRESPONDENCE

## *Turgot to Voltaire*

Paris, August 24, 1761.

SINCE I received the letter which you did me the honour of writing to me, a change that concerns me has taken place: I have had the misfortune to be made intendant. I say the misfortune, for in this age of troubles there is no happiness except in living philosophically among our studies and our friends.

It is to Limoges that I am to be sent. I should have much preferred Grenoble, which would have enabled me to make little pilgrimages to the chapel of Confucius and to sit at the feet of the high priest.[1] But your friend M. de Choiseul has judged that to fill a place so important I have still need of some years of training. Thus I cannot hope to see you for a long time, unless indeed you come to fix your tent in Paris—an event I desire more than I dare to advise.

You would find there certainly nothing so good as your present repose—*rem prorsus substantialem*, said the truly wise Newton. You already enjoy as much glory as if you were dead, while you delight yourself as a man in every sense alive; without being in Paris you amuse it, you instruct it, you make it laugh or weep according to your own good pleasure. It is Paris that ought to visit you.

I thank you for having thought of me in proposing the subscription to the edition you are preparing of the works of the great Corneille, and I have to apologise for having so long delayed in replying to you. My desire to see gathered, first, a greater number of subscriptions, then the duties

[1] At Ferney, Voltaire's seat in the vicinity.

connected with my entrance into the intendancy, and above all, some degree of indolence in writing letters, have been the cause of this delay. I am the more ill-pleased with myself in now being able to ask of you only a small number of copies, the most of my friends having already subscribed on their own account.

But you need not doubt that the public will speedily concur in your enterprise. Independently of the interest which the name of the great Corneille must excite in the nation, the notes and reflections which you promise will render your edition infinitely precious. I have, however, learned from M. d'Argental that you intend to limit these to the pieces which have kept possession of the theatre. I feel that you have in this wished to avoid occasions of criticising Corneille too hardly, while raising a monument to his glory. But I believe that you would have been able to trace with nicety his beauties and his defects, without deviating from the respect due to his memory. You have left things less complete, and I think that an adequate criticism of the very pieces which we no longer act would be really useful to literature, and above all to young men who destine themselves to art. Your analysis would teach them to distinguish the defects springing from the subject, from those belonging to the manner in which it is treated. You would indicate the means of their avoiding some of these defects and of modifying others. You would lead them to regard essays which have failed under new aspects which would display the conditions of success.

The Court is in difficulty which side to take [in the decree of the Parliament against the Jesuits]. For myself, I would wish that we did these poor fathers the good turn of sending each of them back to his family, leaving him a reasonable pension and the distinction of the *petit collet*. The college finances would not be overburdened, the individuals would be made happy, the body would no longer exist, and the State would be tranquil.

Adieu, Monsieur; I repeat all my excuses and I pray

you to be assured that nobody is, with a more real attachment, &c., &c.[1]

### *To Condorcet*[2]

[Condorcet had written to Turgot (June 14, 1773): 'You are very fortunate in being possessed by the passion for the public good and in having the ability to satisfy it; this is a great consolation and of a kind superior to any afforded by literature.' Turgot replies to this]:

Ussel, June 21, 1772.

Whatever you may say, I believe that the satisfaction resulting from literary studies is deeper than any other satisfaction. I am quite convinced that by literature we may be a thousand times more useful to mankind than we can be in any official position, in which we strain ourselves, and often without succeeding, to effect some small benefits, while we are made the unwilling instruments of very great evils. All these small benefits are transient, but the light that a man of letters can shed must, sooner or later, destroy all the artificial evils of mankind, and enable men to enjoy

[1] In *Œuvres de Turgot*, ii. 794.

[2] Condorcet (J. A. N. de Caritat, Marquis de). Born September 17, 1743. In 1758 he commenced his mathematical studies at the College of Navarre at Paris. Within the year he distinguished himself there so highly that D'Alembert predicted his future fame. At twenty-two he presented to the Academy of Sciences an essay on the integral calculus which drew forth general admiration. He was received into this Academy in February 1769. In 1773 he was appointed virtually perpetual secretary, and actually in 1777. His *Éloges* of the Academicians, published over the next twenty years, won for him much renown for many-sidedness, impartiality, and eloquence. He was one of the very earliest publicly to denounce negro slavery (1776). Admitted to the French Academy 1782. His *Life of Turgot* appeared in 1786. During the next five years he published many notable works advocating political reform. In September 1791 he was elected deputy for Paris in the Legislative Assembly, and was President in 1792. He attached himself to the party of the Girondists and shared their fate. He voted against the sentence of death on the king. Proscribed, he was concealed for some months in one house after another of his devoted friends, during which time, faithful as ever to his high ideal, he wrote his *Sketch of the Progress of the Human Mind.* At last he fled in disguise, but was discovered and imprisoned. Utterly hopeless, he took the poison he had carried with him in a ring as his last resource, April 7, 1794. In public life few men have been more noble, in private none more lovable.

all the good offered them by Nature. I know well that in spite of this there will still remain physical evils and moral disappointments which must be endured by bowing the head under the yoke of necessity. But enduring, and yet fighting against these, the human race is strengthened in moral character. I confess to you that my gout has not prevented me from still believing in final causes. I know well that no individual, or even world of individuals, is the centre of the system of final causes, and that the bounds of this system are not and cannot be known by us. To burst blood, to cough, to have the gout, to lose our friends, all these are but in detail the execution of the decree of death pronounced against everything that is born: and if we die only to be born again, it will still be true that the sum of good will be greater than that of evil (always of course setting aside those evils which men bring upon themselves), transient evils, as I believe they are, for the species, and transient also for the individual, if the thinking and feeling individual has successive careers to fulfil.

[Alluding to a reported commentary on the Bible, written by 'Émilie' (Madame du Châtelet, Voltaire's friend), Turgot in the same letter remarks :]

Such a commentary will be an interesting work, but I would wish it written without passion, and in a design to gather from the text commented on all that can be gathered of what is useful as an historical monument precious in many respects. The indulged desire to discover absurdities and things to ridicule, which sometimes are not there, lessens the effect of the incongruities which really are there.[1]

Limoges, December 17, 1773.

. . . My proscription of the *dévotes* is not so general as yours, because I have seen many of them who are very honest persons. Even fanaticism, which leads to very bad actions on some points, does not exclude probity on other

[1] *Corr. inédite de Condorcet et de Turgot.* (Ed. by Charles Henry.) Paris, 1887.

points. There are persons who have a corner for dishonesty, as there are some who have a corner for madness. I do not wish, however, to say that M. du Muy belongs to this. We must know the facts and the circumstances before we can judge persons.

[In reply to some remarks of Condorcet on Helvetius, Turgot writes:]

December 28, 1773.

I do not think that morality in itself should be regarded as *local*. Its principles everywhere spring from the nature of man and from his relations with his fellow-creatures, which do not vary, except in very extraordinary circumstances. But the *judgment* to be passed on the actions of individuals is a problem much more complicated, and infinitely variable, by reason of local opinions and the prejudices of education. In respect to moral judgments, I am a great enemy to indifference, and yet a great friend to indulgence, of which I have often as great need as any other man.

[On this and other questions in moral philosophy connected with it we have a longer letter by Turgot, the date of which is uncertain. Dupont considered it to belong to the pre-Limoges period. But Charles Henry relegates it, we think with more reason, to the period of correspondence marked by the previous letter—December 1773.]

As I do not believe that you yourself could ever write a work in philosophy without logic, in pure literature without taste, and in morals without honesty, I do not see that the severity of my judgment on the book 'De l'Esprit' by Helvetius need displease you. . . . I agree with you that the book is the portrait of the author. But apart from this merit, and that of some passages, written in a kind of poetic eloquence brilliant enough, although usually ill-introduced and also spoiled by some features of bad taste, I confess I cannot see any more in it. It appears to be made and written with the same incoherence that existed in the head of the author. In spite of a pretentious apparatus of definitions and divisions, one finds scarcely an idea analysed with justice, scarcely a word defined with precision. Even with the good maxims which he has stuffed into his work, it is seldom that their effect is not missed or is not spoiled by false applications and by paraphrases which take away all their sharpness or their energy. . . .

I know that there are many good men who are so according to the principles of the book 'De l'Esprit'—that is to say from a calculation of self-interest. To make the work one of merit the author might have concerned himself in proving that men have a real interest in being virtuous. But he seems continually occupied in proving the contrary. He pours floods of contempt and ridicule on all honest sentiments, and on all the private virtues; by the grossest and most absurd errors in viewing morals and politics, he would regard these virtues as worthless in order that he may laud presumed public virtues, much more fatal to men than useful to them. Everywhere he seeks to exclude the idea of justice and morality. Those who concern themselves with these *minutiæ* he confounds with the bigots in religion and hypocrites in morals. Never do we find him founding his morality on justice, and he has not a word tending to prove that justice towards all is the interest of all, that it is the interest of every individual as well as of every society. According to his false method and very false principles, he lays it down that there is no foundation for probity between nations, from which it would follow that the world must be for ever a den of robbers. On no side does he see that the interest of a nation is nothing else than the interests of the individuals who compose it. Nowhere does he rest himself upon any deep knowledge of the human heart; nowhere does he analyse the real needs of men—which appear to him to consist only in their having wives. He has no idea that man may have need to love. But indeed a man who could have felt this need could not have said that *self-interest is the only principle that actuates men.* He would have understood that, in the sense in which this proposition is true, it is a puerility and a metaphysical abstraction from which there is no practical result to be drawn, since it is just equivalent to saying that *men only desire what they desire.* If he alludes to self-interest, reflected upon, calculated upon, by which a man compares himself with others, and prefers himself, it is false to say that men, even the most corrupt, conduct themselves always by this principle. It is false to say that the moral sentiments do not influence men in their judgments, in their actions, in their affections. A proof that they do influence is that men have to make an effort to overcome their sentiment when it is in opposition to their interests. A proof is that they have remorse. A proof is that this interest, which they pursue at the expense of integrity, is often founded on a sentiment honest in itself and only ill-directed. A proof is that they are deeply touched by romances and by tragedies; a romance whose hero acted according to the principles of Helvetius—I mean to those he teaches—would displease readers much. Neither our ideas nor our sentiments are innate, but they are natural, they are founded in the constitution of our mind and of our soul, and on our relations with everything that surrounds us.

I know that there are some deficient in moral sensibility who are at the same time virtuous men, such as Hume, Fontenelle, &c., but all take for the foundation of their virtue *justice,* and even a certain degree of kindness. Thus I make it less a reproach to Helvetius for his having little sensibility than for his representing the quality as a ridiculous folly, or as a piece of hypocrisy, and for his exalting only the passions without fixing the definition of any duty, and without acknowledging any principle of justice. . . .

I forgot to mention the affectation with which he recounts to you the greatest horrors of every kind, the most horrible barbarities, and all the infamies of all the vilest debauchery, in order to declaim against hypocritical or imbecile moralists, who make them, he says, the object of their preachings, without seeing that they are the necessary effects of such or such stated legislation. As regards the most sensual vices of mankind, he reflects complacently on the debaucheries of great men. . . . Doubtless a debauchee, a brigand, a murderer may be a Nadir-Shah, a Cromwell, or a Cardinal de Richelieu—but is that the destination of man? Is it desirable that there should be such men? Everywhere Helvetius finds grandeur only in startling and stunning actions; certainly it is not by this fashion of judging that we can arrive at just ideas of morality and happiness.

I cannot side with his declamations against the intolerance of the clergy, nor with those against despotism. 1. Because I do not love declamations; 2. Because I see in his book, everywhere, the question of intolerance is treated not in a manner that could improve either clergy or princes, but only in a manner to irritate them; 3. Because in his declamations against despotism he confounds all ideas, and adopts the style of an enemy of all government. . . . When we would attack intolerance and despotism, it is before all necessary to stand on just ideas, for the inquisitors have their self-interest in being intolerant, and the viziers and sub-viziers have a self-interest in maintaining all the abuses of government. As they are the stronger, we should not add right to their might. I hate despotism as much as any man does, but it is not by declamations that we ought to attack it; it is by establishing, in an unanswerable manner, the rights of man. And besides, we must distinguish despotism in its degrees; there are a crowd of abuses of despotism in which the princes themselves have no real interest; there are other abuses which they permit only because public opinion has not decided upon their injustice and their evil effects. We should win a better hearing from nations by attacking these abuses with discernment, with courage, and above all by interesting humanity against them, than by indulging in mere eloquent invective. When we do not insult we rarely offend. Men in place are justly shocked by violent expressions which everyone seizes upon, and they attach only a minor importance to the cause provoking the outburst, and to the uncertain or far-distant consequences of philosophic truths, often contested and regarded by most men as problems. There is no form of government without some anomalies to which the governments themselves would not willingly apply a remedy, and without some abuses which they intend to reform sooner or later. We should therefore assist them by treating questions of public good solidly, calmly; not coldly, yet not passionately, but with that touching warmth which arises from a deep feeling of justice and the love of order. It is not necessary to believe that to persecute is a pleasure. See what an interest J.-J. Rousseau has inspired in spite of his follies, and how highly he would have been respected if his self-love had only been reasonable. He has been condemned, it is true, by the Parliament; but, 1, because he had the madness to put his name to 'Émile;' 2, the Parliament was sorry enough to take it up, and if Rousseau had wished he could easily have avoided the storm by concealing himself two or three months. . . . By adopting a proper tone, we may say almost anything, and still more effectively when we add to it the weight of solid reason, along with some slight precautions not difficult to take.

I have a leaning to Rousseau in almost all his works, but what case can I make for a declaimer such as Helvetius, who pours vehement insults and scatters bitter sarcasms on all government, and who undertakes to send to Frederick a company of finance-mongers, and who, while deploring the misfortunes of his country, in which he says that despotism has arrived at the last degree of oppression, and the nation at the last degree of corruption and of baseness (which is not true), holds up as his heroes the King of Prussia and the Empress of Russia? I see in all that nothing but vanity, the spirit of party, an excited brain; I see neither the love of humanity nor of philosophy. . . . I am, I confess, indignant at hearing him praised with a kind of fervour which seems to me an enigma which party-spirit only can explain. . . .

I have received news to the effect that my return is not urgent. I will, therefore, stay here all the month. It is not for any pleasure, nor even for 'interest,' for I should greatly prefer to be with you, my friends. I find there is more substance in this verse of La Fontaine—

> 'Qu'un ami véritable est une douce chose!'—

than in the whole book 'De l'Esprit.' I hope that this will obtain my pardon from you for all the ill I have said of the hero whose glory I have attacked. You know well that it is like trying to obscure the sun by throwing dust into the air.

[Condorcet writes in January 1774: 'There is a degree of character being below which a man is a fool; but, that aside, we can scarcely cultivate one talent except at the expense of another; in like manner in morality we cannot absolutely avoid certain vices of some danger without the risk of losing some great virtues. In general, scrupulous persons are not fit for great things; a Christian will, while subduing the motions of the flesh, lose the time which he might have employed on things useful to humanity. He will not dare to rouse himself against tyrants, fearing that he may have formed a rash judgment, &c.' Turgot replies:]

Limoges, January 14, 1774.

. . . 'I do not lean much to the opinion that virtues may be opposed, one kind to another, unless in the case where by virtues we mean certain active qualities which are perhaps as much talents as virtues. Besides, all these words are taken in different senses, and are almost always so ill-defined that we may easily dispute for ages on those matters without coming to an agreement. Morality turns much more on duties than on these active virtues, which, belonging to characters and to passions, are in fact rarely combined in a high degree in the same individual. But all duties are in accord with themselves. No virtue, in whatever sense we take this word, dispenses with justice, and I do not set much value on the men who do 'great things' at the expense of justice, or on poets who think that they can produce great beauties of imagination without justness. I allow that excessive exactitude dulls in some degree the fire of composition and that of action, but there is a middle point with everything. We have nothing to do in our argument with a monk who loses his time in subduing the movements of the flesh (although, by parenthesis, the time lost in satisfying them might have been really much greater). Nor has our argument anything to do with the case of a blockhead who hesitates to reprobate a tyrant from fear to form a rash judgment.[1]

*To David Hume*

Paris, March 25, 1767.

I profit by the opportunity, through Mr. Francis, to acquit myself of the reply I have so long been owing you, and at the same time to give you my congratulations on the place which you now occupy in the Ministry,[2] so far as there can be a congratulation made to a man of letters upon finding himself thrown into the whirlpool of affairs. As for myself, I should receive much more heartily a congratulation on an event which would set me free from affairs, and would restore me to letters and to liberty. Whatever may be your sentiments on this event, I share them, and I take in it the interest which I shall always take in everything concerning you.

. . . I hesitate to allude to the subject again [the quarrel between Hume and Rousseau], at which you have, with reason, been so much annoyed. Besides, in order to explain oneself at this distance volumes would need to be written, and even after these we might not succeed in understanding each other perfectly, because the slightest circumstance, differently looked upon, suggests interpretations quite contrary to the intention of the writer. I see,

[1] *Corr. inédite de Condorcet et de Turgot.* (Ed. by Charles Henry.) Paris, 1887.

[2] The Under-secretaryship for the Home Department, to which Hume had been appointed the previous year.

for example, by the details into which you enter, and by the pains you take to defend yourself, that you have believed my reflections to be dictated by my attachment for Rousseau, of whom you call me a zealous friend, and of whom you say elsewhere, I am so fond (*engoué*). . . . I can well assure you that no other motive has dictated what I wrote to you than my attachment for you—attachment very real, and founded on personal knowledge, while of Rousseau I have no knowledge personally, for I met him only for half an hour at Baron d'Holbach's more than twelve years ago. I know Rousseau only as an author. Unfortunately experience has dispelled in me the illusion that the man himself is to be loved merely from faith in his writings. I say unfortunately, because this illusion is very sweet, and I have lost it only with much regret. I do not, however, less esteem, and love greatly, the works of Rousseau. Quite independent of the beauty of his language, the eloquence of Rousseau in his moral writings has a charm of peculiar power. I believe that he is one of the authors who have best served morality and humanity. Very far from reproaching him for having in this respect wandered from common ideas, I believe, on the contrary, that he has respected still too many prejudices. I believe that he has not gone far enough forward on his road; but it is by following his path that we shall arrive at the end which is to draw men together into equality, into justice and happiness. You must understand me. You will do me the honour of believing that I do not adopt his ridiculous paradoxes on the danger of literature, and on the destination of man to the savage life. Like yourself, I regard them as a display, a kind of 'feat of strength' of eloquence. Rousseau was not yet known when he set himself on this false track; the body of his ideas was not yet formed. He imagined himself as gaining an advertisement by seizing on the paradoxical sides of the subjects proposed by the Academy of Dijon. This unfortunate pride, which I do not pretend to justify, has led him constantly to heap up paradoxes in order not to have to retract those first made; and his 'Émile' is still spoiled by the twists he sometimes gives in it to truths placed there merely in order to connect them with his crack-brained fads. I believe that in this he is a victim of the charlatanism produced by an ill-conceived self-love. Moreover, I do not believe much in his pretended Christianity. But, in spite of these defects, how many potent truths there are in 'Émile,' how closely the path which he presents to education is drawn from Nature, what fine and original observations there are on the successive developments of the human mind and human heart! He prolongs rather much this development. Nature moves faster than he thinks; but she follows the route which he traces, and he is the first who has known to quicken and advance Nature without hampering her, and for this assuredly the human race is to him under an eternal obligation. And do you count for nothing the *contrat social*? At all events it presents a very luminous truth, which appears to me to fix for ever our ideas on the inalienability of the sovereignty of the people under whatever government may exist. 'Émile' appears to me everywhere to exhale the purest moral lessons ever yet taught, and they might in my opinion be carried into further application; but I guard myself against giving you more of my ideas on this because you would think me perhaps to be still madder than Rousseau. I will not say to you, then, that I find true morality in no book on morals, and that all I recognise of it is scattered here and there *in romances*. I will not say to you that it is precisely because the morality in the writings of Rousseau approaches nearest to that of romances, that I so much esteem it, for I should thus give you too ill an opinion of myself. After this profession of faith in Rousseau considered as author, I confess freely, but not without regret, that there are defects which render his person intolerable in society and which have caused him to fall into odious improprieties. There is no one in the world who can be more indignant than I am at his suspicions against you. Although I have not regarded them quite in the same light as you have, and although I have not believed them to be a mere pretext suggested in bad faith, and deliberately, in order to shake off the obligations which he received from you; although I have regarded them only as the fruit of an imagination excited by pride and by melancholy, I do not the less feel that no honest soul could conceive such suspicions against a benefactor, and that a misbelief so evil-minded proclaims a man in whom we can have no confidence. I believe that at present Rousseau is quite convinced of the falsity of his suspicions, and I hold him to be inexcusable for not having retraced his steps. However, I am less surprised at this second fault than at the first, considering that the excess of his pride and the horror he would doubtless feel to see himself humiliated before you after the manner in which you have treated him. If I have differed from your view of the matter, it was not that I might justify Rousseau, because no one in the world can justify him, but I believed—and I confess to you that I still think the same—that you are mistaken in the manner of regarding his conduct; and I see with pain that in defending yourself on the subject of Rousseau's accusation—on which assuredly you have no need of defence, and which falls by its own atrocity—you have put yourself slightly in the wrong towards him by attributing to him views which I believe he did not hold, and you have given him, so to speak, a means of setting him on his feet again in the fight. It seems to me that by confining yourself to making public the two letters without comment he would have been confounded in the most overwhelming manner. I know well that he is so already; but the partisans of Rousseau still say: 'Mr. Hume has taken this affair too seriously;' besides I think all this ought to disquiet you very little. Men who know you the least of the world have rendered you full justice, in France as well as in England, and I am sure that even among Rousseau's partisans who know you the least no one has been tempted to give the least credence to the absurdities of his letters. If in order to lead Rousseau into England you shortened your stay in France, it is we who suffer the most by the whole affair, since we are deprived of the pleasure to possess you and to live with you. I am one of those who regret it the most. I have dwelt longer than I intended upon this affair, but it shall be certainly the last time of my mentioning it to you. [The remainder of Turgot's letter is given to an argumentative defence of his 'agricultural' doctrine.]

Paris, June 1, 1767.

. . . I am not surprised at your ways of thinking on literature and public affairs, although they are quite opposed to my own. Your passion for Letters is a love used up by long enjoyment, and public affairs are to you a new taste. As to me, on the contrary, I am more than satiated with affairs, and circumstances have never permitted me to give myself up to my taste for literature. It may possibly be that my career will thus become the inverse of yours, and that I shall yet find my relaxation in study as you find yours in affairs.

It is right to say that the affairs with which you meddle are probably less irksome than those occupying me. With us the interior administration is complicated with a multitude of details repulsive and trivial, entangled with the spirit of pettifogging, by the multiplicity and perplexity of forms, &c. . . . However, literature and public life are both *means*—the end is happiness. But it happens too often that the equipments embarrass the march, and prevent the end being reached. I wish very earnestly that you may find everywhere the happiness of which you are so worthy. It will ever be a happiness for me to be counted one of your friends.

Paris, July 3, 1768.

. . . The good government [hoped for in the future] cannot establish itself without creating a crisis, and crises are accompanied by disorder. Must we accuse on that account the light and liberty which force us to pass through these disorders in order to bring about a happier condition? No, certainly no. They make evil on the way to good; but after all do they make more evil than the tyranny and the superstition which would suppress them? You do not think so, I am sure, any more than I do. The people occupied with their necessities, the great occupied with their pleasures, have no time to be wise and to extricate themselves from their prejudices. But in the progress of knowledge it will come about that we need not be so learnedly wise in order to have good sense and to be able to render truths easily popular which to-day exact labour before they carry conviction.[1]

*To Mlle. de Lespinasse* [2]

Limoges, January 26, 1770.

. . . You seem to believe that I think the Abbé Galiani's work ('Dialogues sur le Commerce des Blés') to be a good one; I only find it to be full of wit, of genius, of tact, of depth, of good temper, &c., but I am far from finding it to be good. I think that, on the whole, it is intellect infinitely ill employed, all the worse for its greater success, for it will be a welcome support to all the fools and knaves attached to the old system, which after all the Abbé himself surrenders in his conclusions. He has the art of all those who set themselves to darken things that are clear to the open mind, of the Nollets disputing against Franklin on electricity, of the Montarans against Gournay on the freedom of commerce, of the Caveyracs attacking tolerance. This art consists in never commencing at the commencement, but by rushing into the subject in all its complications, or with some fact which is only an exception, or some circumstance isolated,

[1] *Letters of Eminent Persons addressed to David Hume* (Edinburgh, 1849), pp. 149–64.

[2] Lespinasse (Claire-Françoise), 1731–76. A noted figure in the intellectual society of Paris from the middle of the eighteenth century till her death. Under the fascination of her manners and the brilliancy of her conversation her very plain features were entirely forgot. The great D'Alembert was her constant and devoted friend. Later in life she formed attachments which more deeply moved her heart, and her love-letters, written at this time of inspiration, excel in passionate eloquence all else of their kind known. They have been published.

far-fetched, or merely collateral, which does not belong to the essence of the question and goes for nothing in its solution. The Abbé Galiani, commencing with the case of Geneva to treat of the question of the freedom of the corn-trade, is like the man who, writing a book on the means men employ to procure themselves subsistence, should make his first chapter on 'culs-de-jatte'; or like a geometer who, treating of the property of triangles, should commence by white triangles as the most simple, in order to treat after of blue triangles, then of red triangles, &c. I would state generally that whoever overlooks the fact of political States being separated from each other and being differently constituted will never treat properly any question of Political Economy. Besides, I do not like to see him always so prudent, so much an enemy to enthusiasm, so much in accord with all the *ne quid nimis*, and with all men who simply enjoy the present and are quite satisfied that the world should go on as it does, because it goes on well enough for them, and who, as Gournay said, having their own bed well made, do not wish to be disturbed. These indeed are not the men to love enthusiasm, and they like to call 'enthusiasm' all that attacks the infallibility of men in office. . . .

I believe it possible for a very good reply to Galiani to be made, but it would demand much study and tact. The Economists are too confident in their science to fight against one they consider a merely adroit dealer in old wares. As for the Abbé Morellet, he must not think of it; he would do himself a real wrong by turning again from the work of his dictionary.[1]

*To the Abbé Morellet.*

Limoges, January 17, 1770.

. . . You have been very severe. Galiani's 'Dialogues is not a book to be called bad, although it sustains a very bad cause, but it could not sustain it with more spirit, more charm, more tact in the exercise of its frank pleasantry and

[1] *Œuvres de Turgot*, ii. 800.

of its subtlety in discussion of details. A book written with this elegance, this airiness of tone, this correctness and originality of expression, and by a foreigner, is a phenomenon. The work is very amusing, and unfortunately it will be very difficult to reply to it in such a manner as to dissipate the seduction induced by the speciousness of its reasonings and the piquancy of its style. I wish I had the time, but I have it not. Neither have you. Dupont is absorbed in his paper. The Abbé Baudeau would reply too much as an economist, &c.

[*To same, some time later, same year.*]

. . . I am curious to know what the English have thought about 'L'Histoire des deux Indes' [by the Abbé Raynal]. I confess that while admiring the talent of the author and his work, I have been somewhat shocked by the incoherence of his ideas, and by seeing paradoxes the most opposite brought forward or defended with the same warmth of argument, the same eloquence, the same fanaticism. He is sometimes puritanic like Richardson, at other times immoral like Helvetius . . . irrational in science, irrational in metaphysics, and often in politics. His book brings out no result, except in showing the author to be a man full of thought, well instructed, but without one idea in him properly determined, such a man as would allow himself to be carried away by the enthusiasm of a jejune rhetorician. He seems to have put himself to the task of sustaining successively all the paradoxes which have presented themselves to him in the course of his readings or of his dreams. He has more learning, more sense, and more natural eloquence than Helvetius, but he is in fact as incoherent in his ideas, and as ignorant of the true nature of man.[1]

[1] *Œuvres de Turgot*, ii. 801.

*To Dr. Josiah Tucker.*[1]

Paris, September 12, 1770.

I have not the honour to be personally known to you, but I know that you were pleased with the translation I made, fifteen years ago, of your 'Questions on the Naturalisation of Foreign Protestants.' I have since translated your pamphlet on the wars of commerce ['On going to War for the sake of Trade.' London, 1763]. I have delayed its publication purposing to add some notes, which my occupations have not yet left me time to complete. A translator owes to his author every kind of homage, and I now request of you to accept as such a pamphlet which, while certainly conveying to yourself nothing new, may, I have been told, prove useful in spreading elementary ideas on subjects with which we desire to see the public better acquainted.[2] This little piece was written for the instruction of two Chinese whom I met in this country, in order to let them better understand questions I had put to them on the state and the economical constitution of their empire.

These questions reminded me of others which you had the goodness to send to me by Mr. Hume, but which I never received; for the packet put into the post-office at Paris for Limoges was lost. Mr. Hume no doubt informed you of this accident and of my regrets. I owe you not the less my deep thanks. If a copy should remain to you and you are disposed to repair my loss, the surest way would be simply to put it into the London post-office, to the address of M. Turgot, Intendant of Limoges, Paris.

[1] Born 1711, died 1799. Dean of Gloucester 1758. Was the author of several publications distinguished for great shrewdness in argument and for enlightened views on the great questions of the time in civil government and political economy, between 1748 and 1785. For advocating the extension of political rights to the Roman Catholics and to the Jews Dr. Tucker brought upon himself the odium of the Bristol mob, which, rising in indignation, burnt his effigy amidst much disturbance.

[2] The work thus modestly referred to is the *Réflexions sur la formation, etc., des Richesses.*

I have a regret very much greater, that of not having been able to profit by the visit you made some years ago to Paris, in obtaining the honour of personal acquaintance with you. I should have been all the more flattered by it, for I find by your works that our principles on liberty and on the main objects of political economy are much in accord. I confess I cannot help being astonished that, in a nation enjoying the liberty of the press, you should be almost the only author who has known and felt the advantages of a free commerce, and who has not been seduced by the puerile and suicidal illusion of a commerce fettered and exclusive. May the efforts of enlightened and public-spirited politicians destroy this abominable idol, which still remains after the mania of conquests and of religious intolerance of which the world begins to be undeceived! Think of the millions of men who have been immolated to these three monsters! I see with joy, as citizen of the world, an event approaching, which more than all the books of philosophers will dissipate the phantom of the jealousy of commerce. I allude to the separation of your colonies from the mother country, which will soon be followed by that of all America from mother Europe. Then the discovery of that part of the world will become really useful. Then will it multiply our commercial enjoyments much more abundantly than when we purchased them with streams of blood. The English, the French, the Spaniards, &c., will consume the sugar, the coffee, &c., &c., and will sell their commodities just as the Swiss sell theirs to-day, and these nations will also have, like the Swiss people, the advantage that this sugar, coffee, &c., will no longer serve as pretexts to intriguers to involve their nation in ruinous wars and to burden it with accumulated taxes.

I have the honour to be, &c.

Limoges, December 10, 1773.

I have many excuses to make to you for having so long delayed the thanks I owe you for all the particulars you have been kind enough to send to me at the request of my friend M. Bostock, relating to the production of cereals and their commerce.

I intended to reply to you in English, but at the time I found myself just convalescent from an attack of gout; and as it is to me somewhat of a task to write in your language, I delayed my answer until another time. Since I returned to the province, I have had quite a pressure of occupations, and I take advantage now of my first moment of liberty. But as Mr. Bostock is now in London, he can translate my letter to you, and thus it is I write it in French.

I begin by thanking you for the different pamphlets you have forwarded to me, of your own composition, on this interesting subject. I am entirely of your opinion on the inutility of the bounty which your Government have so long granted on the export of corn. My principles on this matter are: absolute liberty to import, without distinction of vessels of this or that nation, and without any duties on import; similarly, absolute liberty to export in all kinds of vessels without any duties on export and without limitation even in times of scarcity; liberty in the interior to sell to whomsoever we wish, when and where we wish, without being obliged to carry to the public market, and without any authority interfering to fix the price of corn or of bread. And I would extend these principles to commerce in all kinds of merchandise. This policy is, as you know, far distant from the practice of your Government and of our own.

[Turgot then, at considerable length, dwells on the desirability of obtaining reliable statistics on the price of wheat, &c., in France and England, with various suggestions, and then replies to an inquiry by Dr. Tucker on a minor matter.]

I have made several inquiries relative to the question you have put to me on the opportunities which an English farmer would have to establish himself in one of our provinces. To work a farm it would be necessary to have a capital sufficient to develope it in value, and I doubt if capital would return as much in a French farm as in an English one. The reason is that our Government is still very undecided on the principles of the liberty of the corn-trade. It is even still extremely prepossessed against the exportation, and if it does not change its way of thinking by permanently establishing liberty of transit, there is reason to fear that our agriculture will become very slightly profitable. Besides, in the greatest part of our provinces, the land-tax is imposed on the farmer and not on the proprietor, which renders the condition of the farmer much less advantageous. I add that a Protestant would, in certain provinces, often have many disagreeable experiences to endure.[1]

*To M. Devaines.*

['Turgot,' says M. Foncin, 'who tolerated all attacks directed against himself, was wounded in the person of his friend; he avenged his chief clerk, M. Devaines (against a slanderous imputation), by assuring him publicly of his esteem and of obtaining for him the appointment of Reader in the King's Chamber, with the right to the *grandes entrées*.' He communicated to his friend this promotion in a letter dated]

September 18, 1775.

. . . You have no need of justification. . . . It is quite in course that you should be exposed to these calumnies, you and all those who have any share in my confidence, and myself perhaps more than anyone. There are too many persons interested in the maintenance of abuses of every kind not to make common cause against those disposed to reform these. When they employ the only arms they know how to wield, lies and calumnies, we must arm ourselves against them with courage and with contempt. We must say to ourselves what the king said to me on the day of the riot at Versailles: 'We have for ourselves our good conscience; with that we are very strong.' If honest men were to allow themselves to be discouraged by such

[1] *Œuvres de Turgot,* ii. 801–804.

infamies, they would give to bad men free course to become permanently masters to oppress and pillage mankind. It becomes our duty then to brave them.[1]

## *To Dr. Richard Price.*[2]

### On the Future of America.

[This letter is peculiarly interesting for being the last writing of Turgot of any considerable length and importance that remains to us. Two years' retirement from office, the cold neglect of him by the king and his former colleagues, his disappointed hopes of seeing France reformed, had not chilled the warmth of his sympathies in every effort made for the world's progress. The letter is even more interesting for giving the views on the future of America held by a cultured and prominent man in 1778, before the termination of the war, and thus before the constitution of the Republic. Within the scope of more than a century it is not surprising that some of his predictions in the letter have been disproved by events; it is surprising how many of them have been confirmed. In this place it may be proper to allude to the position he took on the question of the American struggle for independence, as far as France was concerned. The question was before the French Cabinet at the beginning of 1776. A Memorial was submitted to the king by Vergennes, the Foreign Minister, giving his views on the best policy to be adopted. It was communicated to Turgot, with a request to have his own views on the matters discussed. These he gives in his own Memorial to the king of April 6, 1776: 'Sur la Manière dont

[1] *Nouv. Biog. gén.* xiii. 934.

[2] Price (Richard), D.D. Born February 23, 1723, died March 19, 1791. Son of an English Dissenting minister. From 1743 to 1756 was tutor, companion, and chaplain in a wealthy private family named Streathfield. In 1757 became minister of an Independent congregation at Newington Green, London. Next year published his *Review of Questions, &c., in Morals*, which at once established for him a high reputation. Admitted to the Royal Society in 1765. In 1776 appeared his *Observations, &c., on the War with America*, of which sixty thousand copies were sold in a few months. The American Congress invited him to reside in the United States and to superintend the establishment of their financial policy, but he declined. Lord Shelburne, in his short administration of 1782, appointed him one of his private secretaries. His works on questions of the time, in morals, political economy, and finance, were numerous, and in all of them he proved himself a sagacious thinker and a constant friend of liberty in every sphere of action.

la France et l'Espagne devraient envisager les Suites de la Querelle entre la Grande-Bretagne et ses Colonies.' It is one of his longest State Papers.[1] The conclusion drawn in it coincided with the decision in favour of neutrality of Vergennes himself at that period. 'My views,' says Turgot, 'are exactly the same as those of M. de Vergennes on the necessity of rejecting every plan of aggression on our part. . . . I believe it essential to precipitate nothing.' Only in certain circumstances would he advise intervention—'when we shall have reason to believe, by the conduct of England, that this power intends really to attack ourselves.' M. Tissot has put the question: 'Would Turgot's policy have been more favourable to France than the one which was adopted, and which drifted to its outlet at the Peace of 1783, when the humiliated Britannic pride conceived in consequence a resentment which was later to break out? It is perhaps useless to make the inquiry. But we must at least acknowledge it was the policy of a man prudent and pacific, who in principle admits only defensive war, and who knew how to prepare for it.'[2] But a reflection more serious than this may be made. It was the cost of the American war to France that still further upset her finances and led directly to her bankruptcy. In a state of bankruptcy, it was no longer gradual reform but only revolution that was possible. Since the Revolution France has never yet found her equilibrium. Her history has been a series of fresh revolutions and repeated reactions. Events have made her no wiser. She still exists under a bureaucratic tyranny, the principles of real personal liberty being scarcely understood.]

Paris, March 22, 1778.

Mr. Franklin has forwarded to me, on your part, the new edition of your 'Observations on Civil Liberty, &c.' I owe you a doubly grateful acknowledgment. 1. For your work, of which I have long known the value, and which I had read with avidity at the time of its first appearance, in spite of the onerous duties that then pressed upon me; 2. For the kindness and sincerity in which you have withdrawn the imputation of 'awkwardness' (*maladresse*) which you had mingled with the good you had said of me elsewhere in your 'Observations.' I should indeed have deserved the imputation

[1] *Œuvres de Turgot*, ii. 551–85.

[2] J. Tissot, *Turgot, sa Vie, etc.* (Paris, 1862), p. 3?6.

if you had had in view no other *maladresse* than that of my being unable to untwist the secret springs of the intrigues directed against me by men much more adroit in this kind of work than I am—than I shall ever be, or ever wish to be. But at first it seemed to me that you imputed to me the *maladresse* of having rudely offended the general opinion of my nation, and in this respect I believe that you did justice neither to me nor to my nation, where there is much more enlightenment than your countrymen generally suppose, and where, perhaps, it is easier to lead the public to reasonable ideas than it is with yourselves. I judge thus by the infatuation of your nation on the absurd project of subjugating America which so long endured, until the result of Burgoyne's adventure began to open its eyes. I judge thus by the spirit of monopoly and exclusion which prevails among all your political writers on commerce (I except Mr. Adam Smith and Dean Tucker), a spirit involving the very principle on which your separation from your colonies took effect. I judge thus by all your polemical writings on questions which have agitated your nation for the last twenty years, and among which, until your own appeared, I can scarcely recollect to have read one in which the real point of the question was seized.

I cannot conceive how a nation which has cultivated with so much success all the branches of natural science, should remain so completely below itself in the science the most interesting of all, that of public happiness; in a science in which the liberty of the press, which your nation alone enjoys, would give to it prodigious advantage over all the other nations of Europe. Is it national pride that has prevented you from turning these advantages to account? Is it because you are somewhat less ill than others that you have employed all your speculations to persuade yourselves that you are perfectly well? Is it the spirit of party, the desire to find a support in [uneducated] popular opinions, which has retarded your progress by inducing your politicians to treat as vain metaphysics all those speculations which tend to establish fixed principles on the rights and the true interests of individuals and of nations? How has it happened that you are almost the first among your men of letters who has advanced just notions of liberty and who has exposed the falseness of the idea, again and again pronounced by almost all public writers, that liberty is secured if men are only subject to *laws*—as if a man oppressed by an unjust law could be free? This would not be true, even supposing all the laws were the work of the assembled nation; for beyond all, the individual has also his rights, and the nation cannot deprive him of them, except by violence and by an illegitimate use of the general power. Although you have, indeed, yourself dwelt upon this truth, perhaps it still merits from you a fuller development, considering the little attention that has been given to it, even by the most zealous advocates of liberty.

Again, it is a strange thing that in England it should not be held as a common truth that one nation has never any right to govern another nation; that such a government can have no other foundation than physical force, which is also the foundation of brigandage and of tyranny; that the tyranny of a people is of all tyrannies the most cruel and the most intolerable, and the one which leaves the fewest resources to the oppressed nation; for after all a despot is limited by his own interest, he is checked by conscience or by public opinion, but a multitude [in a fit of ascendency] never calculates, is checked by no conscience, and awards to itself glory while it more deserves disgrace.

Events are, for the English nation, a terrible commentary on your book. For some months they have rushed on with an accelerated rapidity. The end is reached in respect to America. She is independent now for ever. Will she be free and happy? Is this new people, placed so advantageously to give to the world the example of a constitution by which man may enjoy all his rights, freely exercise all his faculties, to be governed only by nature, reason, and justice?—will this people be able to form such a constitution?

Will they be able to establish it on permanent foundations, and to ward off all the causes of division and of corruption which can undermine it, little by little, and destroy it?

I confess that I am not pleased with the constitutions that have been drawn out by the different American States up to this time. You reproach with reason that of Pennsylvania for the religious oath exacted from members of the representative body. The case is even worse in other States; there are several which exact, by oath, specified belief in certain dogmas. I observe in a great many instances an imitation, without any real necessity, of the usages of England. Instead of radiating all the authorities to one centre, that of the nation, different bodies have been established, a body of representatives, a council, a governor, just because England has a House of Commons, a higher chamber, and a king. They think of balancing the different powers; as if this equilibrium of forces, which was believed to be necessary to balance the great preponderance of royalty, could be of any use in republics founded on the equality of all the citizens, and as if the establishment of so many different bodies would not be a source of so many divisions! In wishing to prevent chimerical dangers, they have created real ones. It was desirable to have nothing to fear from the clergy; they have united them under their banner of a common proscription. By excluding them from the right of eligibility [to the representative body], they have made of them a body by themselves, a body foreign to the State. Why should a citizen, who has the same interests as others in the common defence of liberty and its possessions, be excluded from contributing to the State his enlightenment and his virtues, because he belongs to a profession which itself exacts these virtues and this enlightenment? The clergy is dangerous only when it exists as an organised body in the State, when we attribute to this body special rights and private interests, and when we attempt to have a religion established by law—as if men could have any right or any interest in regulating the conscience of others; as if the individual man should sacrifice, for the advantages of civil society, the principles to which he believes his eternal salvation to be attached—as if a people were to be saved or to be damned *in a lot*! Wherever tolerance, that is to say the absolute neutrality of the Government in dealing with the conscience of individuals, is established, there the ecclesiastic, in the midst of the national assembly, when he is admitted, is but a citizen; he becomes an ecclesiastic only when he is excluded.

The framers of American constitutions cannot study enough to reduce to the smallest number possible the kinds of affairs of which the Government of each State should take charge; to separate the objects of legislation from those of general administration and from those of local administration, and to constitute minor local assemblies which by fulfilling the functions of Government in local matters would exclude these from the general assemblies, and remove from their members every opportunity, means, and desire of abusing an authority which should be confined to general interests, and kept free from the petty local passions which agitate people. . . .

No fixed principle is established in respect to taxation; it would seem that each province could tax itself according to its fancy, could establish personal taxes, taxes on consumption, and on importation—that is to say, would maintain an interest of its own, contrary to the interest of the other provinces.

The right to control commerce is everywhere taken for granted; exclusive bodies, or the governors, are even authorised to prohibit the exportation of certain commodities in certain circumstances. So far are people yet from realising that the law of complete freedom of all commerce is a corollary of the right of property—so deep are they still immersed in the fog of European illusions.

In the general union of the provinces with each other I do not see a coalition, a fusion of all parties, in order to make a body one and homogeneous. It is only an aggregation of parties, always too separated, and which will always maintain a tendency to separate, by the diversity of their laws, of their manners, of their opinions, by the inequality of their actual forces, and still more by the inequality of their eventual progress. It is only a copy of the Dutch Republic, which had not to guard, like the American Republic, the possible extension of some of their provinces. The whole edifice at present rests on the false basis of a very ancient and very vulgar policy, on the prejudice that nations and provinces have an *interest*, as nations and provinces, other than the interest of the individuals composing them, which is to be free and to defend their property against invaders; that they have an interest, not in buying merchandise from the foreigner, but in compelling the foreigner to consume their productions and the works of their manufactures; an interest in having a vaster territory, in acquiring such and such a province, such an island, such a village; an interest in gaining an ascendency over other peoples. . . . Some of these prejudices are fostered in Europe, because the ancient rivalry of nations and the ambition of princes obliged all States to hold themselves armed to defend themselves against their armed neighbours, and to regard the military force as the principal object of Government. But America has the happiness to have no enemy to fear (unless she creates a division within herself); thus she can and should appreciate at their real value those presumed interests, those subjects of discord which would threaten her liberty. By the sacred principle of the freedom of commerce, regarded as a consequence of the right of property, all the presumed interests of national commerce disappear, also the interest to possess more or less territory will vanish, by the principle that the territory belongs not to the nations but to the individual proprietors of the land [and other inhabitants]; that the question whether such a canton, such a village ought to belong to such a province, to such a State, ought not to be decided by the presumed interest of that province or that State, but by the interest of the inhabitants of that canton or village themselves.

I imagine that the Americans are yet far from feeling the force of these truths to the degree necessary to insure the happiness of their posterity. I do not blame their leaders. They had to provide for the necessity of the moment by a Union, such as it is, against a present and formidable enemy; there was no time to think of correcting the vices of constitutions and deciding upon the composition of the different States. But they ought to beware of making these defects permanent. They ought to set about uniting opinions and interests, and placing them under uniform principles in all the provinces. They have in this respect great obstacles to overcome. . . .

In the Southern colonies there is a too great inequality of conditions, and above all, the great number of black servants, whose slavery is incompatible with a good political constitution, and who, even when their liberty is granted, will cause embarrassment by forming almost a second nation in the same State.

In all the States there prevail prejudices, an attachment to established forms, the use and wont of certain taxes, the fear of taxes of a better kind that should be substituted for them, the vanity of those colonies which think themselves to be the most powerful, and most unhappy symptoms beginning of national pride. I believe that the Americans are bound to become great, not by war but by culture. . . . If they leave neglected the immense fields that stretch to the sea on the west, there might be formed there a mingling of their outlaws, of their scamps escaped from the severity of the law, with the savages there, from which would rise hordes of brigands to ravage America as the barbarians of the North ravaged the Roman Empire; hence another danger, the necessity of holding themselves armed on the frontier and of being there in a state of continual war. The colonies on the frontier will in consequence become more inured to war than the others, and this inequality in military strength may become a terrible spur to ambition. The remedy for this possible inequality would be to maintain a standing military force, to which all the colonies will contribute in proportion to their population. The Americans, who harbour still all the fears that prevailed in England, dread more than anything a permanent army. They are wrong. Nothing is easier than to connect the constitution of a standing army with the militia, in such a manner as to improve the militia and to make liberty even more assured. . . . There are thus many difficulties for the future, and perhaps the secret self-interest of powerful individuals will be joined to the prejudices of the multitude to frustrate the efforts of the truly wise and good citizens.

All right-thinking men must pray that this people may arrive at all the prosperity of which they are capable. They are the hope of the human race. They should be the model. They must prove to the world, as a fact, that men can be both free and peaceful and can dispense with the trammels of all sorts which tyrants and charlatans of every costume have presumed to impose under the pretext of public safety. They must give the example of political liberty, of religious liberty, of commercial and industrial liberty. The asylum which America affords to the oppressed of all nations will console the world. The facility of profiting by it, in making escape from the consequences of bad governments, will compel the European powers to be just, and to see things as they are. The rest of the world will, by degrees, have its eyes opened to the dispersion of the illusions amidst which politicians have been cradled. But, for that end, America herself must guarantee that she will never become (as so many of your ministerial writers have preached) an image of our Europe, a mass of divided powers disputing about territories or the profits of commerce, and continually cementing the slavery of peoples by their own blood.

All enlightened men, all the friends of humanity, should at this moment contribute their lights and join their reflections to those of wise Americans, in order to concur in the great work of their legislation. This would be well worthy of you, Sir; it has been my desire to excite your zeal; and if in this letter I have given myself up, perhaps too much, to the expression of my own ideas, this desire has been my only motive, and will excuse me, I hope, for the weariness I may have inflicted on you.

I would that the blood which has been shed and which will yet be shed in this quarrel, should not prove useless for the happiness of mankind.

Our two nations have done each other much evil, without either of them probably having gained any real profit. The increase of national debts and expenditure, and the loss of many lives, are perhaps the only result. England, it seems to me, has incurred that even more than France. If, instead of pursuing this war, you had only acted with a good grace at the beginning, if you had allowed policy to dictate then what it was inevitably compelled to do later, if national opinion had permitted your Government to have been beforehand with events, and to have consented at first to the independence of America, without making war on anyone, I firmly believe that your nation would have lost nothing by such a policy. She will lose now all that she has spent, and she will spend more; she will suffer for some time a great falling off in her commerce, and suffer many internal troubles, if she is forced to bankruptcy; and whatever happens, she must suffer a great loss in her influence abroad. But this last point is of very little importance for the real good of a people. . . . Your present misfortunes are the effect of a necessary amputation, which will make for your future happiness; it was perhaps the only means of saving you from the grangrene of luxury and corruption.

If in your political agitations you could reform your Constitution by making elections annual, by granting the right of representation in a more equal manner and one more proportionate to the interests of the represented, you would gain as much perhaps as America herself by this Revolution; for your liberty would remain to you, and your other losses would be soon repaired with that and by that.

You can judge, Sir, by the frankness with which I have expressed myself on these delicate points, of the esteem with which you have inspired me, of the satisfaction I have in feeling that there is some resemblance between our ways of thought. I need not remind you that this confidence is intended only for yourself. I must request of you not to reply to me in detail, *by the post*, for your letter would certainly be opened at the office, and they would find me much too great a friend of liberty for a minister—even for a disgraced minister—to be!

I have the honour, &c.[1]

[1] *Œuvres de Turgot*, ii. 805–11.

# MISCELLANEOUS EXTRACTS

# MISCELLANEOUS EXTRACTS

*Great Questions to be discussed philosophically.*—It seems to me that it is only by treating the matter in its whole length and breadth, and by developing in their natural order all the principles involved, that we can determine what is the best; for it is always with the *best* that we must concern ourselves in theory. To neglect this research, under the pretext that the best is not practicable in existing circumstances, is attempting to solve two questions at one operation; it is to miss the advantage of placing the questions in the simplicity that can alone render them susceptible of demonstration; it is to throw ourselves without a clue into an inextricable labyrinth, or rather it is to shut our eyes wilfully to the light, by placing ourselves in the impossibility of finding it. (Memoir 'Sur les Impositions' (1764), *Œuv.* i. p. 898.)

*Freedom of Thought.*—In directing the forces of your mind to the discovery of new truths, you fear to go astray. You prefer to remain quietly in the opinions most generally received, whatever they may be. That is as much as to say that you should not walk beyond doors, for fear that you might stumble and break your legs. But in that case you are in the position of him whose legs are *already* lamed, for yours are useless to you. And for what has God given limbs to man, if not to walk with them; or given him reason, if not to make use of it?

It is not error that opposes so much the progress of truth; it is indolence, obstinacy, the spirit of routine, everything that favours inaction.

I do not admire Columbus merely for having said: 'The earth is round; then in advancing towards the west I shall meet the land again,' because the most simple things are often the most difficult to find. But what characterises a great soul is the confidence in which it abandons itself to an unknown sea on the faith of a reasoning. What genius and enthusiasm there would be in that man to whom a recognised truth gave such courage! In many other careers the tour of the world is still to be made. Truth is for us everywhere, in like manner, on our road; glory and the happiness of being useful are at the end. ('Pensées' (1750), *Œuv.* ii. pp. 672–75.)

*Mere Physical Courage.*—We err in judging the merit of actions by their apparent difficulty, and in preferring the courage of a soldier, who exposes his life, to that of a man who follows reason in spite of prejudice. We do not realise that the effort of the latter comes entirely from himself. He walks, and often alone; the former is carried, and along with others. Men are children, who cannot take a step quite alone on the smoothest road. And whither may they not be led, through what dangerous paths, to what precipices, by the leading-strings of fashion and of public opinion! One may have sufficient courage of mind, and yet not desire to expose himself to a useless death. And those who have enough good sense not to desire a useless death for themselves, and enough virtue not to inflict it on other innocent people, are generally the most fit to brave death and to receive it nobly when the service of their fellow-creatures and the defence of their country are really concerned. ('Observations,' &c., *Œuv.* ii. p. 779.)

*Exaggerated Language a Failure.*—What we call bombast is but, so to speak, a sublime counterfeit. True eloquence uses the strongest and most animated figures, but they must come from real enthusiasm. One does not move others without being first moved himself, and the language of enthusiasm has this in common with all the passions, that it is ridiculous when it is only assumed. . . . An arrow justly drawn rises to the level of the mark and there is fixed; shot too high it falls to the ground. Such is the image of a figure of speech, the one natural, the other exaggerated. (On 'Universal History' (1750), *Œuv.* ii. 659.)

*Study of Languages the best Lesson in Logic.*—The study of languages, well carried out, would be perhaps the best of logics. In analysing, in comparing the words of which they are composed, in following them from their formation up to the different significations which have been afterwards attributed to them, we recognise the thread of ideas, we see by what degrees, by what shades of meaning, men have passed from one to the other; we seize the connection and analogy which exist between them, we succeed in discovering which of them were presented first to man's thought, and what order they kept in the combination of the primitive ideas. This kind of experimental metaphysics is at the same time the history of the mind of the human race and of the progress of its ideas, always proportioned to the needs which have called them forth. ('Réflexions sur les Langues' (1756), *Œuv.* ii. 753.)

*Geography and History.*—If we include in geography the state of nations, as the title of political geography seems to require, there is very little to add to geography of the different epochs, to form from them universal history, beyond the names and actions of some special men. In a word, history and geography place men in their different distances. The one expresses the distances of space, the other those of time. The bare description of a country on the one side, and the dry record of successive years on the other, are as the canvas on which objects are to be represented. Ordinary geography and chronology determine their situation; history and political geography paint them in their true colours. Political geography is, if I may call it so, the *coupe* of history. ('Géographie politique' (1750), *Œuv.* ii. 613.)

*The highest Pagan Philosophers gave no Enlightenment to the People.*—A few philosophers had, by exercise of their reason, learned to despise the religion of the people, but they felt it no duty to enlighten them. Indifferent to the gross errors of the multitude, they were carried away by errors of their own, which had only the frivolous advantage of subtlety. The greatest geniuses had still greater need of the Christian religion than the people, because they bewildered themselves in the obscurity, the absurdity, and the instability of their reasonings. ('First Discourse at the Sorbonne' (1750), *Œuv.* ii. 587.)

*How Christianity extended the World's Education.*—Christianity, by establishing a body of pastors for the instruction of the people, made study necessary for a great number of persons, and thus stretched out her hands to all men of genius among the mass of mankind. More men having applied themselves to literature, we had thus the more great men. ('First Discourse at the Sorbonne' (1750) *Œuv.* ii. 587.)

*Honour to Constantine.*—It was not to the good Roman emperors like Titus, Trajan, or the Antonines, that the world owed the abolition of the combats of gladiators—those sports where the flowing of human blood was greeted with popular applause. It was to Constantine (or rather it was to Jesus Christ), it was by the hands of a prince whom history reproaches for his cruelty, that religion conferred benefits on mankind much greater than could be accomplished by the 'good emperors' who were destitute of Christian spirit and enlightenment. ('First Discourse at the Sorbonne' (1750), *Œuv.* ii. 591.)

*A great Blot on Christendom.*—[Referring to the early conquests.] O America! vast countries! Have you been revealed to our knowledge only to be the miserable victims of our ambition and our greed? To what horrors and cruelties have we subjected you? Nations entirely swept from the earth, or buried in the mines; destroyed at one time in murderous executions, at another in prolonged punishments by a slavery harder than death! But religion was only the pretext for those horrors, which indeed she reprobated with vigour; it was one of her apostles, the pious Las Casas, who, denouncing them to Europe, mitigated somewhat the calamities. ('First Discourse at the Sorbonne' (1750), *Œuv.* ii. 591.)

*New America. A Prediction.*—Let us turn our eyes away from those sad sights, let us cast them on the immense plains of the interior of America. Here we see no longer conquerors impelled by self-interest or ambition, we see the missionaries whom the Spirit of Christ animates. . . . Innumerable colonies form themselves day by day; by slow degrees, these savages, permitted now to be men, may be disposed to become Christians. The soil, hitherto uncultivated, is made fruitful by industrious hands. Laws faithfully observed maintain henceforth tranquillity in these favoured regions. The ravages of war are there unknown. Equality has banished from them poverty and luxury, and preserves there, with liberty, virtue and simplicity of manners; our arts will spread themselves there without our vices. Happy peoples! Thus have you been brought, in a short time, to a happiness greater than that of the oldest and most polished nations. Vast regions of America cease to complain of the ferocity of Europe. She has given you her religion, fitted to enlighten the mind and to soften manners. Europe, faithful herself to religion's laws, shall spread amongst you all the virtues and all the happiness that follows them. Europe shall find in you the perfection of her political societies and the firmest support of her well-being. ('First Discourse at the Sorbonne' (1750), *Œuv.* ii. 592.)

*Decline of Ancient Eloquence.*—I am not surprised at the decline of eloquence in Greece and Rome. After the division of the empire of Alexander, the kingdoms that were established on its ruins eclipsed all the little republics in which eloquence had shone with such brilliancy. Alexandria and Antioch became the centres of commerce and arts. Athens was only a town in Greece, without authority, to which young men were sent to study, but in which no career was open to abilities. Ambitious men frequented the courts of kings, but there it was intrigue that was necessary and not eloquence. . . . After the fall of the republics there were declaimers but no longer orators. At Rome, where the same causes had produced the same effects, some emperors, passionately fond of eloquence, did not disdain to set the example of composing discourses, but they could not create Ciceros, because they could not repeat the circumstances which had produced them. ('Universal History' (1750), *Œuv.* ii. 658–59.)

*Art; Apology for Mediocrity.*—No art can well subsist if it does not succeed in engaging a number of men sufficient to cultivate it as a simple trade. [Turgot here adds as a note :] The English for many years have spared nothing in order to acquire fine paintings, but they have not been able to produce a single great painter of their own nation—the reason is that the English pay for only *good* paintings. In banishing images from their churches they have deprived of the means of living bad artists and even mediocre ones. In any trade where the worst workman cannot live or where the mediocre is not tolerably comfortable, the greater men cannot be formed. ('Universal History' (1750), *Œuv.* ii. 657.)

*Art and Fashion.*—Exaggerated luxury, or the vanity of accumulating ornaments because it considers them less as ornaments than as signs of opulence, deadens fine taste. The pleasure which the things afford to the senses or to the mind is no longer sought, one no longer reflects, he consults only the fashion. The sure means of judging ill in matters of all kinds is not to judge with our own eyes. . . . Another cause of bad taste has often been the very progress made in the mechanism of art. In everything men are prone to mistake the elaborate for the beautiful. ('Universal History' (1750), *Œuv.* ii. 657.)

*Discoveries made by Accident.*—The observation, by a thinking man, of a fact which strikes him, and from which he knows how to draw the useful consequences—this is what produces discoveries. We call the meeting of this fact with this man a *chance.* It is evident that these chances would be always more frequent if men were better instructed and had their reasoning powers more cultivated. . . . It is 2,500 years since medals were struck by first engraving, the reverse way, the inscriptions desired to be made on them, and it is only three hundred years since it was thought of to print on *paper*, with characters engraved, in the same way. The step seems very short; it took twenty-two centuries. ('Pensées,' &c. (1750), *Œuv.* ii. 672.)

*Bacon and Descartes.*—Bacon was the first who felt the necessity of bringing back all notions to a strict examination. . . . We may pardon him for having himself proceeded only with timidity. He is like a man walking trembling on a road scattered with ruins. At length Galileo and Kepler by their observations laid the true foundations of philosophy. But it was Descartes who, bolder, meditated and made a revolution. The system of occasional causes, the idea of reducing everything to matter and motion, constitute the spirit of this vigorous philosopher, and assume an analysis of ideas of which the ancients had given no example. . . . One is astonished that a man who had dared to doubt of everything he had learned did not try to follow the progress of his new light from his first sensations. . . . He realises, like the ancients, pure abstractions. . . . He is overcome by the very same old prejudices which he combats. If I were not withheld by the respect and gratitude due to so great a man, I would compare him to Samson, who in overturning the temple of Dagon was crushed under its ruins. ('Universal History' (1750), *Œuv.* ii. 650.)

*Newton.*—It is said that M. Frenicle anticipated that the law of gravitation, by which bodies fall to the earth, holds also the planets in their orbits. But the distance from an idea, so vague and uncertain, to that piercing view, to that glance of genius which penetrated the immensity of combinations and relations of all the heavenly bodies, to that inflexible intrepidity, deterred neither by the extreme difficulty of the problems nor by the [necessity of inventing a] profounder calculus for their solution, to the genius which was to rise to such perfection as to weigh in the balance the sun, the stars, and the forces of Nature—that is the distance from M. Frenicle to Newton. ('Universal History' (1750), *Œuv.* ii. 651.)

*Certainty attainable in all Sciences.*—We are never deceived in mathematics. If by inadvertence a geometer falls into an error, it is easy to convince him of it, or at least no one will be deceived after him. I venture to believe that, with more pains taken, we may arrive at the same point in the other sciences; that there is no dispute on which, in time, men cannot come to an agreement—for a dispute would be at an end when demonstrated to be incapable of decision. . . . There is no reason to doubt that new discoveries or further advancement of the human mind will some day render very clear the contested points and will, over them, arrive at evident and irresistible science. ('Observations,' &c., *Œuv.* ii. 778.)

*The End of Government.*—Since it is admitted that the interests of nations and the success of a good government reduce themselves to a sacred respect for the liberty of persons and of labour, to the inviolable maintenance of the rights of property, to justice between all, from which conditions necessarily result a greater production of things useful to man, the increase of wealth, and of enjoyments, and of enlightenment and all the means of happiness, may we not hope that some day all the present chaos will evolve into some distinct cosmos, in which the elements will have become co-ordinated, and that the science of government will then become easy, and will cease to be beyond the reach of men endowed with only ordinary good sense? This is the term to which we should arrive. ('Penseés,' &c., *Œuv.* ii. 675.)

*Paternal Government.*—The comparison between the magistrate and the father of a family, legitimate in some respects, ought not to be pushed too far. The father is necessarily the tutor of his children, he ought not only to direct them in all things belonging to social duties, but in those things which belong to private life. The magistrate leaves, and ought to leave, to private individuals the choice of the advantages personal to them. They have no need of him, and it would be impossible for him rightly to direct them there; the exercise of his authority is limited [to checking the encroachments of the individual upon the rights of others]. Besides, in those things having no relation to general society, where the private happiness of children is concerned, I shall always maintain that the duty of parents is limited to simple advice. It is the fashion of thinking otherwise which has made the young so unhappy for the rest of their life, which has brought about so many forced marriages, without reckoning the many unsuitable vocations. Every exercise of authority that goes beyond what is really necessary is a tyranny. ('Lettres sur la Tolérance' (1753), *Œuv.* ii. 685.)

*Clerical Intolerance.*—The dogma of infallibility is certainly false, or inapplicable, when the exercise of infallibility is conferred on those who are certainly not infallible, that is to say, on princes or on governments, for then spring forth two necessary consequences, intolerance and the oppression of the people by the clergy, and the oppression of the clergy by the Crown. The Albigensian wars and the Inquisition established in Languedoc, the St. Bartholomew, the League, the Revocation of the Edict of Nantes, the raid against the Jansenists,—see what has come from that maxim : one law, one faith, one king. I acknowledge the good that Christianity has given to the world, but the greatest of its benefits has been in having enlightened and propagated natural religion. Besides, the greatest number of Christians maintain that Christianity is not Catholicism, and the most enlightened, the best Catholics, admit that it is still less intolerance. They are in this in accord with other sects truly Christian, for the characteristic signs of Christianity are, and are bound to be, gentleness and love. ('Lettres sur la Tolérance' (1753), *Œuv.* ii. 687.)

*Church and State.*—You ask me to what I reduce *protection* which the State ought to accord to the dominant religion. I reply that, to speak accurately, no religion has any right to exact any other protection than liberty. It follows from the principle of tolerance that no religion has any right except on the submission of the [individual] conscience. The interest of each man is isolated with regard to salvation, he has in his conscience only God for witness and for judge. The laws of society have no relation but to those interests in pursuit of which men can help each other, where they can balance one interest against another. But in [actually determining one's own] religion the help of other men is impossible, and the sacrifice of one's own interest in this respect is a crime. The State, society, men incorporated, have as such no right to adopt arbitrarily a religion, for a religion is founded only on a personal conviction. ('Lettres sur la Tolérance' (1753), *Œuv.* ii. 676.)

*The Religion of Humanity.*—Natural religion formed into a system and accompanied by a worship. ('Lettres sur la Tolérance' (1753), *Œuv.* ii. 678.)

*Individual Freedom.*—Laws (according to some thinkers) are the articles of a treaty by which the parties who form it are united. The laws are the result of the interest of the greater or the stronger number, who compel the smaller or the weaker number to observe these laws, that is to surrender themselves to the will of the stronger. Laws, they say, approach the nearer to perfection by the degree in which they embrace the interests of the greater number of men, and in which they favour all more equally, because it is only then that the equilibrium is established between all the interests and all the forces. According to this system, to say that a man has not the right to oppress another man is to say that this other has the strength to resist the oppression. True morality knows other principles. It regards all men with the same eye. It recognises in all an equal right to happiness, and recognises this equality of right, not as founded on the struggle of forces between different individuals, but as founded on the destination of the nature of man and on the goodness of Him who has formed man. Hence, whoever oppresses another opposes himself to the divine order. The use he makes of his power is but an abuse. Hence the distinction between might and right—in a word, all intelligent beings have been created for an end; this end is happiness, and on this is founded the right of everyone to the heritage. It is according to the exercise of these divine rights to fulfil man's destiny that God judges men, and not according to their powers. . . . Thus the strong has no right over the weak. . . . Every convention contrary to these natural rights has no other authority than the right of the stronger; it is a real tyranny. We may be oppressed by a single tyrant, but we may, quite as much and as unjustly, be oppressed by a multitude. . . . Liberties, like properties, are limited, the one by the others. The liberty to injure has never been sanctioned by conscience. The law ought to interdict it, because the conscience of mankind condemns it. On the other side, the liberty to act while not injuring can be restrained only by laws really tyrannical.

In matters of government we are too much given to sacrifice the happiness of individuals to the presumed rights of society. We forget that society is made up of individuals, that it is instituted to protect the rights of *all*, by insuring the fulfilment of all the relative duties. ('Lettres sur la Tolérance' (1753), *Œuv.* ii. 680–87.)

*Political Doctrines subject to Modification.*—Every kind of light comes to us only through time. The slower its progress is, the further the object (carried along by the rapid movement that distances or approaches all existing things) is already distant from the place in which we think we see it. Before we have learned to deal with things in a fixed position, they have already changed several times. Thus we always perceive events too late, and policy has always the necessity to foresee, so to speak, the present. ('Pensées,' &c. (1750), *Œuv.* ii. 673.)

*Injustice of Indirect Taxation.*—Because the indirect tax imposes a multitude of inconveniences upon commerce. It involves actions at law, condemnations, the loss of many men [engaged in contraband], a war of the government with its subjects, a disproportion between crime and its punishment, a continual and irresistible temptation to fraud even while cruelly punished. Because indirect taxation attacks liberty in a thousand ways. Because it greatly lessens consumption and by that means destroys itself. Because by it the expenses of the State are increased, since the State has to pay not only its own expense but that of all its agents. . . . Because the same tax has to be paid on productions of the same nature, of which some are precious and others not, the same on some from rich land, cultivated at little cost, as on others from poor land, the cultivation of which scarcely pays itself. Because it is a disproportionate burden on the poor consumer; [the rich man's consumption of the taxed article not being proportionate to his greater wealth]. ('Sur les Impositions' (1764), *Œuv.* i. 396.)

*Free Trade.*—The idea that the duties we put, either on our own commodities exported, or on foreign commodities imported, are paid by the foreigner is a chimera, for the foreigner sells his merchandise to any one nation at the same price he gets for it from other nations, the duty of import resting necessarily at the charge of the nation establishing it. A government intending to establish certain national manufactures by laying duties on merchandise or raw materials imported, favours these manufactures only at the expense of all others of the nation [and of all consumers]. The manufacturing interest in general is not promoted, because, by placing obstructions to commerce, the development of manufactures is restrained. . . . All the presumed advantages of these combinations of duties in favour of national commerce against foreign commerce are illusory; all their disadvantages are reciprocal and are increased, the one side by the other. Foreigners employ the same means against our commerce. This 'mercantile' and jealous policy is injurious to all States, without being useful to any; it makes of commerce, which should be a tie between nations, a new source of divisions and of wars. It is the interest of all peoples that commerce should be everywhere free and exempt from duties. The first nation giving to others the example of this enlightened and humane policy, by liberating its productions, its industry, its commerce from all prohibitions and all duties, will raise herself rapidly to the very highest prosperity, and will soon compel other nations to imitate her, to the great advantage of the whole world. ('Turgot's last written State Paper' (1776), *Œuv.* ii. 358–68.)

*The American War.*—M. de Vergennes places the problem before us, whether France and Spain should desire to see the subjection or the independence of the English colonies, and he observes that it is not within ordinary human foresight to prevent or to divert the dangers that must result from either event. This remark appears to me to be very just, because

I believe that whatever may be, in this respect, the desire of the two crowns, nothing can hinder the course of events which must certainly lead, sooner or later, to the absolute independence of the English colonies, and by an inevitable consequence to a total revolution in the relations of Europe and America. ('Turgot's last written State Paper' (1776), *Œuv.* ii. 551.)

*All Colonies must sooner or later make their own Laws.*—To this all European nations with colonies must come, sooner or later, by agreement or by force. The independence of the English colonies will precipitate this inevitably. Then that delusion, which for two centuries has rocked the cradle of our politicians, will be dissipated. It is then we shall appreciate the exact value of colonies, called *par excellence* 'Colonies of Commerce,' all the wealth of which European nations believed they would appropriate by reserving for themselves the selling to them and buying from them exclusively. We shall see how precarious and how fragile was the power founded on this system of monopoly. . . . Wise and happy will be that nation the first to bend its policy to the new circumstances, to see in its colonies only allied provinces, and no longer subject to the mother-country. Wise and happy the nation the first to be convinced that all policy in point of commerce consists in employing all lands in the ways most advantageous for the possessors of the land, all hands in the way the most useful to the individual who works—that is to say, the way in which each man, guided by his own interest, would employ them if let alone—and that all else is illusion and vanity. When the total separation of America shall have compelled all the world to recognise this truth, and shall have corrected European nations of the jealousy of commerce, there will exist among men one great cause of war the less, and it is difficult not to desire an event [the independence] which must bring about this benefit for the human race. ('Turgot's last written State Paper' (1776), *Œuv.* ii. 559–64.)

*The Future of Colonies.*—I firmly believe that all the mother-countries will be forced to abandon all empire over their colonies, to leave to them entire freedom of commerce with all nations, to content themselves in partaking along with the others this liberty, and in maintaining with their colonies the ties of friendship and fraternity. If it be an evil, I believe there exists, at all events, no means of preventing it, and that the only part to take is to submit to absolute necessity and to make the best of it. For those powers who should be so obstinate as to resist the course of events, there would be the very great danger that, after having been ruined by efforts beyond their means, they would see their colonies escape them all the same, and become their enemies instead of remaining their allies. ('Turgot's last written State Paper' (1776), *Œuv.* ii. 581–82.)

*A Warning for Spain.*—Unhappily there is reason to fear that Spain has less facility than any other power to abandon a road which she has followed for two centuries, and now to form a new system, adapted to a new order of things. Until now she has given her whole policy to maintain the multiplied prohibitions with which she has harassed her commerce. . . . Neither the ideas of her ministers, nor the opinions of the nation, nor the actual condition of her agriculture and her commerce, nor the constitution and administration of her colonies, nothing, in short, is prepared in advance in order to seize upon that opportunity of power of resolving to change, while change can be made, and of modifying the shock of change, and of the consequences it entails. . . . Nothing would be worthier the wisdom of the King of Spain and his council than to fix at present their attention on the possibility of this forced separation and on the measures to be taken to prepare for it.[1] ('Turgot's last written State Paper' (1776), *Œuv.* ii. 565.)

[1] The warning was neglected for half a century, and was then vindicated upon Spain by the loss of nearly her whole colonial empire.

*Confidence in the Public Spirit of British America.*—It is possible, if the war is prolonged, that the generals may take too much ascendency by the glory they have acquired, by the enthusiasm they have inspired in their army. It is possible that, not daring to form projects to master a people intoxicated with liberty, recently gained through their courage, the leaders may still try to perpetuate their power and to prepare for a higher fortune at a future time, by insinuating the taste for conquests into their young republic. . . . We can, however, predict from the prudence that has as yet presided at the conduct of the Americans, from the courage and enlightenment diffused among them, and from their confidence in the wise counsels of the celebrated Franklin, that they have foreseen that danger, that they mean to protect themselves against it, and that they have decided, before all, to give a solid form to their government, and that consequently they will love peace and will seek to preserve it. ('Turgot's last written State Paper' (1776), *Œuv*. ii. 557.)

*Reform for France depends, 'perhaps for ever,' on War being now avoided.*—The king knows the situation of his finances. He knows that in spite of the economies and the ameliorations already made since the commencement of his reign, there is between the revenue and the expenditure a deficiency of twenty millions. . . . There are three means of clearing off this deficit: an increase of taxes; a bankruptcy, more or less decided, more or less disguised; and a considerable economy in the expenditure as well as in the cost of tax-collection. The first economy ought to be that of expenditure. . . . While the king finds his finances involved and in disorder, his military and his marine are in a state of weakness difficult to be imagined. . . .

By making a premature use of our strength we risk the perpetuating of our weakness. . . . War we ought to shun as the greatest of evils, since it will render impossible for a very long time, and perhaps for ever, the reform which is absolutely necessary for the prosperity of the State and for the relief of the people. ('Turgot's last written State Paper' (1776), *Œuv.* ii. 571.)

[We conclude our extracts with two taken from the earliest essay of Turgot, his first discourse at the Sorbonne, delivered when two-and-twenty. To see life made easier and nobler for the people was ever the yearning of his heart. Through his public career, from first to last, and after his disgrace as well, we have seen how true he was to the aspiration of his youth.]

*A Word to Monarchs and Courtiers.*—Religion, indeed, still repeats, 'Peoples, submit yourselves to the lawful authority;' but she does not cease to say, on the other hand, 'and you who rule the world, you kings, learn that God has entrusted you with power only for the happiness of your people. Learn to regard no longer your authority as the sole end of government, and no longer to sacrifice the end to the means. . . . And you, servile courtiers, who would flatter kings by betraying the cause of humanity, by persuading them that they have to consider only themselves, that the people are only created to be the basis for their grandeur, and to bear its weight, learn that your shameful adulations are an outrage to all kings worthy of the name.'

*Well-timed Reform, to avert Revolution.*—Unhappy are those nations in which false principles of government have actuated their legislators. . . . Almost all have neglected to keep open the door for the improvements of which all the works of man have need, or have neglected to make the means for these easy. . . . The only remedy for abuses that remains—Revolution—is one sadder than the abuses themselves. ('First Discourse at the Sorbonne' (1750), *Œuv.* ii. 593.)

# INDEX